Access to God
in Augustine's *Confessions*

Access to God in Augustine's *Confessions*

Books X–XIII

Carl G. Vaught

State University of New York Press

Published by
State University of New York Press, Albany

For information, address the State University of New York Press,
90 State Street, Suite 700, Albany, NY 12207

Production by Michael Haggett
Marketing by Michael Campochiaro

Library of Congress Cataloging-in-Publication Data

Vaught, Carl G., 1939–
    Access to God in Augustine's Confessions : books VII–IX / Carl G. Vaught.
      p. cm.
    Includes bibliographical references and index.
    ISBN 0-7914-6409-1 (alk. paper)
    1. Augustine, Saint, Bishop of Hippo. Confessiones. Liber 7-9. 2. Augustine,
Saint, Bishop of Hippo. 3. Spirituality—History—Early church, ca. 30-600.
4. Christian saints—Algeria—Hippo (Extinct city)—Biography—History and
criticism. I. Title.

BR65.A62V37 2004
270.2'092—dc22   2004043451
[B]

10 9 8 7 6 5 4 3 2 1

For Lauren, Kristen, and Rebecca

Contents

Preface

Augustine's *Confessions* is a fascinating book. The author begins by praising the greatness of God, confesses his sins by writing an autobiography, and defends his faith by describing the conditions that make memory, temporal experience, and existential transformation possible. In each case, the dynamism of his discourse takes us beyond the surface of the text into the presence and absence of the one to whom he speaks. The richness of the language Augustine uses permits him to stand before God as a unique individual, and it enables him to make even the most theoretical issues accessible in the last four books of the text. The author comes to himself, not only by describing the story of his life in Books I–VI, and by giving an account of his encounter with God in Books VII–IX, but also by describing the conditions that make his transformation possible in Books X–XIII.

How shall we respond to a book as rich and complex as this? What approach should we take? What questions should we ask? What answers should we expect? What purposes should undergird our inquiry? Without trying to answer these questions prematurely, at least this much should be clear from the outset: we cannot plunge into the *Confessions* without calling ourselves into question. Augustine speaks as a psychologist, a rhetorician, a philosopher, and a theologian; but even in the so-called "theoretical Books" of the text, he speaks most fundamentally from the heart. If we are unwilling to probe the depths of our souls, we will never understand Augustine; for he makes insistent demands that we trace out the path he has traveled in our own spiritual and intellectual development.

No one undertakes a project of this kind alone, and I want to thank my students and colleagues who have participated in it and have helped make it possible. First, I express my gratitude to the students at Baylor who have attended my lectures and seminars about the *Confessions*, and two of whom have been my research assistants. Natalie Tapken prepared the notes for the book; and Christi Hemati assisted me with changes in the final version of the manuscript and with the copyedited manuscript. She also proofread the penultimate copy of the text and prepared the index for the book. I am also grateful to the thirteen philosophers who came to Penn State for a week in 1992 to study the *Confessions* with me. We thought and talked until we were exhausted; but in the process, the text opened up in ways that none of us could have anticipated. Some of the papers from this conference and from my graduate seminars appeared in a two-part issue of *Contemporary Philosophy*, published in 1993.[1] In 2001, Baylor University sponsored a Pruitt Memorial Symposium devoted to the topic, "Celebrating Augustine's *Confessions*: Reading the *Confessions* for the New Millennium"; and Professor Anne-Marie Bowery and I were the codirectors of this conference. Finally, I am grateful to President Robert Sloan, Provost David Lyle Jeffery, our former Provost Donald Schmeltekopf, and my colleagues in the Philosophy Department at Baylor for providing me with a supportive and exciting academic environment in which to bring this project to completion. However, I am grateful most of all to Robert Baird, the Department Chair, who read the penultimate version of the manuscript. He not only made valuable suggestions about what I have written, but also encouraged me to turn the project loose after more than a decade of work.

I have presented parts of chapter 2 at a number of institutions and philosophical meetings: the Graduate Christian Forum at Cornell, the Convocation Lecture Series at Bethel College, the Distinguished Lecture Series at Baylor, the Philosophy Department Colloquium at the University of Essex, the Faculty of Divinity in the University of Edinburgh, the "D" Society at Cambridge, the School of Philosophy at the Catholic University of America, the Philosophy Department Colloquium at Penn State, the Baptist Association of Philosophy Teachers at Furman University, the Interdisciplinary Program at Valparaiso University, and the Kenneth Konyndyk Memorial Lecture to the Society of Christian Philosophers in New Orleans. I want to thank those who attended these lectures for comments and criticisms that have helped me sharpen some of the issues in this final version of the book. I have also published parts of chapter 2 in an essay entitled, "Theft and Conversion: Two Augustinian Confessions," in *The Recovery of Philosophy in America: Essays in Honor of John Edwin Smith*.[2] I want to thank State University of New York Press for permission to reprint parts of this paper and to express my appreciation to John Smith for helpful comments about it.

I am grateful to Colin Starnes and James O'Donnell for their encouragement. I met Colin at his farmhouse near Halifax in the summer of

1992 soon after his book about Augustine's conversion appeared; and I participated in a session of James's NEH Seminar at Bryn Mawr the following summer, where teachers from a variety of disciplines discussed a wide range of problems and raised questions about his three volume text and commentary about the *Confessions*. I value the work of these classical philologists because it is the most encouraging sign that Augustinian scholarship is beginning to move beyond the place where Pierre Courcelle left it in 1950. I am pleased to add my philosophical voice to their attempts to reorient the discussion of Augustine's most influential book.

Finally, I want to express my gratitude to Professor Richard Swinburne in Oxford, who helped me find an academic home at Oriel College while the first draft of this book was written. I also want to thank Professor Rowan Williams at Christ Church for allowing me to participate in his course about Augustine, Christopher Kirwan at Exeter College for discussing some philosophical problems about the *Confessions* with me, and Robert Edwards, a medievalist and colleague at Penn State, for making detailed comments on an earlier version of the manuscript. I am grateful. I want to thank my wife, Jane, who has stood beside me for more than fifteen years while the three volumes of my books about Augustine have been written, often listening and sometimes calling what I have said into question. I am also proud of our granddaughters, Lauren, who is six, Kristen, who is four, and Rebecca, who is one. They have brought great joy to their parents and to the rest of our family, and I hope they will be willing to read the *Confessions* when they are older. This book is for them.

Introduction

This book is a detailed analysis of Books X–XIII of Augustine's *Confessions*, and it comes to focus on the conditions that make his access to God possible. The first of these conditions is the structure of memory, the second is the nature of time, and the third is the meaning of creation *ex nihilo*. Looking back on the first thirty-three years of his life, and writing from the perspective of adulthood, Augustine develops the view that memory is a pathway to God; and having established the relation between God and the soul along this pathway, he turns to the confession of his present sins. Then he gives an account of the nature of time, bringing time into relation with eternity by claiming that God not only produces things in time, but also creates time itself as the context in which he remembers, encounters, and anticipates the stages of his quest for fulfillment. Finally, Augustine commits himself to a Christian community of interpretation, where literal and allegorical interpretations of the first chapter of Genesis issue in a new way of understanding the relation between God and the soul.

Augustine's attempt to deal with the problems of memory, time, and creation presupposes a metanarrative of creation, fall, conversion, and fulfillment in the light of which he believes that the lives of all his readers can be understood. However, this does not mean that each of us moves through every stage that Augustine traverses, that all of us do so in the same way, or that the particularity of our unique situations can simply be subsumed within a universal pattern. Augustine is convinced that the pattern is there, and one of his most important tasks is to call our attention to it. However, the author of the *Confessions* not only addresses us as tokens of a type, but also as unique individuals. In doing so, he stands in between the global human situation and the particular modifications it exhibits. The *Confessions* thrusts us into the hyphenated place between the universal and the particular, the past and the future, the community and

1

the individual, and God and the soul, challenging us to listen, not only to what God says to Augustine, but also to what God says to us.

The problem of God and the soul and the language appropriate to it are intertwined in a variety of ways. First, the interaction between God and the soul unfolds within a temporal, spatial, and eternal framework, mobilizing the language of the restless heart as a way of bringing space, time, and eternity together into a metaphorical and analogical unity. The relation between time and eternity is expressed most adequately in metaphorical discourse, while the relation between eternity and space requires analogical uses of language for its appropriate articulation. In both cases, figurative discourse is the key for binding God and the soul together. Second, this pivotal relation involves both unity and separation and expresses itself in creation *ex nihilo*, in the fateful transition from finitude to fallenness, and in the quest for fulfillment that attempts to reestablish peace with God. All these stages of the cosmic drama require figurative discourse for their adequate expression, but they also involve a performative use of language that reflects the dynamism of God, the discord of our fragmented spirits, and the vibrant interaction that can develop between the soul and the ground of its existence. Performative discourse is the language of creation, the language of the restless heart, and the language that permits God and the soul to confront one another in the space that opens up between them. Finally, the two strands of our inquiry come together because the interaction between God and the soul has a linguistic dimension and involves speaking and hearing as its fundamental expression. However important seeing may be, speaking and hearing generate the context in which the ultimate issues of life can be addressed. If these issues are to be dealt with adequately, the language of God and the soul must not only be figurative and performative, but also sufficiently intelligible to bring stability to the human situation.

Figurative language points to the mystery of God and to the separation between God and the soul; performative utterances point to the power of God and to the space between the creator and the creature in which they can disclose themselves; and intelligible discourse points to the Word of God, to the self-transcendent structure of consciousness, and to the hope that both God and the soul will have something to say when they meet. In this book, this hope is grounded in Augustine's existential and ecstatic language about God and the soul and in the conviction that its figurative, performative, and intelligible dimensions will enable it to leap across the centuries to speak decisively in the postmodern world.

Augustine stands like a colossus for more than a thousand years, casting his shadow over the development of the Middle Ages. As one of the translators of the Confessions reminds us, "every person living in the Western world would be a different person if Augustine had not been or had been different."[1] The story of Augustine's life reveals the secret of its impact: though he is one of the most original philosophers and theologians in the Western tradition, he is also a person in whom powerful feelings, strength of will, and greatness of intellect converge. Augustine is one of the greatest psychologists since Plato, the greatest rhetorician since Cicero, and the greatest Christian thinker before the birth of Thomas Aquinas. In all three domains, the greatness of his soul expresses the complexity of his life, the power of his spirit, and the profundity of his thinking.

The most important fact about Augustine is that he combines philosophy and passion in equal proportions. Yet his passion pours into his philosophy, not to confuse or distort it, but to give it impetus. Augustine not only gives us his thought, but also gives us himself. "He does not skim the truth off the [surface of] experience and give us that"; instead, "he gives it [to us] in the [concrete] context in which he learned it."[2] Augustine's head and heart interpenetrate and sustain one another, and his experience and his thinking are equally important because they express inseparable sides of the same person. Though he presents himself as a rhetorician, a psychologist, and a philosopher with unquenchable passions, what he wants most is truth about God. Augustine seeks the ground of truth as the light in which all other truth exists; and to find it, he not only undertakes a philosophical journey, but also speaks to God from the center of his being.

Despite its intrinsic interest and its lasting significance, Augustine's account of his development is perplexing. It begins with infancy and childhood, but has nothing to say about either stage that could not have been said about any other person. This leads Courcelle and others to move quickly through this part of the text, focusing instead on matters of historical interest peculiar to Augustine.[3] Yet even from an historical point of view, the *Confessions* is not his complete life story. Augustine finishes writing the book when he is forty-six, and the narrative portion of the text concludes with the death of his mother thirteen years earlier. This leaves the reader with a truncated account of his life, and it leaves commentators philological and historical room to speculate about the disparity between what actually occurs and Augustine's recollections of events more than a decade afterwards.

Between Books IX and X, Augustine passes over ten to thirteen years of his life in silence, opening up a chasm in his story that swallows up more than a decade of his life, leaving only a trace. Yet standing on the other side of the hiatus he creates, Augustine deals with philosophical and theological problems in Books X–XIII only to interrupt his reflections with a detailed description of his present spiritual condition. This suggests that even in the most intricately philosophical section of the text, he is structuring the book around the interplay among the experiential, the reflective, and the eternal dimensions of his existence. If we take these dimensions as a clue, we can transcend the modern preoccupation with the opposition between the knower and the object of knowledge; and in moving from there to the relation between space, time, and eternity, we can begin to understand how Augustine's experience, reflection, and developing awareness of God intersect.

After Augustine describes his experiential development, he focuses his attention on the nature of memory, the problem of time, and the hermeneutics of creation. As a consequence, a fissure breaks the linear pattern of his narrative, permitting it to give way to philosophical reflection and to the dialectical subtlety appropriate to it. Though the power of Augustine's rhetoric leads us to the heart of his experience, it also carries us beyond it to his longing to understand the relation between God and the soul. This understanding can be achieved by reflecting on the story of his life, by probing the significance of what he remembers and what he forgets, by standing in the open space between time and eternity, and by attending to the written Word of God, where God has spoken so richly that his discourse can never be exhausted by a finite sequence of interpretations.

On more than one occasion, Augustine says that he is not telling the story of his life to inform God about it, but to speak to other men and women in God's presence. Though he could have scarcely foreseen the impact his book would make on future generations, in addressing "that small part of the human race who may come upon these writings," he makes it clear that he wants to bring his readers into the vertical relationship between God and the soul from which he speaks (2.3.5).[4] Augustine's deepest wish for the *Confessions* is that those who read it may understand "what depths there are from which we are to cry unto thee" (2.3.5). Thus, he asks us to join him, not only by reflecting on his experiential journey, but also by plunging into the problems of memory and forgetfulness, time and eternity, and creation and interpretation, where we can make confessions of our own, and where we can embrace the existential and philosophical depths to which these problems call our attention.

THE FRAMEWORK OF THE ENTERPRISE

Augustine's *Confessions* develops within a three-dimensional framework: the first is temporal, the second spatial, and the third eternal. These dimensions generate three axes along which he moves, and each axis exhibits two orientations that point in opposite directions. The temporal aspect of Augustine's life moves forward and backward; the spatial side of his existence points outward and inward; the eternal horizon in which he lives stretches upward and downward; and when these axes converge, they establish a place where his life and thought unfold, both for himself and for his readers.[5]

The two orientations of Augustine's temporal development are important because they allow him to embrace the future and to recover the past. His life is a sequence of episodes that develops toward a culmination, but he also plunges beneath the flow of his experience in a courageous effort to remember the most significant stages of his psychological, spiritual, and philosophical development. He does this, not because he loves the past or because he is proud of his achievements, but because he wants to remember the sins that separate him from God, and by reliving them, to allow himself to be gathered up from the fragments into which he has fallen (2.1.1). Augustine's recollection of the past and his expectation of the future are ways of finding God, where what he remembers and what he anticipates give him access to what would otherwise remain beyond his grasp.

The spatial side of Augustine's life also develops in two directions, not only moving outward toward the cosmos, but also moving inward toward the soul. The story of his life begins with his parents, nurses, friends, and education and culminates in a philosophical and theological framework that makes his experiential and reflective development intelligible.[6] This development permits him to transform the narrow spatial context with which he begins into a way of thinking that gives him access to a larger world. Yet the most crucial episodes of his life occur within the depths of his soul,[7] where it is not so much what happens to him, but how he responds to his circumstances that matters.[8] The internal space in which Augustine comes face to face with himself, the marks his interactions with others make upon him, and the ways in which these encounters point toward God are the most important elements of his spatial development.

The eternal axis along which Augustine moves makes the interplay between the soul and the ground of its existence possible, pointing upward toward God and pointing downward to his fruitless attempts to flee from his presence. In the first case, Augustine seeks to transcend his limitations and to bring himself into relation with the source of power that creates and sustains him. In the second, he tries to flee from God in a downward movement that implicates both his will and his intellect. The upward movement begins as an intellectual ascent and culminates in a response to a divine command that he surrender his will to a source of power that transforms his life. By contrast, the flight from God is an intellectual attempt to escape the searching light of truth and a desperate effort to insist on his own willfulness in opposition to the will of God.

This upward and downward development reflects a double movement in Augustine's soul. In the first case, he transcends himself to find God (7.10.16; 7.17.23), opens himself to the expression of God's grace (8.12.29), and attempts to understand the gift he has received (10.1.1). In the second, he flees from the center of his being, falls toward the earth, squanders his possessions in a far country, and attempts to escape the voice of God by embracing the nothingness from which he comes. The upward development expresses Augustine's faith that seeks to understand its ground, while the downward spiral reflects his abiding identification with the plight of the Prodigal Son (1.18.28). The *Confessions* is a battleground between these two directions, and it is only as he attempts to overcome the conflict between them that he finds God in the heights and in the depths of his soul.

An adequate attempt to understand the *Confessions* must move within temporal, spatial, and eternal dimensions simultaneously. The temporal side of the discussion gives us access to Augustine's historical development, to the narrative devices he uses to express it, and to the reflective problems of memory, time, and creation, where the writer and what he writes about become contemporaneous for the first time. The spatial aspect of the inquiry allows us to take up the relation between Augustine and his surrounding context, leads to the problem of the individual and the community, and permits us to understand the relations among remembering and the structure of memory, temporal episodes and the structure of time, and the created order and the act of creation *ex nihilo*. The eternal horizon of the enterprise enables us to deal with Augustine's journey toward God, the pivotal moments when he finds him, and the ways in which the nature of memory, the problem of time, and the hermeneutics of creation make God accessible. Finally, in the place where time, space, and eternity intersect, Augustine sees the light of truth with his intellect, responds to the voice of God with his will, and expresses the unity of God with his being, where his being, his will, and his intellect interpenetrate to become a transformed image of the ground of his existence.[9]

The concepts of time, space, and eternity that undergird Augustine's experience are related in a variety of ways to his attempts to deal with the problems of memory, time, and creation. Memory is related to time because it puts us in touch with past experiences; it is related to space because it has infinite depths into which we must plunge to make access to its riches (10.12.19); it is related to eternity because it gives us access to God (10.17.26; 10.24.35) making it possible for the (finite-infinite) structure of the soul[10] to reach beyond itself to the sustaining ground of its existence. In an analogous way, time is "temporal" because it can be understood as a dynamic process of remembering, apprehending, and expecting temporal events (11.20.26); it is spatial because it can be divided into "tracts" or "periods" that can be measured and compared with one another (11.23.30); and it can be brought into relation with eternity because it stretches out, is gathered together, and stretches forth toward God (11.30.40). Finally, the hermeneutics of creation is temporal because it points to the alpha and omega of history (8.3.8); it is spatial because it depicts the created order as a hierarchy of levels of being (7.16.22); and it exhibits an eternal dimension because it points to cosmological and soteriological relations that bind God and the soul together (7.15.21; 7.17.23; 8.12.30). In all these cases, the framework that makes Augustine's journey toward God possible makes the discussion of memory, time, and creation possible as well.

Augustine writes the story of his life from the perspective of adulthood, and his evaluation of the book in the *Retractations* places a stamp of approval upon it from the standpoint of its aging author. Two years before his death, he speaks more persuasively than any other commentator about his most influential book:

> [Here are the] thirteen books of my *Confessions*, which praise the just and good God in all my evil and good ways, and stir up towards him the mind and feelings of men: as far as I am concerned, they had this effect on me when I wrote them, and they still do this, when now I read them.[11]

In one of his final sermons, Augustine epitomizes the project he completes thirty years earlier:

> Whoever does not want to fear, let him probe his inmost self. Do not just touch the surface; go down into yourself; reach into the farthest corner of your heart. Examine it then with care. . . . Then

only can you dare to announce that you are pure and crystal clear, when you have sifted everything in the deepest recesses of your inner being.[12]

The Bishop does not give this advice to others without following it himself; in the *Confessions*, he has already undertaken a searching examination of his soul by exploring the crucial stages of his experiential and reflective development.

When Augustine deals with the problems of memory and time, he is not raising psychological questions, but initiating philosophical investigations. Augustine does this because the recollection of the past and the temporal development it presupposes make it appropriate for him to ask about the conditions that make them possible. In *Time and Narrative*, Paul Ricoeur suggests that the paradoxes generated by Augustine's concept of time stand in radical opposition to the continuity displayed by his capacity to remember his temporal development.[13] However, the deeper truth is that Augustine's life displays both continuous and discontinuous dimensions and that the concepts of memory and time contain both harmonious and dissonant elements that reflect the vacillations of his temporal journey. These concepts are related to the temporal stages of his life, not as a cluster of paradoxes to a process of continuous development, but as reflective images of the process of development and discord that he describes in the experiential sections of the book.

Augustine's philosophical accounts of the nature of memory and the problem of time are imbedded in a comprehensive theological conception of four levels of memory and temporality that are discontinuous with one another. First, he tells us that memory is a pathway that makes a divine disclosure possible (10.26.37), and that time is a created matrix (7.15.21) that can be bound together in a unity (11.31.41). In this case, the positive relation between God and the soul is reflected in the continuity of memory; and the beauty of creation is reflected in the goodness of time. Second, Augustine suggests that when human beings fall away from God, memory is transformed into forgetfulness (10.16.24–10.16.25), and time becomes an unstable existential medium in which our lives are distended in a negative way (11.24.31).[14] The problem of forgetfulness and the paradoxes of time are not simply philosophical puzzles, but theoretical indications that both memory and time are intractable contexts in which life falls apart into fragments, raising a theological question about how they can be gathered up into a unity (12.31.42). Third, though memory and time are problems that reflect our intellectual and volitional separation from God, they can also become ecstatic pathways that give us access to God (10.26.37; 11.31.41). At this level, temporal beings who have forgotten their origins need to be converted, and both the act of recollection and the temporal medium in which conversion occurs need to be converted as well. Finally, if Augustine's responses to the problems of memory and time are ways of showing how they can be converted, conversion in both cases makes it possible for us to reach existential and reflective fulfillment in relation to God (10.26.37; 11.31.41). In this case, created, fallen, and converted temporality seek fulfillment; and time becomes the existential and the theoretical matrix that leads us back to the sustaining ground of our existence.

At the beginning of Book X, Augustine exclaims, "Let me know thee, O my Knower; I shall know thee even as I am known" (10.1.1). This single sentence establishes the framework for Books X–XIII and introduces the distinctively philosophical and theological aspects of his enterprise. At this stage of the book, the writer and what he writes about become contemporaneous; the ten-year chasm between the first nine Books of the text and the last four collapses; and Augustine's temporal perspective coincides with the reflective present in which he attempts to express its significance. In this new context, Augustine deals with the nature of memory, the problem of time, and the hermeneutics of creation; and in the process, philosophy and theology converge to give us access to eternity.

Unity and Separation in Augustine's Thinking

Though the relation between God and the soul is Augustine's central theme, his attempts to deal with this issue reveal a tension in his thinking that pervades every stage of his reflective development. This tension surfaces most clearly as an interplay between Neoplatonic and Christian strands in his thought. Neoplatonists maintain that a continuous series of levels connects God and the soul, while orthodox Christians insist that an act of creation *ex nihilo* holds them apart.[15] Augustine exploits the Neoplatonic dimension of continuity by inverting the downward path of emanation and by participating in the soul's ascent to God;[16] but he also emphasizes the Christian dimension of separation by insisting that God and the soul are not different in degree, but different in kind (12.11.11). Another place where Augustine does this is in Book X, where his upward journey toward God, and the recollection of God that makes it possible (10.20.29)[17] is counterbalanced by God's self-manifestation that undergirds the doctrine of illumination that Augustine develops (10.26.37).[18]

Augustine speaks in both ways to express his fundamental insights about the relation between God and the soul (12.6.8; 6.16.26); but when he states his cosmological views with the greatest precision, a metaphysical chasm separates God from the world in such a radical way that a Neoplatonic continuum can never mediate it. According to Augustine, God creates the world from nothing (12.3.3; 12.19.28); according to Plotinus, the One creates the world out of itself. As Augustine suggests in Book XII, the nothingness with which he struggles is absolute (7.1.1) and is more elusive than the lower limit of a Neoplatonic continuum.[19] The author of the *Confessions* not only joins the Neoplatonist in equating evil with the privation of goodness, but also insists that evil is a distorted tendency of the soul to seek annihilation as it attempts to flee from God.[20] Thus, the Augustinian contrast between being and nothingness differs fundamentally from the Plotinian distinction between the One and the privation of which the concept of matter is the clearest expression.

When Augustine rejects the emanation theory by insisting that God creates the world *ex nihilo*, and when he elaborates the significance of this distinction for Christian theology, he baptizes Plotinus just as successfully as Aquinas baptizes Aristotle. Indeed, the first baptism is superior to the second because Augustine grafts the richness of Platonic discourse onto the Christian doctrine of creation rather than imposing Aristotelian categories upon the dynamism of creation *ex nihilo* that they inevitably obscure. Augustine suggests that after God creates the world, the world participates in God by reflecting his infinite richness. This dimension of participation presupposes a continuum between God and the world along which Augustine moves; but it also presupposes the act of creation that brings the continuum into existence in the first instance.

As *Vere Esse*, God is the upper limit of a continuum that finite beings can approach but never reach; and as creator *ex nihilo*, he is infinitely beyond them as the source that brings them into existence. Yet it is important to emphasize the fact that discontinuity comes before continuity in Augustine's thinking and that it is the foundation upon which the ontological continuum between God and the world is established. To repeat: an ontological continuum permits Augustine to appropriate the linguistic flexibility of Platonism, moving back and forth between metaphorical unity and analogical separation between God and the soul. However, the successful baptism of Plotinus hinges on the fact that creation *ex nihilo* comes first and is the metaphysical foundation upon which the relation between God and the soul depends.

When Augustine occupies the middle ground between God and the soul, the place from which he speaks displays several important characteristics. First, it is a region in which the soul is an image of God and where this imagistic relation connects and disconnects them. The original is prior to the image and expresses itself in creation *ex nihilo*, but the image that emerges from it is a being with its own integrity and reflects the richness of the source that generates it. Second, the image of God is not only a thinking being, but also a center of power that expresses itself in the freedom of the will. In the *Confessions*, the will is a dimension of the soul that is distinct from both thinking and feeling; and it is the moving principle that allows it to transcend itself by embracing a positive relationship with God. Third, though the will is a center of power that can exercise its freedom, it sometimes degenerates, leading from a positive orientation toward God to a radical separation from him that raises the problem of sin and redemption. Along the vertical axis that defines the relation between God and the soul, the will sometimes turns away from its source and plunges into an abyss that threatens to destroy it. Fourth, though the redemption that liberates the soul from this predicament is mediated by the intellect, it also depends upon a transformation of the will. Knowing God is a necessary condition for finding the transformation Augustine seeks, but deciding to follow him requires an act of the will that reorients the soul. Finally, as Books VII, VIII, and X indicate, Augustine's alienation from his origins can be overcome only when God speaks; for though an intellectual vision opens him to a source of intelligibility that transcends him (7.10.16; 7.17.23), it is equally clear that the transformation of his will requires a divine interjection (8.12.29). Indeed, it is only when this transformation occurs that the intellect and the will are bound together as a recreated image of the source that generates them.

It is customary to claim that we are images of God because we are rational creatures; for unless this were so, we could never raise the question of our relation to the origin that transcends us. Augustine commits himself to the view that the intellect sets us apart from the rest of creation and makes it possible for us to understand what is at stake in the relation between God and the soul. However, Augustine's position is much more sophisticated than this: to be an image of God is not only to think, but also to reflect God's infinite richness. The difference between God and the soul is not primarily a distinction between finite and infinite centers of reason, but a contrast between God as an infinite ground and a creature that is both finite and infinite.[21] We could never be related to God if we were merely finite beings separated from him by an infinite chasm. The soul is both a finite and an infinite reflection of its creative ground, and the restless heart displays both finite and infinite dimensions that allow it to move beyond its natural limitations toward the source that creates and sustains it. It is the interplay between these finite and infinite dimensions that allows us to move up and down the ontological continuum generated by creation *ex nihilo*,[22] using metaphorical language to bind God and the soul together, and analogical language to hold them apart.

By describing the stages of his spiritual development, Augustine not only appeals to our intellect, but also puts our souls in motion. His technical term for the motion of the soul is *voluntas*—a volitional faculty that cannot be reduced to feeling or cognition and that expresses the self-transcendence of the person that can bring it into a positive relation with God. Without pointing to this aspect of our nature, we would be unable to distinguish one individual from another. Individuals differ, not only because they exhibit different characteristics, but also because they express distinctive wills. The structure of our finitude and the power of our wills distinguish us from one another; and taken together, they enable us to reach beyond ourselves toward the ground that sustains us.

Augustine not only describes the soul as an intersection of intellect and will, but also as a center of willfulness. Willfulness emerges when we deny our limitations and when the infinite dimension of our souls attempts to become divine. When this occurs, we make the fatal transition from a center of power that is both finite and infinite into an infinite center of self-accentuation. Willfulness stands over against God as a negative imitation of omnipotence and attempts to cancel its finitude by mastering both itself and the world. Yet when the will becomes willful and attempts to control its own destiny, it falls into an abyss from which it is unable to emerge without divine intervention.

Augustine develops two definitions of willfulness that he uses throughout the *Confessions*: first, it is an infinite attachment to a finite good rather than an appropriate attachment to what is infinite; second, it is a negative act we perform for its own sake. In the first case, sin is curiosity or sensuality; in the second, it is pride that separates us from God. All three kinds of sin generate a problem from which the soul is unable to extricate itself, and they have negative personal and social consequences because they shatter our relation to ourselves and to the relationships that bind us to others. The attempt to enjoy what we ought to use as a way of making access to God produces what a later Augustinian monk describes as "the bondage of the will,"[23] where bondage of this kind separates us from God, paralyzes the soul, and destroys the community in which it is embedded.

Augustine often describes the bondage of the will in sexual terms. In a crucial passage at the center of the book, he tells us that will becomes lust, lust becomes habit, and habit becomes necessity (8.5.10). When we are caught in the chains of necessity, sexuality becomes an addiction that not only enslaves the individual, but also has disastrous consequences for the community. Augustine sometimes focuses on the sins of the flesh as if the flesh and sexual activity were the same. However, we must remember that he has a more profound understanding of the body than this. He does not regard sexuality as inherently negative, but only as the most obvious way in which willfulness can manifest its destructive consequences. Augustine struggles with sexual addiction so persistently because it points beyond itself to a more serious problem: the addiction that binds him reflects a degeneration from will to willfulness, symbolizes the stain that defines the human predicament, points to the idolatry of exclusively finite attachments, and produces a disorientation of the will that destroys the community in which it is embedded.

A profound experience of absolute nonbeing undergirds Augustine's account of this process of degeneration. When he moves beyond the Neoplatonic account of evil as privation, he commits himself to a radical way of understanding nothingness that must be distinguished from its relativized and domesticated counterpart. Nonbeing depends on Being as the primary concept, but it also becomes absolute when the freedom of the will breaks beyond the ontological continuum on which it is located and affirms its infinite dimension for its own sake (2.4.9–2.10.18). Having begun to undertake it, Augustine finally turns away from a systematic discussion of the problem of evil because nonbeing and the willfulness that seeks to embrace it cannot be understood by placing them within a larger context. The kind of nonbeing with which Augustine struggles is absolute, and its absoluteness suggests that the problem to which it points has no logical resolution.

Augustine attempts to escape the bondage of the will and the nothingness that makes it possible by embracing the transforming power of what is infinite. A necessary condition for transformation is the positive self-concern that is natural to the psyche (1.20.31). This implies that the image of God has not been effaced altogether and points to the truth of the Neoplatonic thesis that a memory of God binds us to the source that generates us.[24] However, the continuity of Neoplatonic ontologism is not enough to bring redemption to the disoriented will. Just as the continuity that makes linguistic flexibility possible presupposes the discontinuity of creation *ex nihilo*, so an external source of deliverance is necessary that will restore the image of God to its original condition.

The descent from will to willfulness is not primarily intellectual, but volitional; and the character of this descent forces Augustine to move beyond his intellectual conversion to Neoplatonism to his more profound Christian conversion that transcends it. Like the Prodigal Son who takes a journey into a far country and squanders his inheritance, he must come to himself before he can go back home (1.18.28).[25] This radical reversal of the human predicament not only involves a refocusing of the intellect, but also requires a reorientation of the will that allows Augustine to reestablish an imagistic relation with God.[26] The recreation of the image of God that occurs along the vertical axis of experience binds Augustine's intellect and will together and makes it possible for his being, his will, and his intellect to recover their relation to their Trinitarian origins.

The goal Augustine pursues is not identical with knowledge: intellectual deliverance presupposes that to know the good is to do it, while the reorientation of the will requires him to turn away from the willfulness that separates him from the source that creates him. Augustine's conversion to Christianity is not an exoteric expression of an esoteric doctrine, but an intellectual and moral transformation that requires a distinctive philosophical response. As Alfred North Whitehead says, Christianity is "a religion in search of a metaphysics."[27] Our fundamental task is to develop an Augustinian version of this metaphysics. The kind of philosophical system we need is not a metaphysics of presence, but a metaphysics of the present that not only presupposes the Neoplatonic image of the fallen soul that returns to its origins (8.6.3), but also requires the Christian image of a divine interjection that bridges the infinite chasm between God and the soul (8.12.29; 10.25.36–10.26.37). Augustine's experiential and reflective journey is not simply an odyssey of the soul along an ontological continuum of emanation, but a way of living in the present that presupposes creation *ex nihilo* and that redeems human beings from the abyss into which we have fallen.[28] If one ever encounters God, it must always be now; and it is only out of the richness of this encounter that faith seeking understanding can develop the metaphysics it needs.

SPEAKING AND HEARING AS PRIMORDIAL PHENOMENA

Augustine's journey toward God unfolds within a temporal, spatial, and eternal framework; presupposes the centrality of the relation between God and the soul; and exhibits unity and separation as crucial features of the interplay between them. Yet what more should we say about the

linguistic pathway the author traverses in binding God and the soul together and about the figurative uses of language that make it possible for
him to do so? These questions are important, not only because they focus
on the language of God and the soul, but also because they call our
attention to speaking and hearing as primordial phenomena.

The most important thing to notice about Augustine's use of language is that he often employs sensory metaphors to point beyond the
fragmentation of time toward the stability of eternity. In doing so, he
establishes a linguistic pattern that ties language about God to sense
perception rather than to the cognitive or transcendental categories preferred by the scholastics. As his frequent reliance on the category of
substance and on the concepts of being and truth suggest, Augustine is
not indifferent to the power of categorial and transcendental discourse.
However, in following the Platonic rather than the Aristotelian tradition,
he is aware that the richest language about God is rooted in the senses,
linking the lowest level of cognition to the highest place the soul can
reach in its efforts to give an adequate description of eternity. In this
coincidence of opposites, the depths of experience meet the heights of
eternity, and the language of God and the soul becomes the language of
the heart.

Augustine follows the Platonic tradition by emphasizing the importance of visual metaphors. In his intellectual conversion, he catches a
glimpse of God and longs to transcend the place where he sees "through
a glass darkly" so he can see the ground of his existence "face to face"
(10.5.7). The vision of God and the metaphors that permit Augustine to
express it are present in both Neoplatonic and Biblical texts, pointing in
each case to the blinding light in which the philosopher wants to live and
to receive divine illumination. However, most commentators assume that
seeing is Augustine's primary mode of access to eternity, while only a few
have noticed that auditory images are equally important in his account of
the relation between God and the soul. This is evident even in his early
book about the freedom of the will, where Augustine places seeing and
hearing side by side because they are the only senses for which the corresponding object is accessible to everyone who seeks it. Publicity is one
of the most important marks of truth, and the fact that seeing and hearing open out upon a public world, and upon the creative source to which
it points, suggests that they are privileged modes of access to what lies
beyond us.

Augustine uses auditory images throughout his writings, but their
crucial role in his search for God is especially evident in the *Confessions*.

Some critics have claimed that the predominance of auditory language in Augustine's most well known book derives exclusively from his numerous quotations from the Psalms. Yet he uses auditory symbols, not only when he echoes the words of the Bible, but also when he speaks in his own voice. The problem is not whether auditory images saturate the *Confessions*, but how we are to relate them to the more familiar visual metaphors that are so clearly present there. Indeed, the problem of relating visual and auditory ways of speaking is a linguistic version of how to connect Neoplatonism and Christianity in Augustine's thinking.

The Neoplatonic path to God depends upon visual metaphors and produces a vision of unity, while Augustine's Christian conversion allows him to respond to the voice of God with the voice of his heart. Augustine uses visual metaphors to express the significant role of the intellect in the search for God. He speaks of "the light of truth," of "inner vision," of "seeing with the eye of the soul rather than the eye of the flesh," and of the "trembling glance" that finally gives him access to God (7.17.23). He also begs God not to hide his face from him and says, "Even if I die, let me see thy face lest I die" (1.5.5). Yet the great rhetorician uses equally powerful auditory symbols to express the longing of his soul for transformation. First he asks, "Let me learn from thee, who art Truth, and put the ear of my heart to thy mouth" (4.5.10). Then he writes: "Accept this sacrifice of my confessions from the hand of my tongue. Thou didst form it and hast prompted it to praise thy name" (5.1.1). Finally, he implores God to "trim away" all "rashness and lying" from his lips, to hearken to his soul, and to "hear it crying from the depths" (11.2.3).

One way to describe the distinction between visual and auditory language is to suggest that visual metaphors are active, intellectual, and a way of bringing the journey toward God to completion, while auditory images are passive, volitional, and expressions of the pilgrimage involved in the quest for unity by the fragmented soul. According to this account, the eye sends out a "visual ray" that touches its object, gives the soul an intellectual apprehension of it, and moves beyond glimpses of God to the capacity to gaze upon him with steadfastness and stability. In fact, some commentators suggest that when the soul makes the transition from time to eternity, the "eye of the mind" and the "eye of the body" converge and that we see God face to face in an intellectual and aesthetic apprehension of truth that mobilizes the soul and the body as a unified being. By contrast, the ear waits passively for someone to address it; the soul decides how and whether to make a volitional response to what it hears; and having made a positive response, the entire person attends to the voice of

God as a preliminary step to seeing his face. In this final moment, hearing the call of God gives way to the vision of God, and faith that leads us toward him is transformed into sight that permits us to stand in his presence.

This way of proceeding suggests that the auditory dimension of Augustine's figurative use of language is preliminary and that he joins his Neoplatonic predecessors in giving pride of place to the eye of the mind. However, several important considerations count against this relatively straightforward picture of Augustine's conception of the language of God and the soul. First, though the visual ray of the eye makes contact with its object, their interplay with one another is mediated by a third term that not only binds the knower and the known together, but also holds them apart. The will connects and disconnects the eye from its object, driving the volitional element of Augustine's journey into the heart of its intellectual dimension. In addition, the brightness of the light he encounters sometimes overwhelms the eye of the mind that seeks to make contact with it. When this occurs, the pervasive discontinuity between God and the soul is more important than the visual continuity between them. Second, the will expresses its crucial role, not only by permitting us to glimpse and gaze upon God, but also by transforming the vision of God into the love of God. In this special case, seeing issues in contemplation; and contemplation produces love that brings our knowledge of God to completion in a fashion that transcends intellectual comprehension. Third, though seeing and hearing are separated in finite contexts, they converge and interpenetrate in the journey toward God. On such occasions, the pilgrim hears and sees voices, just as the Light and the Word are dual aspects of the essence of God. Finally, metaphors of vision point toward a continuity between God and the soul, while analogies of hearing point toward an irreducible discontinuity between them. Even in the final vision of God, unity is not identity, but is the richer community of similarity, likeness, and analogy in which a fundamental difference of essence remains between God and the soul. In this moment of unity, there is an imagistic correspondence between the soul and God that brings visual and auditory elements together and that permits the finite being to become a picture of both the word and the light that come from God. When this correspondence occurs, the knowledge of God that fulfills our intellect, and the love of God that fulfills our will, becomes the praise of God that fulfills our being. In this final moment, the intellectual and volitional dimensions of the encounter between God and the soul express themselves as an auditory phenomenon, in which the voice of the body unites with the voice of the heart in a song of praise that never ends.

The complex semantics Augustine develops to express the relation between God and the soul unfolds on four levels. In the moment of creation, man is a (finite—infinite) reflection of God, where the finite dimension holds the creator and the creature apart, while the infinite dimension binds them together. In the Fall, the (finite↑infinite) creature turns away from its finitude and attempts to embrace its infinite dimension without qualification, causing it to become a negative reflection of the creative source that brings it into existence. In the incarnation, the infinite God becomes finite, and having emptied himself, enables the (finite-infinite) creature to come back to itself by embracing its finitude. And in the resurrection, the (finite—infinite), being returns to its infinite source as a reflection of the original infinitude from which it has fallen away. Creation, fall, conversion, and fulfillment are the four pivotal moments in the cosmic drama Augustine reenacts; these moments are bounded by God, on the one hand, and by absolute nonbeing on the other; and each of these moments involves unity and separation between God and the soul that requires metaphorical and analogical discourse for their adequate articulation.

We can understand Augustine's account of his life most adequately by reading it aloud rather than by moving our eyes from place to place along a printed page. This way of proceeding allows the cadences of his discourse to resonate in our ears, reflecting the original linguistic situation in which he speaks, and mirroring the linguistic interaction between God and the soul to which he responds. The richness of Augustine's rhetoric and the power of his thinking moves us most when we hear him speaking; the oral culture in which he lives and the circumstances in which he dictates the *Confessions* come to life as we listen to his story; and the conversation between God and his soul become accessible to us when we repeat the words he speaks and hears as he enters God's presence. The *Confessions* is not a theoretical account about God that Augustine formulates from a distance, for he knows that God has spoken to him directly and that he must respond to the voice of his creator from the center of his being. The response he makes to what he hears presupposes two kinds of word: on the one hand, it is the intelligible structure of the world that makes his reflections about God and the soul possible; on the other hand, it is an act of speaking in which God reveals himself to Augustine's fragmented heart.

The *Confessions* is a sequence of acts of speaking, some of which are divine and some of which are human. Augustine says, "Speak that I may hear" but he also exclaims, "Who shall bring me to rest in thee? Have mercy that I may speak" (1.5.5). The author of the *Confessions* responds to the voice of God not only by listening to what it says, but also by presenting himself to God as a person who has something to say. What sets human beings apart from other creatures is their capacity to transcend their finitude. One of the most important ways in which this dimension of Augustine's nature expresses itself is the forcefulness with which he responds to the utterances of God. The resulting conversation allows him to plumb the depths of creation, to confront the human predicament, to embrace the new creation that brings reconciliation to his soul, and to anticipate the resurrection in which he will not only see God, but will also be like the incarnated word that makes this vision possible.

Augustine writes the *Confessions* so we can overhear his conversation with God. In a poignant passage in which he refers to his past, his present, and his future companions, he speaks to his Christian readers directly:

> This, then, is the fruit of my confessions . . . , that I may not confess this before thee alone, in a secret exultation with trembling and a secret sorrow with hope, but also in the ears of the believing sons of men—who are the companions of my joy and sharers of my mortality, my fellow citizens and fellow pilgrims—those who have gone before and those who are to follow after, as well as the comrades of my present way. Thus, therefore, let me be heard (10.4.6).

Augustine lays bear his feelings before God, not only to make linguistic contact with the ground of his existence, but also so the one who has created him can set him free. Thus he concludes what he says about the purpose of the *Confessions* by pleading, "And do not, on my account whatever, abandon what you have begun in me. Go on, rather, to complete what is yet imperfect in me" (10.4.5).

PROBLEMS OF ACCESS TO THE TEXT

With the framework for interpreting the *Confessions* before us, and with the problem of unity and separation at the center of our attention, two important problems about Augustine's enterprise require special consideration. The first pertains to the attitudes of typical readers toward the book, and the second raises crucial questions about the unity of the text. Let us consider each of these issues in turn.

The most important thing to say about our initial attitude toward the text is that we are perhaps too close to what Augustine has written or too far away from it. On the one hand, we have heard his story before and believe we understand it without further reflection; on the other hand, his problems are unfamiliar or offensive, turning us away from them toward other questions that seem to be more pressing or congenial. As a consequence, a radical opposition emerges between positive and negative attitudes in almost any audience he addresses. When we read the *Confessions* for the first time, read it again because we know that it has an indispensable place in the Western tradition, or return to it with philosophical and theological maturity, it either arouses or irritates us by bringing us face to face with the inescapable relation between God and the soul.

Augustine deals with this problem by finding a middle ground between the divine and human realms and by speaking from it. In the process, he challenges his readers to find a place of their own between pious fascination and intellectual antagonism. Augustine encourages his readers to move back and forth between the immediacy of his experience and his attempts to describe it as a series of intelligible stages; and when he discusses the problems of memory, time, and creation, he invites us to engage in the philosophical and theological reflection they generate. By doing this, he makes it clear that the problem of God and the soul is not only an existential question, but also a theoretical issue of considerable complexity.

The second question that we must consider pertains to the difficult problem of the unity of the text. For many interpreters, the *Confessions* is a bifurcated document, divided almost equally between experience and reflection. Indeed, Augustine himself divides it into two parts: in the *Retractations*, he says that the first ten Books are about himself, while the last three focus on the interpretation of Scripture.[29] This characterization of the book by its author prompts one of his critics to suggest that the *Confessions* is dictated haphazardly and that Augustine is never able to forge it into a unity:

> The entire work is divided into two parts which seem to have nothing whatsoever to do with each other. The biography of the first ten books is suddenly resolved into a dry exposition of the first chapter of Genesis. Who has not been compelled to shake his head and ask what purpose Augustine could have had in mind when he brought together such diverse materials?[30]

However overstated this evaluation may be, the transition from the first nine Books of the *Confessions* to the last four reveals a fundamental discontinuity in the text that threatens to dissolve it into fragments. One indication that this is so is a radical shift of tone in the book, which suggests that Augustine has moved away from the account of his journey toward God, and from the depiction of the self-transcendent experiences in which he finds him, to the theoretical language that he needs to describe the conditions that make his quest for transformation possible. Because this shift in tone is so abrupt, the last four Books of the text not only stand in contrast with the first nine, but almost seem to be a different document.

Another indication that there is a basic discontinuity in the text is that Augustine shifts his attention at the beginning of Book X from experience to relatively autonomous reflection. In Books I–IX, reflection is either part of a developmental stage or an attempt to clarify the significance of a particular experience; but in Books X–XIII, philosophical reflection emerges as a significant factor in its own right. The last four Books of the *Confessions* are the reflective center of the text; but as we begin to immerse ourselves in them, the task of bringing them into an intelligible relation with Books I–IX emerges as a difficult problem.

The final indication that there is a radical discontinuity in the text is that there is a ten to thirteen year chasm between the death of Augustine's mother, which he describes at the end of Book IX, and what he writes about in Books X–XIII. When he turns away from the story of his life to the problems of memory, time, and creation, Augustine makes an unexpected transition from the past to the present; and the writer and what he writes about become contemporaneous for the first time. This transition shifts our attention from what he remembers about the earlier stages of his life to the stage of adulthood in which the book itself is written. Yet having made this transition, we find that the relation between unity and separation is not only a serious problem in Augustine's life and in the relation between God and the soul, but an equally serious problem in what he writes about these issues.

One way of dealing with this problem is to turn away from it, permitting the *Confessions* to become a bifurcated document. Many readers have proceeded in this way, focusing their attention on the experiential Books to the exclusion of the theoretical ones or moving in the opposite direction. Those who prefer the first nine Books usually do so because of the existential and linguistic richness of this part of the text,[31] while those who prefer the last four often point to the important pedagogical function that Augustine intends for them to serve.[32] Though he describes the experiential dimension of his quest for wholeness in Books I–IX, Augustine gives instruction to those who have already undertaken it in Books

X–XIII; and depending on the temperament or the stage of development of the reader, it is tempting to focus on one of these aspects of the text to the exclusion of the other.

Though Augustine divides the text into two parts, this fact does not lead him to emphasize one part in contrast with the other. He not only plunges into the depths of his experience in Books I–IX, but also deals with the philosophical problems that have a bearing on his journey toward God in Books X–XIII. One of the ways in which he brings these two dimensions of his enterprise together is to suggest that the transition between them is an example of faith seeking understanding. According to this way of approaching the problem of unity, faith seeking understanding binds the text together, where the account of his journey toward God unfolds in Books I–VI, the description of his encounters with God emerges in Books VII–IX, and the interpretation of his quest for understanding develops in Books X–XIII.[33]

Augustine deals with the discontinuity between Books IX and X, not only by moving from faith to understanding, but also by giving a confessional account of his present spiritual condition in the second part of Book X. In this way, he extends the experiential dimension of his enterprise into the most theoretical part of the book. This allows him not only to commit himself to a quest for reflective fulfillment in Books X–XIII, but also to continue his quest for experiential fulfillment in the most theoretical part of his inquiry. In moving from the first nine Books of the text to the last four, Augustine does not exchange an existential for an exclusively reflective frame of mind, but is still a pilgrim engaged in a journey that tilts first toward experience and then toward reflection. This suggests that the *Confessions* is autobiographical in a suitably broad sense of the term, where what Augustine experiences is the central element in Books I–IX, and where what he thinks is the most important aspect of Books X–XIII.[34]

In the vast literature on the subject, many interpreters have tried to uncover other principles of unity that bind the text together. Some have claimed that the interlocking meanings of *confessio* unify the *Confessions*, allowing Augustine to bring the confession of praise and the confession of sin in Books I–X into relation with the confession of faith in Books XI–XIII.[35] Others take their point of departure from Augustine's theory of time. These interpreters maintain that Books I–IX presuppose memory, Book X focuses on present experience, and Books XI–XIII point toward the expectation of eternal rest. Some suggest that this way of dividing the text presupposes the doctrine of the Trinity and that references to the first, the second, and the third persons of the Trinity appear most clearly in Books I–IX, Book X, and Books XI–XIII respectively.[36] Still others claim that Books I–VI involve a quest for truth. This quest culminates in the intellectual conversion of Book VII, the Christian conversion of Book VIII, and the shared mystical experience of Book IX; and these experiences finally lead to the enjoyment of truth Augustine achieves in his reflections about memory, time, and creation in Books X–XIII.[37] Some interpreters suggest that the *Confessions* is unified by the doctrine of the odyssey of the soul,[38] while Frederick VanFleteran counters this interpretation by claiming that the most important element of the text is the ascent of the soul toward God.[39] Finally, the unity of the text can also be established by the interplay of the scriptural elements of curiosity, sensuality, and pride.[40]

It should go without saying that no single principle of interpretation is an adequate way of binding Augustine's text together. The Books of the *Confessions* are so complex and overlap in so many ways that we must use every device at our disposal to give an adequate account of it. However, this does not mean that a new approach to the *Confessions* is neither necessary nor warranted. This new way of bringing unity to the text begins by claiming that the nature of memory, the problem of time, and the hermeneutics of creation are conditions that make Augustine's experiential journey possible. According to this way of unifying the text, the structure of memory makes it possible for him to remember the stages of his journey; the nature of time makes the temporal episodes in which he participates possible; and the interpretation of creation *ex nihilo* makes the understanding of his quest for fulfillment possible. In the first case, remembered episodes presuppose the self-transcendence of memory as a pathway to God; in the second case, temporal episodes presuppose the ecstatic structure of time as a way of stretching out and stretching forth toward God; and in the third case, cosmological and soteriological interpretations of creation *ex nihilo* indicate how it is possible to cleave to God instead of falling into the abyss out of which we have been created.

It is important to notice that in moving from remembered episodes to memory, from temporal episodes to time, and from existential fragmentation to creation *ex nihilo*, Augustine not only makes a transition from experiential episodes to the ontological conditions that make them possible, but also moves to a reflective domain that mirrors the structure of his earlier experience. The structure of memory as a pathway to God is an image of the process of remembering in which Augustine engages; the nature of time reflects the temporal episodes Augustine describes; and the allegorical account of creation is a reflective image of the process in which God gathers up the fragments of Augustine's fragmented life into a unity. In all of these cases, the conditions that make his experience possible are also images that reflect the structure of his experience at the distinctively reflective level.

Though the structure of memory, the nature of time, and the hermeneutics of creation help us unify the text, it is important to notice that crucial aspects of Augustine's experience and reflection break beyond the categorial analysis of his religious and philosophical intentions. This is especially evident in relation to God and absolute nothingness, which are not only the upper and lower limits of an ontological continuum, but are also positive and negative ways of transcending the continuum altogether. A dimension of transcendence is expressed in Book X, where God is the divine teacher,[41] who exists beyond Augustine's mind (10.17.26), and where his volitional orientation toward the absolute *nihil* expresses itself in a forgetfulness of God (10.16.24–10.16.25) that the fall precipitates and that can only be overcome by responding to the voice of God (8.12.29). In Book XI, God is the creative source of existence toward which Augustine stretches; and the absolute *nihil* points to a radical separation from God into which he is distended (*distentio*) as he falls away from him (11.29.39). Finally, in Books XII and XIII, God is the creator that is infinitely beyond all finite creatures (7.11.17); and the *nihil* is the abyss from which the world is created (7.12.18), and to which it attempts to return as it falls away from God (2.10.18; 7.3.4; 7.13.19).

The interplay between God and the soul that unfolds in time, space, and eternity, and that expresses itself in the "space" between God, on the one hand, and the absolute *nihil* on the other points to speaking and hearing as primordial phenomena and to the Place of places where the voice of God reverberates. In his discussion of the nature of memory, Augustine suggests that he overcomes his forgetfulness of God and secures a stable mode of access to the knowledge of God by responding to the voice of the divine teacher (11.8.10).[42] In his discussion of the biblical account of creation, he claims that God creates the world by speaking through the Word with which God himself is identical (11.7.9). And in his account of the first chapter of Genesis, he says that God not only speaks episodically, but also speaks through the written words of the Bible to make his nature and intentions intelligible (11.6.8). In all three cases, speaking and hearing lead us to the Place of places where vertical transactions occur between God and the soul. This suggests once more that even in the most theoretical part of his book, Augustine does not abandon the existential dimension of his enterprise, but continues to speak from his heart by placing the language of God and the soul at the center of his thinking.

1

The Nature of Memory (Book X)

At the beginning of Book X, Augustine makes a transition from the death of his mother in 387 A.D. to the time at which he writes the *Confessions* some ten to thirteen years later. This transition from the past to the present permits him to move from the episodes that he records in Books I–IX to memory as an ontological condition that makes these recollections possible. It also permits him to turn his attention to memory as an ecstatic dimension of consciousness that mirrors his recollection of ecstatic experiential episodes. The episodes in question not only include the three pivotal experiences in which Augustine finds God (7.1016; 7.17.23; 8.12.29; 9.10.24), but also the occasions upon which he falls away from God along the vertical axis of experience. The two most memorable occasions of this kind are the pear-stealing episode in Book II (2.4.9) and the encounter with absolute nonbeing that the death of his closest friend precipitates (4.4.7).

The transition from the past to the present has a spatial dimension that expresses itself in a new kind of community that Augustine addresses in Book X. Having dealt with the public aspect of his life in Books I–IX, he points to the new community he has in mind by praying for the soul of his mother at the end of Book IX (9.13.37). In this prayer, Augustine begins to shift his attention from the external world of Books I–IX, about which he could have provided many more details, to the internal world of his mother, which according to the demands of Christ, must be free from contradiction.[1] Augustine knows that despite the exemplary behavior of

Monica, she might have committed hidden sins that he does not know about or is in no position to know. Thus, he prays for her, asking his readers to pray for his mother and father as well (9.13.37).

At this point, a door swings open to the inner world of every believer, giving us access to the place where Augustine encounters God in Books VII–IX.[2] It is here that the most important and difficult questions for the Christian are played out; and it is in this context that Augustine confesses the sins with which he struggles, even as Bishop of Hippo (10.1.1). Augustine knows how important confession of this kind can be, since he also knows that if the demands of Christ that regulate the inner life can be met, appropriate external behavior will follow.

In the first nine Books of the text, Augustine speaks to a universal audience, where his purpose is to stir up the hearts of unbelievers by pointing to the depths from which we they must cry out to God and to delight the souls of believers because their sins have been covered by the waters of baptism (9.6.14). By contrast, in Book X, he begins to address the Christian community, whose members he asks to believe what he says because they love him. This request presupposes a community of charity, the members of which believe that Augustine's confessions are true because he is a fellow Christian (10.4.5). In this case, what he confesses is not intended to stir up the heart toward God, or to delight the ones who have been converted, but to express the struggle of a convert as he joins other Christians in moving from conversion to fulfillment at both the experiential and reflective levels.

The eternal dimension of Augustine's journey toward God emerges in the soul's attempt to move toward the knowledge of God through memory understood as a pathway. As Augustine understands its structure, memory is the mind's way to God (10.17.26); and forgetfulness is a cognitive and volitional reflection of the fall from Paradise that separates us from God (10.16.24–10.16.25). When God speaks to overcome our forgetfulness, he appears as the divine teacher;[3] and when we listen, our temporal and reflective presents not only coincide in time, but are also brought together in relation to eternity. Since God is not in time, and since the memory of God emerges along the vertical axis of experience, the memory of the past becomes what Gilson has called, "the memory of the Present."[4] Memory of this kind makes it possible for Augustine to bring himself into relation with the eternal present, not only by confessing his sins, but also by moving along the pathway of memory to recover his original relation to God.

The structure of Book X is a mirror image of the book as a whole, for after five introductory chapters that correspond to the first five chapters of Book I, the central part of the book is divided almost equally between theoretical and experiential sections. Having discussed the nature of memory as a pathway to God in Section II, Augustine gives a detailed account of his present spiritual condition in Section III. It should not be surprising that the writer moves so abruptly from the discussion of memory to the confession of his present sins; for as James O'Donnell reminds us, sin has always been the primary threat to the kind of mysticism displayed in Augustine's intellectual conversion, which is recorded in Book VII (7.10.16).[5]

The confession of Augustine's sins in the second half of Book X is an embarrassment to Neoplatonists, who believe that he is converted completely to chastity and continence in the garden in Milan.[6] If this is so, it is astonishing that he is still struggling to live up to his ideals so many years after the fact. However, his preoccupation with the sins described in Book X becomes intelligible if we realize that the task of an embodied soul after its conversion is not to separate itself from the body, but to engage in the difficult task of seeking fulfillment in relation to God. In confessing the sins that continue to beset him even after he becomes Bishop of Hippo, the saint who is recovering from sexual addiction[7] undertakes a painful journey from conversion to fulfillment that only the grace of God will make it possible for him to achieve.

Augustine focuses on his need for grace when he considers the criteria that a mediator must fulfill in making grace accessible. At the end of Book VII, he realizes that he needs a mediator (7.18.24), and he finds the one he seeks in his conversion in the garden in Milan (8.12.29). Yet now he needs to make the transition from conversion to fulfillment, and he also needs to understand how mediation is possible at the distinctively reflective level. At the end of Book X, Augustine deals with the problem of fulfillment by indicating how the mediator can bring experiential and reflective stability to his soul (10.43.68–10.43.69); and he points to the way in which fulfillment can be anticipated by participating in the sacramental dimension of the Christian community (10.43.70).

THE MEANING OF CONFESSION (10.1.1–10.5.7)

Just as Augustine provides an introduction to the book as a whole in the first five chapters of Book I, he provides an introduction to this stage of his inquiry in chapters one through five of Book X.[8] In both places, he begins with a prayer (1.1.1; 10.1.1). Yet in the second introduction, he expresses his longing to know God (10.1.1) and no longer claims that his heart is restless until it comes to rest in God (1.1.1).

On the basis of the three pivotal experiences that bring Augustine's existential journey to completion,[9] Augustine wants to know the one he has been seeking; and he wants to understand the one he has found. Thus, he says at the beginning of Book X, "Let me know you, I shall know you," "even as I am known" (10.1.1). The subjunctive ("Let me know you") expresses a request addressed directly to God, and the future indicative ("I shall know you") expresses confidence that Augustine will find the knowledge that he seeks.[10] Faith seeking understanding must neither abandon the trust with which it begins, nor turn away from the knowledge of God to which it is oriented. Thus, Augustine brings faith and understanding (*intellectum*) together when he asks God to reveal himself, and when his faith assures him that this understanding will one day be achieved.

It is important to notice that at this stage of the *Confessions*, Augustine is not seeking objective truths about God's nature and existence of the sort that he has found by reading the books of the Platonists (7.9.13) or the pathway that leads to God, which he has found by reading the Epistles of the Apostle Paul (7.21.27). Rather, he is seeking knowledge of himself that only God has and that he can have only by knowing God. Augustine needs this knowledge in order to obey the mandate of Christ to fulfill the Law inwardly.[11]

Augustine asks God to enter and transform his soul so that the one who has brought him into existence may possess it "without spot or wrinkle" (10.1.1).[12] In somewhat different terms, he wants the transcendent power of God to become immanent within his soul, where the basis for this request is that he has loved and done the truth by coming to the light (10.1.1). In Book VII, Augustine sees an unchangeable light and moves toward it (7.10.16), where "doing the truth" (*facio*) does not mean "making the truth," as the Latin verb permits,[13] but "acting in accord with the Truth," as the context demands. At this later, more theoretical stage of the book, Augustine wants to continue to act in accord with the Truth by engaging in confession, not only in his heart, but also before God and in his "writing before many witnesses" (10.1.1).

Augustine's confessions in Books I–IX are a public account for a public audience about matters in the public sphere. By contrast, the confessions of the thoughts and feelings of his inner life are a private matter between himself and God.[14] Yet if he refuses to confess the hidden sins with which he continues to struggle, even though he does not hide himself from God, he hides God from himself (10.2.2). In addition, when

God is hidden from us, we lose our positive orientation toward him; and our failure to know God becomes a volitional orientation in the opposite direction. The only way to overcome this problem is to renounce oneself and choose God, where one can be pleasing either to oneself or to God only because of God (10.2.2). Once more Augustine places confession before profession (10.2.2), suggesting that confession is the only way to speak to God, and to speak to others about the source of power that creates and sustains us.

Augustine's primary mode of speaking uses the words of the soul and the "outcry of thought" to address God directly rather than bodily words and sounds that he might utter in the presence of other people (10.2.2). The soul and the body are separated by the distinction Augustine makes here, but it is important to notice that there is a semantical solution to the problem of their unity.[15] When he distinguishes the words of the soul from the words of the body, this distinction not only separates two kinds of entity, but also binds them together by extending the concept of discourse as it pertains to the body to discourse as it pertains to the soul. The analogical distinction between the soul and the body that holds them apart is an important dimension of Augustine's thinking, but the language of the soul as a metaphorical extension of the language of the body is important as well. It is this metaphorical extension of discourse from one context to another that permits Augustine to bind the soul and the body together in semantical terms.

Augustine begins to formulate the meaning of the kind of confession in which he intends to engage in Book X by claiming that when he is evil, confession is nothing else but being displeased with himself, and that when he is upright, it is nothing else but refraining from attributing goodness to himself (10.2.2). As they stand, these formulations are problematic because they seem to eliminate all reference to God and to suggest that confession is little more than the conversation of the soul with itself. However, Augustine reintroduces a transcendent dimension into the discussion by claiming that God blesses the just man and that he justifies the one who has been ungodly (10.2.2). Even though he avoids ontological references to God at this point, Augustine makes a soteriological reference to him by drawing a distinction between the one who is justified and the one who justifies. Thus, what appears to be a way of collapsing the relation between God and the soul into an identity between them opens out into a dimension of difference that confessional discourse evokes.

To underscore the crucial role God plays in the *Confessions*, Augustine speaks about the order in which the language of the text unfolds. First, he says that God speaks to him; then he says that he speaks to God; and finally, he says that he speaks to us (10.2.2). The *Confessions* is an expression of the language of God and the soul, not primarily because it is language about God or about God's relation to us, but because it attempts to teach us how to listen and how to speak to God, where this, in turn, permits us to speak to one another. The language of God and the soul is language addressed to Augustine before it becomes language addressed to God and other people, where the fundamental purpose of this kind of discourse is to point to the priority of God and to renounce authorial control over the confessional enterprise.

Augustine expresses his reluctance to speak to many of those who are anxious to hear his confessions, even though he is required to do so (10.3.3). Part of the reason for his reluctance is that his audience is unable to cure him of his disease and feebleness (10.3.3). People of this kind are eager to know about another human being's life, but are reluctant to correct their own. As a consequence, they are curious about Augustine,[16] but are unwilling to display a confessional openness of their own. Finally, those who approach Augustine in this way are unable to know whether what he says about himself is true, since no one knows "what goes on within a man but the spirit of man which is in him" (10.3.3). Since this is so, Augustine suggests that the best thing for his readers to do is not to ask him about himself, but to ask God to speak to us (10.3.3). If we do this, we can join his confessional enterprise, not as curious bystanders, but as individuals prepared to engage in confessions of our own.

If we turn away from curiosity to enter the same vertical space that Augustine occupies, there is at least one way in which we can listen to the confession of his present sins that transcends curiosity. Knowing that it is part of the Christian life for Augustine to confess his sins to other members of the Christian community, and recognizing that he cannot prove that what he says is true, we can approach him with charity and listen to what he says in love. Augustine suggests that we will have a reason for believing him only if we love him, where the community into which he is attempting to lead us is a community of love. Across the chasm of suspicion that might otherwise separate us from him, Augustine asks us to listen to what he says about himself in the spirit of charity (10.3.3). Thus, the trust with which faith seeking understanding begins becomes a principle of communication in terms of which we can believe what Augustine says, where members of the community in which this occurs overcome the suspicion that often separates us with the love that binds us together.

Augustine's appeal to a community of love as a way of moving beyond the hermeneutics of suspicion[17] is especially relevant to the reception the *Confessions* has been received in the twentieth century. This reception has often reflected the conviction that Augustine does not mean what he says at many places in the text and that he even fabricates incidents in order to enhance the rhetorical power of his story.[18] The most interesting fact about this view is not that it casts doubt on Augustine's veracity, but that Augustine anticipates the kind of critical spirit that gives rise to it. In appealing to a community of charity, he admits that his audience has no way of knowing whether what he says is true unless charity opens the ears of its members to what he is attempting to communicate. Yet if this occurs, Augustine says that we will realize that he is not lying by speaking out of the source of himself, but pointing instead to the truth that is grounded in God. Thus, a willingness to participate in the vertical dimension of experience becomes a necessary condition, not only for finding God, but also for embracing the Truth of Augustine's confessions as he stands in the presence of God.

Besides stirring up the hearts of unbelievers to cry out to God from the abyss into which they have fallen, the profit that arises from confessing past sins is that good people enjoy hearing about misdeeds that no longer trouble the one who makes the confession. In this case, the audience recognizes the fact that the deeds in question are not present evils, but sins that no longer trouble the individual who confesses them (10.3.4). However, Augustine wonders about what benefit (*fructus*) accrues from confessions that focus on what he is rather than on what he was. In this case, he suggests that the benefit of his confessions is that his readers will give thanks for the extent to which he is able to approach God and will pray that he will not be held back from God by his own weight (10.4.5). Thanksgiving and prayer are marks of the fact that Augustine and his audience are parts of the same community, where this community is bound together by the principle of charity that makes it possible for us to love Augustine in God.

Even though the community to which Augustine commits himself is founded on the principle of love, its members will not be uniformly positive in their appraisals of what Augustine confesses. Rather, they will love those things in Augustine that ought to be loved and will lament those things in him that ought to be lamented. Yet members of this community will not be hostile to him, even when they blame him for some of his actions (10.4.5). This community draws a radical distinction between positive and negative behavior, but they rise above the binary logic of the

Law and the perpetual conflict between good and evil by placing them both within the context of love.

Rejoicing over what can be approved expresses love, but sadness over what must be disapproved expresses love as well. Though the love that binds the community together sometimes manifests itself in negative terms, the opposition between good and evil that Augustine struggles for so long to transcend never splits the community apart. Thus, he says that it is men like these to whom he is willing to reveal himself and that anyone else is a stranger (10.4.5). Finally, in laying bare his feelings before God, Augustine says, "And do not, on any account whatever, abandon what you have begun in me. Go on, rather, to complete what is yet imperfect in me" (10.4.5).

Augustine confesses his present sins to "the believing sons of men," who partake in his joy, who share his mortality, and who are fellow pilgrims and citizens of the City of God (10.4.6). The band of pilgrims to which he refers in this passage is forged at the end of Book IX, where he prays for his father and mother and asks the servants of God to remember them at the altar of the Church (9.13.37). The audience to which Augustine is appealing is not simply readers who are willing to respond to what he says with open minds, or readers who are sympathetic with theism as a general philosophical position, but the community of the Church whose members are bound together by the cords of love (10.4.6).[19]

It is important to notice that the community to which Augustine refers in this context is not identical with the visible Church. The first arises out of the second through the public confession of our inner life. In the course of the *Confessions*, Augustine creates it by giving encouragement and warning to every Christian struggling with problems similar to his. The community in question is identical with those who seek Augustine's help and seek to help him with charitable intent. Augustine responds by making the example of his own life available to those whom God has commanded him to serve.[20]

The perils in confessing private sins are great: shading the truth, leaving something out, and making some additions, all of which are possible because the kind of truth under discussion is unobservable. As a consequence, Augustine confesses his present sins, not only in words, but also in deeds. He writes:

> . . . Your Word would be but little to me, if he had given his precepts in speech alone and had not gone on before me by deeds. I do this service by deeds as well as by words. . . . (10.4.6)

Standing under that shadows of God's wings, Augustine knows that members of the Church will be able to conclude that he is telling the truth, not only by listening to what he says, but also by attending to what he does. Action is the fruit by which Augustine wants to be judged, where what he says and what he does must never be separated from one another. Thus, he reveals the details of his present spiritual condition to the people that God has commanded him to serve, and he does this on the basis of deeds as well as words (10.4.6). Yet in doing this, he depends upon God for stability and is never able to judge himself; and this leads him to say, "In this manner . . . let me be heard" (10.4.6).

When Augustine confesses his sins in the second half of Book X, it is easy to believe that the audience he has in mind is made up of fellow Christians. Who else would have the patience to listen to the lengthy and often tedious confession of his present spiritual condition? But does Augustine intend to address this same audience in the first part of the book that focuses on the problem of memory? This section deals with many technical problems that only a philosopher would be likely to appreciate, leading us to wonder whether the discussion of these issues is intended exclusively for members of the Church, or for members of a wider philosophical community.

Had Augustine not committed himself so explicitly to the Christian community in the opening paragraphs of Book X, we might be warranted in concluding that his discussion of the nature of memory is addressed to the purely philosophical intellect. Yet as things now stand, we must open ourselves to the possibility that his discussion of this issue, and of the other philosophical problems with which he deals in Books XI–XIII, is addressed to the intellect that begins with faith. Augustine claims again and again that understanding completes faith;[21] but if this is so, Christian philosophers who begin with faith and move toward understanding are the audience to which Augustine is speaking in the reflective part of his inquiry.

The purpose of Augustine's discussion of the nature of memory is to retrace the pathway to God that he has traveled in his own experience (10.8.12). It is important to do this because memory is both an ontological condition and an imagistic reflection of Augustine's experiential journey. As a consequence, one of our most important tasks in this chapter is to indicate how Augustine's discussion of the nature of memory is not simply a theoretical examination of a philosophical problem, but a way of instantiating his journey toward God in distinctively reflective terms.

Augustine refines the concept of the kind of confession he intends to undertake in Book X by claiming that even though no one knows the things of a man but the spirit of man that is in him, there is something in man that even the spirit of man does not know (10.5.7). He also tells us that he knows something about God that he does not know about himself: he knows that God is not subject to violation, but he does not know which of the temptations that encroach upon him can be resisted and which cannot. Thus, Augustine wants to confess not only what he knows about himself, but also what he will not know until his darkness is made as noonday in God's sight (10.5.7). The confessions that Augustine is about to make to the community of love to which he has committed himself is complete, not only because it includes what is evil as well as what is good, but also because it includes what he does not know as well as what he knows. What Augustine does not know will prove to be just as important as what he knows, since his ignorance is a window that permits him to move beyond himself to the transforming source of power that manifests itself in the reflective context to which he now turns his attention.

THE MIND'S WAY TO GOD (10.6.8–10.27.38)

Augustine begins his account of the mind's way to God by claiming that he knows that he loves God, saying that the Word of God has transfixed his heart and that he loves God because he has responded to what he has heard (10.6.8). Heaven and earth and everything in them say that he should love God, and Augustine claims that they never cease to say this to all of us. On the other hand, hearing the voice with which nature speaks presupposes the mercy of God that allows us to hear what it says. Otherwise, the voice of nature would speak about God to "deaf ears" (10.6.8). Once more, Augustine begins with speaking and hearing as primordial phenomena,[22] claiming that nature plays an important but derivative role in giving us access to God. As he has discovered from his own experience, God transforms the soul directly (10.6.8), while nature mediates our cognitive access to God by providing us with a realm of symbols that point beyond themselves to a transcendent source of transformation (10.6.9).

Having begun by claiming that he loves God, Augustine turns abruptly from what he knows to what he does not know by asking, "What is it then that I love when I love . . . [God]?" (10.7.11). This transition from confidence in the existence of God to a lack of confidence about the nature of God is typical of Augustine; for even at relatively early stages of his development, he believes in God's existence without understanding

God's nature (10.6.9). However, the fact that he raises a question about the nature of God at this juncture might seem strange in light of the fact that he has encountered God already in the mystical experiences of Books VII and IX (7.10.16; 9.10.24). The identification of God with Truth in both these contexts should lead us to expect that this concept of God will govern the present discussion, making us wonder why Augustine asks what he loves when he loves God.

The answer begins to emerge when we notice that even though Augustine has identified God with Truth, he has not been able to place God in a systematic relation with everything else. It is one thing to claim that God is identical with Truth and quite another to say how Truth is related to all the elements of the cosmos that stand in contrast with it. In the account of his mystical experiences in Milan and Ostia, we find informal sketches of Augustine's answer to this question (9.10.24). However, he does not give a systematic answer to it until he describes the stages of the mind's ascent toward God.

Augustine begins to answer it by moving through a series of negations, claiming first that God is not bodily beauty, temporal glory, or the radiance of the light. Then he says that God is not the melody of songs, the fragrance of flowers, the taste of honey, or the limbs that we embrace in physical love. Yet having begun with negations, he moves to symbols that point beyond themselves by saying that he loves "a certain light, a certain voice, a certain odor, a certain food, and a certain embrace when [he loves] God"; for God is "a light, a voice, an odor, a food, [and] an embrace for the man within me" (10.6.8).

This extension of bodily predicates to God serves to bind God and the soul together, where the soul is bound already to the body by the metaphorical transfer of bodily predicates to it. Of course, both God and the soul have no body; but this does not prevent Augustine from speaking as though they do by binding them together in metaphorical terms. Augustine says that our senses, and the metaphors that cluster around them, give us access to God by pointing to light that "no place can contain," to words that "time does not speed away," to an aroma "that no wind can scatter," to food "that no eating can lessen," and to a "satiety" that "does not sunder us" from him. Finally, he brings this figurative description of the relation between God and the soul to a conclusion by saying, "This is what I love when I love my God" (10.6.8).

Having moved from what he knows to what he does not know, and from what God is not to what he is, Augustine passes the entire natural order in review, asking every part of it from the earth to the stars whether it is God, and hearing in each case the reply, "I am not he!" (10.6.9). Then he asks the things that he perceives to tell him something about God; and all of them cry out: "He made us" (10.6.9). According to Augustine, Creation is the fundamental relation between God and the world (10.6.9); and having come to know God through direct experience, he is able to understand that God is the creator by observing the beauty of nature (10.6.9). The question that Augustine puts to nature and the beauty with which it responds allow him to hear the voice with which the natural order speaks about the ground of its existence.

Unlike Aquinas, Augustine does not give a cosmological argument for the existence of God that begins with a premise about the natural order and that ends with a conclusion about God the creator.[23] Instead, he begins with the existence of God and turns to nature as a domain of symbols that gives him access to the nature of God (10.6.9). In doing so, he embraces a dialogical context rather than an argumentative framework, where his gaze is the question that he puts to nature, and where the answer is the beautiful forms that the natural order displays. Augustine already knows that God exists before he turns his gaze toward nature, and the answer that nature gives him about its relation to God points toward God the creator rather than requiring us to make a mediated inference to him. Formulated in somewhat different terms, Augustine's question leads to an immediate inference that God is the creator, not asking us to begin with nature and to move away from it toward the existence of God by means of an argument.[24]

At this crucial juncture, Augustine turns away from nature and turns inward to continue his account of the journey toward God (10.6.9). He has traveled this pathway before by participating in self-transcendent experiences that have given him access to God (10.6.9), but now he begins to generalize the pattern of those experiences by giving a systematic account of it. The structure of the journey toward God is a condition for and an image of his earlier experiences; and as he reflects upon this structure, the one who asks nature where God is to be found begins to ask questions about himself. In doing so, he attempts to find a place of access to the one who transcends him infinitely.

When Augustine asks himself, "Who are you?" the answer he gives is "A man!" (10.6.9). However, at the more abstract level of philosophical analysis, he also claims that the body and the soul are in him and ready to serve him, one exterior and the other interior. This means that he has both a soul (*anima*) and a body (*corpus*), that both principles make him what he is, and that these principles are to be distinguished from one another in terms of their distinctive functions. Thus, Augustine asks which of these principles ought to be his point of departure in seeking God, whom he has sought already among bodily things by sending out "beams from his eyes" as far as he has been able to project them (10.6.9).[25]

Augustine answers this question by suggesting that the soul (*anima*) is the principle through which the search for God should be conducted, claiming that the inner man is better than the outer man because it rules and judges (10.6.9). When Augustine asks where God is to be found, his senses report the answers of heaven and earth to the inner man by saying, "We are not God!" and "He made us!" Thus, "the inner man" is higher than "the outer man" in the order of being; and Augustine expresses the importance of the distinction between them by claiming that the inner man knows what the heavens and the earth say about God through "the ministry of the outer man" (10.6.9). Yet then in one of the most important but most misleading sentences in the *Confessions*, he says, "I, the inner man, know these things: I, the mind (*animus*), by means of my bodily senses" (10.6.9).

If we are to avoid misunderstanding at this juncture, it is important to notice that Augustine's identification of himself with his soul (*animus*) is derivative upon his identification of himself as a man. His initial answer to the question, "Who am I?" is "A man!," where to be human is to be a composite of a soul (*anima*) and a body. From an ontological point of view, this means that when he uses the word "I," he is talking first about himself and only derivatively about his soul or his body. The true man is not the soul, but the composite of the soul and the body, where the concepts of the inner and the outer man involve metaphorical extensions of the concept in question to the soul and the body considered in themselves.[26]

When Augustine claims that the soul is better than the body, this does not mean that the soul is the true man, but simply that the inner man is higher than the outer man. The true man is the soul and the body taken together, where the soul is the higher part of man understood as a composite. On this basis, it is possible to distinguish three Augustinian concepts of what it means to be human against the background of his initial identification of himself as a man. First, to be a human being is to be a composite of a soul and a body. Second, to be human is to be a soul, which Augustine calls "the inner man." Finally, to be human is to be a body, which Augustine calls the outer or the exterior man. Augustine's strong identification of himself with his soul (*animus*) at this stage of his inquiry does not cancel the fact that he is a composite, but points to the distinctive function of his soul in the journey toward God.

Augustine suggests that the soul (*animus*) uses the bodily senses as instruments to understand the answers of the natural order to the questions he raises about where God is to be found (10.6.9). In doing so, he begins with the soul (*anima*) as it is engaged in the act of sensation; but in understanding what the senses teach, he moves beyond the *anima* to the *animus*. This does not mean that there are two souls, the *anima* and the *animus*,[27] but that the same soul has different roles to play in the journey toward God. As partially constituting a human being, the soul is called the *anima*; as the starting point for an inquiry about God, it is called the *anima* again; but in judging what the senses teach, it is called the *animus*. Yet even though Augustine identifies himself with his soul (*animus*) for the purpose of ascending toward God, he continues to be a composite of a soul (*anima*) and a body (*corpus*) that God has created.

The priority of the composite to both the soul and the body is not merely linguistic, but points to an ontological priority in virtue of which the composite is more fundamental than its constituents. When Augustine identifies himself as a man, he is claiming that he is a human being fundamentally, and that he is a soul and a body derivatively. This explains the fact that he answers the question, "Who are you?" with the exclamation, "A man!" where to be a man is to be a composite of a soul and a body. However, it is important to notice that from a metaphysical point of view, Augustine understands the soul, the body, and the composite as substances, all of which display a certain measure of independence.[28]

As his argument progresses, Augustine moves back and forth between the unity and the separation of the soul and the body, saying on the one hand that he is a man, and hence a soul (*anima*) and a body, while claiming on the other that he is a soul (*animus*) using a body to understand what the senses teach. This does not mean that Augustine is confused about the relation between the soul and the body,[29] but that he has a subtle and fundamentally rhetorical way of articulating the identity and the difference between them.[30] When he is emphasizing a function that the soul or the body is playing, Augustine subordinates them to the human being of which they are constitutive elements; but when he points to properties in terms of which the soul and the body can be distinguished, he construes them as substances in their own right. It is the subtlety with which he moves back and forth between these two ways of speaking that enables Augustine to unify and to separate the human being, the soul, and the body.

Augustine begins to develop the epistemic side of his thinking by reclimbing the Neoplatonic ladder from sensation to higher levels of cognition that he first introduces in Book VII (7.5.7). In doing so, he suggests that the beauty of nature is apparent to everyone whose senses are sound (10.6.10). Augustine also claims that though animals know beauty because they see it, they are unable to ask questions about what they see or judge the validity of the evidence that the senses report. By contrast, human beings are able to ask questions about the natural order, where the "answers" nature gives permit us to understand the invisible things of God through the things that he has created (10.6.10). Once more, Augustine uses nature, not to frame an argument for the existence of God, but to understand the nature of God on the basis of the things he has made (7.5.7).

Though human beings can reason about the validity of evidence, we are often no better than animals. We sometimes love created things too much; and when we subject ourselves to them, we are unable to pass judgment upon them. As Augustine formulates the point, some of us only look at things, while others both see and ask questions about them (10.6.10). The author of the *Confessions* claims that though nature speaks to both classes of individual, only those who compare what nature teaches with "the truth within" understand it (10.6.10). Thus, the capacity to consult Truth as a standard of judgment not only separates men from animals, but also permits us to distinguish those who know God tacitly from those who know him explicitly.

The voice of Truth says to us, "Your God is not heaven and earth, nor any bodily thing." Indeed, the nature of things says this; for we see that the physical world is a mass in which the parts are smaller than the whole. This property differentiates the world from God, permitting Augustine to appeal to what is self-evident in drawing a radical distinction between God and the visible world (10.6.10). At the beginning of Book VII, Augustine sees that God is incorruptible, inviolable, and immutable, where these concepts follow immediately from the concept of God (7.1.1). Now the voice of Truth teaches him that God is not to be identified with heaven and earth, where this conclusion is equally clear on the basis of the concepts involved.

Having pointed to the fact that bodies are not to be identified with God because they are finite,[31] Augustine says that the soul (*anima*) is better than the body because it animates and gives life to it, and that God is better than the soul because he is the life of life (10.6.10). When these two claims are taken together, it is evident that the three substances to which Augustine refers are ordered hierarchically, beginning with God, moving to the soul, and concluding with the body. It is also true that the soul (*anima*), insofar as it quickens the body, is to be distinguished from the soul (*animus*), insofar as it thinks and judges. However, we must understand once more that there are not two souls, but that the soul plays two characteristically different functions in contrast with the body.

Augustine begins to bring the epistemic and the metaphysical strands of his thinking about the relations among God, the soul, and the body together by emphasizing self-transcendence. He writes:

> What therefore do I love when I love my God? Who is he who is above the head of my soul (*anima*)? Through my soul (*anima*) will I ascend to him. I will pass beyond that power of mine by which I adhere to the body and fill the body's frame with life. Not by that power do I find my God. For "the horse and the mule in which there is no understanding" would likewise find him, since in them there is that same power, and by it their bodies also live. (10.7.11)

When Augustine asks what he loves when he loves God, and when he wonders about the identity of the one who is above his soul (*anima*), the one who loves and wonders is Augustine, the man, understood as a composite of a soul and a body. And when he says that he will ascend toward God through the soul (*anima*), passing beyond the power by which he adheres to the body and gives life to it, the one who ascends is Augustine himself, insofar as he identifies himself with his soul (*anima*). In claiming that he will ascend toward God by means of his soul (*anima*), Augustine implies that he will continue to be embodied, even though he must transcend the body in his upward journey toward God.[32]

The power of the soul by which Augustine begins to ascend is the power of sensation, and he describes this power in the following way:

> But there is another power, by which I not only give life but sensation as well to my flesh, which the Lord has fashioned for me, commanding the eye that it should not hear, and the ear that it should not see, . . . and [giving] . . . to each of the other senses powers proper to their organs and purposes. I, who am one single mind (*animus*), perform these diverse things through the senses. But I will pass beyond this power of mine, for this too the horse and the mule possess. They too sense things by means of the body. (10.7.11)

In this formulation, Augustine claims that he gives sensation to his eyes, his ears, and all his other senses, which God has fashioned to sense the world through "powers proper to their organs and purposes" (10.7.11). Thus, the soul is bound to the body, not only because it animates it, but also because it senses by means of it.

Augustine does not understand the soul as the passive recipient of images that external objects inscribe upon it, but as the active agent that generates images in accord with changes in the body that the outer world produces. This fact follows from the claim that the soul is higher than the body and from the general epistemological principle that what is lower can never act on what is higher.[33] However, the power to generate images is not the means Augustine uses for reaching God; for as he indicates once more, animals share the power of sensation with us. Augustine concludes that if having a soul that animates the body and that senses the world by means of it were sufficient to find God, even the horse and the mule would be able to do so (10.7.11).

At this stage of the argument, Augustine identifies himself with the *animus* and claims that he performs diverse functions through the senses (10.8.12). However, this claim should not lead us to conclude that he exercises these capacities *qua animus*; for it is not necessary to have a rational soul in order to encounter the world by means of the senses. This is evident from the fact that the lower animals have the power of sensing without being able to engage in reflection about what they have seen. What then does Augustine's reference to the *animus* mean at this juncture, and how is it related to the mind's way to God?

In establishing the framework in which he undertakes his journey toward God, Augustine identifies himself in a variety of ways. First, he claims that he is a composite of a soul (*anima*) and a body, where the two constituents are distinct ontologically (10.7.11). Then he says that he is a soul (*anima*) adhering to the body and sensing by means of it (10.7.11). Finally, he tells us that he is a soul (*animus*) engaged in the distinctive epistemic functions of thinking and knowing (10.8.12). Augustine's first way of identifying himself points to the ontological unity of the soul (*anima*) and the body of which he is a composite. His second way of identifying himself points to the ontological unity of the soul (*anima*) and the body to which it adheres, but also calls our attention to the epistemic separation between the soul (*anima*) and the body that it uses to make cognitive access to the world. Finally, his third way of identifying himself points to the epistemic separation between the soul (*animus*) and the body, since no reference to the body is required in saying what is distinctive about the act of thinking. However, since the *anima* and the *animus* are not two separate souls, but one soul with different functions, the epistemic separation between them does not cancel their ontological unity.

The unity and the separation of the soul (*anima*) and the body in Augustine's thinking are not only expressed ontologically and epistemically, but also semantically. From a semantical point of view, the soul and the body are separated by the fact that they have distinctive properties. For example, the soul is in time but not in space, while the body is in time and space as well. On the other hand, the soul and the body are unified by the fact that properties of the one can be transferred metaphorically to the other. For example, Augustine sometimes speaks about his bones as if they could cry out to God, and he sometimes speaks about his soul as if an arrow had transfixed it. When we put these two dimensions of Augustine's approach to the problem of the soul and the body together, we find that they are not only unified ontologically and separated epistemically, but also unified and separated in semantical terms. This does not betray confusion on Augustine's part, but is one of the facts that gives his language about God and the soul so much of its richness.

One of the things that makes Augustine's treatment of the problem of the soul and the body so difficult is that he speaks ambiguously about the senses. Sometimes he treats them as if they were parts of the body (10.8.13); but on other occasions, he regards them as dimensions of the soul (10.7.11). However, he has good reasons for doing this; and they are analogous to his reasons for moving back and forth between the unity and the separation between the soul and the body. Sensation has a physiological basis; and for this reason, Augustine links perception to the eyes, the ears, and other organs of sensation (10.8.13). Yet he also believes that if sensing is a way of knowing, the senses must be dimensions of the soul as well. This leads him to distinguish the eyes and the ears as parts of the body from seeing and hearing as epistemic acts (10.8.13).

The eyes and the ears register changes in the world at the physiological level; and when the soul attends to these changes, it produces images that allow it to make cognitive contact with its environment. More accurately, the eyes send out visual rays to their objects that permit the body to be modified at a distance; and sensations result when the soul makes images that notice and correspond to these modifications.[34] As Augustine moves back and forth between these two conceptions of sensation, we are led once more to the need for subtle uses of language that bind these conceptions together and also hold them apart.

The next and most important step Augustine takes in tracing out his journey toward God is to move beyond the power of sensation, and ascending step by step to his creator, to enter "the fields and spacious palaces of [his] memory" (10.8.12). This way of formulating the nature of his journey is important because it points to the orderly progression of the stages involved in his ascent toward God. By moving toward God in stages that are arranged in a hierarchy, Augustine makes it clear that he is now attempting to give a systematic picture of the mystical experiences that have been recounted already in Books VII and IX (7.10.16; 9.10.24). The hierarchy of stages to which this picture calls our attention is both a condition that makes these earlier experiences possible and an image of the ascent toward God understood in reflective terms. It is also important to notice that when Augustine refers to "[his] memory" in the passage before us, the one who has the memory in question is a man rather than a soul. This will become clear when we find that Augustine virtually identifies his memory with his soul (*animus*) (10.8.12).[35] Once this identification has been made, the only one left to "possess" the memory in question is Augustine himself rather than his soul (*animus*).

The transition that Augustine makes at this stage of the discussion allows him to move beyond the dimensions of the soul (*anima*) that he shares with the animals to the rational side of the soul (*animus*) that is distinctively human. It is the *animus* rather than the *anima* that will allow the language of God and the soul to be developed as Augustine moves upward toward God in a series of stages. When he turns to the spacious halls of his memory as a place where this language can unfold, he finds countless images of a great variety of things that have been brought there from objects perceived by the senses (10.8.12). In addition to images generated by the activity of the senses, he also finds products of the activity of thinking when he turns inward toward the soul (*animus*). The mind generates these products by increasing, lessening, or altering the images that sensation produces (10.8.12). Finally, Augustine's soul finds "whatever else has been entrusted" to his memory which "forgetfulness has not yet swallowed up and buried away" (10.8.12).

In these reflections about what he finds when he turns inward, the word Augustine uses for image is *imago* rather than *phantasma*. The images he has in mind give him access to what stands in contrast with him, and they differ from the phantasms that imprison him at earlier stages of his development (7.1.1). The images Augustine remembers allow him to take up the disjoint moments of his experience and to reorder them into a coherent pattern. Yet his memory also brings him face to face with the problem of forgetfulness, where memory is important to him, not only because of what it allows him to remember, but also because of what he forgets.

Augustine's description of the way in which his memory functions is one of the classic passages in the *Confessions*, and it is of special significance because it reflects the process he undergoes in writing a book that requires him to remember so many things about his past. In this connection, Augustine says,

> When I am in that realm, I ask that whatsoever I want be brought forth. Certain things come forth immediately. Certain other things are looked for longer, and are rooted out as it were from some deeper receptacles. Certain others rush forth in mobs, and while some different thing is asked and searched for, they jump in between, as if to say, "Aren't we perhaps the ones?" By my heart's hand I brush them away from the face of my remembrance until what I want is unveiled and comes into sight from out of its hiding place. Others come out readily and in unbroken order, just as they are called for: those coming first give way to those that follow. On yielding, they are buried away again, to come forth when I want them. All this takes place when I recount anything from memory. (10.8.12)

This passage points in three directions. First, it emphasizes Augustine's active role in remembering: he does not remain passive when he turns inward to the storehouse of memory, but asks what he wants to remember to reveal itself. Second, some of the things he seeks are harder to find than others: some of them come forth immediately; others bury themselves in secret cells; and still others rush forth in crowds, even when Augustine does not ask them to appear. Finally, some images suggest themselves without effort and in continuous order, where the linear dimension of the *Confessions* depends upon Augustine's capacity to remember his experiences in this way.

Having pointed to the way in which acts of remembering occur, Augustine tells us that the images we remember are kept distinct and are organized under categories. This is the finite, structural dimension of memory, which permits him not only to give a chronological account of events, but also to collect images from the storehouse of memory to reconstruct the story of his life. Collecting the images he needs for this purpose is made possible by the fact that they do not exist in his memory haphazardly, but according to kinds. Augustine also claims that every image comes into his memory in its own way. Light, colors, and bodily shapes come in through the eyes; sounds impinge on the ears; odors come in through the nostrils; flavors enter "by the portal of the mouth"; and what we touch reaches us through the sensation of the whole body (10.8.13).

Having called our attention to the finite dimension of memory, Augustine points to its infinite dimension by claiming that it has "hidden and inexpressible recesses within it" (10.8.13). Memory as a context in which we can attempt to find God is finite and infinite at the same time; and in this respect, it reflects the (finite-infinite) structure of the soul as it journeys toward God. Once more, we find that the structure of memory is the condition that makes the journey toward God possible, and it is an image of this journey at the distinctively reflective level.

In addition to claiming that every image enters the memory by its own gateway, Augustine says that objects themselves do not enter the mind, but only through images perceived by the senses. These images are kept ready for us to recall and to think about them when appropriate occasions arise. Yet instead of returning to the problem of sensation, or raising the question of the relation between sensation and thinking, Augustine points to his own spontaneous activity in the production of images. Thus he tells us that even when he dwells "in darkness and silence," he brings forth whatever images he wishes and distinguishes between them (10.8.13). He also says that though sounds are hidden in his memory, they do not rush in and disturb him as he reflects on the images upon which he fastens his attention.

Augustine says that the sky, the earth, and the sea are present to him in his memory, together with all the things that he perceives in them. Yet he adds a crucial phrase that points beyond the presence of images to a mysterious dimension of the memory that must also be taken into account. Augustine alludes to this dimension when he says that many things are present to him "except what I have forgotten" (10.8.14). This apparently innocent reference to forgetfulness stands in contrast with the power of memory to give us access to things, and it points to the contrast between presence and absence in Augustine's thinking. As we shall soon discover, the interplay between these elements is one of the most important aspects of Augustine's discussion of the nature of memory.

The interaction between presence and absence begins in an unlikely place. When Augustine turns inward, he not only remembers external objects, but also encounters himself. However, the content of what he knows about himself depends upon what he does and how he feels on previous occasions. This suggests that though recollections that mediate self-knowledge are present, their content points to what is absent. Augustine also includes among his memories what he takes on trust from others; and in this case, he remains at a distance from what he knows in a twofold way. First, his recollections depend upon what others say rather than on what he has experienced directly (10.8.15). Second, these recollections present themselves only as if their contents were present. If recollections were absent, Augustine could say nothing about their contents; but in all these cases, the presence of recollections presupposes the absence of their contents.

The interplay between presence and absence becomes even more crucial when Augustine says that he often combines likenesses of things that he experiences or learns from other people with past events and future actions as if all of them were present. This stage of the inquiry is important because it is a precursor of Augustine's analysis of the nature of time in Book XI (11.11.13–11.31.41). In that familiar but complex analysis, the past, the present, and the future are equated with memory, present experience, and expectation and are held together in the present (11.11.13). Yet as we shall discover in the following chapter, Augustine's claim about the way in which we hold the past, the present, and the future together points beyond the metaphysics of presence to which we might be tempted to reduce it.[36]

The most important aspect of the interplay between presence and absence arises when Augustine confronts the enigma of self-consciousness. He tells us that memory is "vast and unbounded" and that it is not possible to penetrate it "to its very bottom" (10.8.15). In doing so, he points once more to the infinite dimension of memory that makes the journey toward God possible. On the other hand, he says that memory is a power of his soul (*animus*) and that it belongs to his nature. This suggests that he does not comprehend all that he is and that his soul (*animus*) is unable to possess itself (10.8.15). Yet if the infinite power of the soul (*animus*) is within Augustine rather than outside him, how is it possible that he is unable to comprehend it? The answer to this question is that Augustine is not only finite and infinite, but also present and absent at the same time.

"Great wonder" arises within Augustine, and "amazement seizes [him]" as he confronts the phenomenon of self-transcendence (10.8.15). This phenomenon implies that self-consciousness is not self-contained, and that as a consequence, it points beyond itself toward a higher principle.

The interplay between presence and absence and between finite and infinite dimensions of the soul calls our attention to the fact that we transcend ourselves by moving from one level of cognition to another. The journey toward God begins by turning inward toward the soul, but it can be brought to completion only when the soul's knowledge of itself leads to a self-transcendent knowledge of the ground of its existence.[37]

Augustine continues to express amazement at the way in which his memory functions by comparing his knowledge of the world with his failure to pay attention to himself. In this connection, he says:

Men go forth to marvel at the mountain heights, at huge waves in the sea, at the broad expanse of flowing rivers, at the wide reaches of the ocean, and at the circuits of the stars, but themselves they pass by. They do not marvel at the fact that as I was speaking of all these things, I did not look upon them with my own eyes. Yet I would never have spoken of them, unless within me, in my memory, in such vast spaces as though I were looking at them outside, I could gaze upon mountains, waves, rivers, and stars, which I have seen, and that ocean, which I believe to be. Yet when I saw them with my eyes I did not draw them into myself by looking at them. Nor are the things themselves present to me, but only their images, and in each instance I have known what has been impressed on me by each bodily sense. (10.8.15)

As this passage indicates, objects are absent while images are present, pointing to the fact that objects transcend the images that give us access to them. However, Augustine is even more amazed because images themselves are self-transcendent, where the space in which they are contained appears to be as vast in the context of consciousness as space in the external world. The images that Augustine produces in response to objects are not merely two dimensional, but have sufficient depth to stretch out indefinitely far. Thus, the self-transcendence of the image points once more to the (finite-infinite) structure that undergirds the self-transcendence of consciousness and that makes it possible for Augustine to undertake his journey toward God.[38]

Augustine continues to point toward the infinite side of himself by speaking about the immeasurable capacity of his memory to store up knowledge. In doing so, he tells us that his memory contains all the things that he has learned from the liberal arts that he has not forgotten. In this case, he does not carry about the images of things in his memory, but the things themselves. As a consequence, what Augustine knows about logic, literature, and rhetoric is in his memory in such a way that he has "not retained the image while leaving the reality outside" (10.9.16).

Augustine illustrates the difference between knowledge by means of images and the kind of knowledge to which he wants to call our attention with one of his favorite auditory examples. The realities that he apprehends directly are not like the sound of a voice that has passed away, making an impression through the ears and leaving only a trace of itself by which it may be recalled. Instead, they are present as they are in themselves, rather than as images that are stored within the "wondrous cells" of the memory and that are brought forth by acts of remembering (10.9.16).

When Augustine hears questions that remind him of what he has learned from the liberal arts, he retains the sounds from which the questions have been fashioned, knows that they pass in an orderly way through the air, and knows that they exist no longer. Yet the things that are signified by these sounds are not "touched" by any bodily sense, nor are they "seen" anywhere except within the soul (*animus*). Thus, he stores these things in his memory rather than their images; for none of them have entered his soul by means of the senses (10.10.17).

Since the realities that he apprehends directly do not enter his soul through the senses, Augustine wonders whence and how they enter his memory; and in a much-disputed passage of the *Confessions*,[39] he replies,

> How, I do not know, for when I first learned (*discere*) them I did not give credence to another's heart, but I recognized (*recognoscere*) them within my own, and I approved them as true, and I entrusted them to my heart. It was as if I stored them away there, whence I could bring them forth when I wanted them. Therefore they were there even before I learned (*discere*) them, but they were not in memory. Where, then, or why, when they were uttered, did I recognize (*agnoscere*) them, and say, "So it is; it is true," if not because they were already in memory, but pushed back as it were in more hidden caverns that, unless they were dug up by some reminder, I would perhaps have been unable to conceive them. (10.10.17)

The obviously Platonic dimension of this passage suggests that Augustine does not learn truths *from* the liberal arts, but that he learns them by recollection when he is placed within a context where the liberal arts are "taught." In addition, the Latin words that are translated by the word *recognition* (*recognoscere, agnoscere*) point toward a doctrine of recollection; for the meaning of the first word is "to know again," and the meaning of the second is "to know on the basis of previous acquaintance." Finally, Augustine seems to confirm this interpretation by moving back and forth between the dimensions of presence and absence as they pertain to the acquisition of knowledge. First, he claims that the truths of the liberal arts are present in his heart even before he learns them. Then he says that these truths are not in his memory. Yet when he asks where and why he recognizes them as true when they are uttered, he concludes that they are present in his memory after all. This conclusion points to the hypothesis that these truths have been pushed back into "hidden caverns" of the memory and that unless they are drawn forth by some reminder, he would perhaps have been unable to conceive of them (10.10.17).

Despite the fact that these considerations point toward a doctrine of recollection, it is important to remember that Augustine says that he does not know how the truths of the liberal arts enter his memory. As a consequence, he turns away from telling a recollection myth as a way of undergirding the claim that learning is recollection of what we have "known" before. In using words for "recognition" within the context of learning, Augustine also points beyond the Platonic doctrine of recollection to the distinctively Augustinian doctrine of illumination, where a direct recognition of the truth can be identified with immediate insight that the light of truth makes possible.[40]

Within the context of illumination, Augustine gives an account of how we learn the truths of the liberal arts apart from images, and as they are in themselves. By acts of thinking, we collect (*colligere*) things that memory contains here and there without any order; and we observe them and place them near at hand so they may occur easily to the mind (*animus*) that is familiar with them already (10.11.18). We know many things of this kind, where in every case, the things that we have learned have been placed ready at hand. However, the process of coming to know these things must occur repeatedly; for if I cease to recall them for only a short period of time, they are forgotten and must be called forth again as if they were new. As Augustine formulates the point,

> They must be brought together (*cogenda*) so they may be known. That is, they must be collected together (*colligenda*) as it were out of a sort of scattered state. (10.11.18)

In giving an account of the process of learning, Augustine fails to mention a state of preexistence in which our knowledge is complete, but confines himself to the scattered condition of what we are attempting to learn and to the process of collecting what is scattered that makes learning possible. The scattered dimension of our epistemic condition is a theoretical reflection of the fall by which we are fragmented (2.10.18; 10.11.18), and the process of collection that brings these scattered pieces together reflects the process of conversion in which the dispersed elements of our lives are bound together in a unity (8.12.29; 10.11.18). Augustine says that the epistemic contents that we are attempting to learn are within our memories before we come to know them but that they are there in a scattered and neglected state. This use of "before" points to the scattered and neglected status of the contents of cognition in our memories rather than to a state of preexistence in which we have perfect knowledge of the contents in question. Finally, in claiming that recollection of what is scattered and neglected occurs repeatedly, Augustine points to the temporal character of the kind of recollection to which he is calling our attention. Recollection of this kind stands in radical contrast with the kind of recollection to which a Platonic recollection myth points,[41] where in the case before us, recollection is a sequence of transitions from the scattered and neglected state of our knowledge to the act of collection that makes knowledge possible.

At this juncture, Augustine makes an explicit connection between the concept of collection and the epistemic context into which he has just been extending it. He says,

> *Cogo* (I bring together) and *cogito* (I cogitate) have the same mutual relation as *ago* (I do) and *agito* (I do constantly) and *facio* (I make) and *factito* (I make often). But the mind has appropriated this word to itself, so that what is collected together (*colligitur*), that is, brought together (*cogitur*), in the mind but in no other place, is now properly said to be cogitated. (10.11.18)

This passage is important, not only because it extends an important concept from one context to another, but also because it contains a cluster of analogies between the experiential and the reflective dimensions of Augustine's enterprise.

The dispersion and gathering of the meanings of words is analogous to the fragmentation and the unity of Augustine's soul, where the unity in question is made possible by the fact that knowing, doing, and making are connected in the relation between God and the soul. When God gathers (*colligere*) the fragments of Augustine's life together, he does (*agere*) something; and what he does is to make (*facere*) Augustine into a new creation. The etymology of *cogitare* and its similarities with doing and making reflect Augustine's conversion, where collection (*colligere*) at the theoretical level is one of the ways in which Augustine imitates the transforming activity of God. Just as God does and makes something in transforming Augustine's soul, so Augustine does and makes something in collecting the scattered and neglected contents of his consciousness together into a cognitive unity.

Augustine continues to develop his analysis of the nature of memory by telling us that it contains the laws and principles of numbers and dimensions. None of these things are identical with images or with the sounds that signify them; for these sounds are one thing in Greek, and another in Latin, while the things themselves are not in one language as opposed to another. Mathematical lines are also different from the lines that builders draw or spiders make, for they are apprehended directly in the soul (*animus*) rather than by means of images. In a similar way, the numbers by which we count are different from the numerals we use in counting; for we know the former by mental apprehension and have access to the latter by perception (10.12.19). As in earlier cases, perception in the customary sense presupposes physiological changes in the body, while the laws and principles of numbers are apprehended by internal "perception." Intellectual apprehension is analogous to perceiving as a mental activity; and Augustine relies upon the analogy in question, even when he draws distinctions between the terms it connects. Once again, an analogy to which he appeals binds dimensions of his inquiry together, while it also holds them apart.

In the next stage of his account of the mind's way to God, Augustine turns away from mathematical principles considered in themselves and turns inward toward himself in relation to them. He not only remembers numbers, but also recalls how he learns them; and he remembers that he has distinguished truths about numbers from objections certain philosophers have urged against them (10.13.20). Yet distinguishing these truths from philosophical objections and remembering that he has done so differ radically. In the first case, there is a distinction at the level of consciousness between one content and another; in the second, there is a contrast at the level of self-consciousness that permits Augustine to make epistemic access to himself. In this case, memory turns back upon itself; for Augustine not only remembers mathematical principles, but also remembers that he remembers them.

Augustine's transition to self-transcendence permits him to focus his attention on the affections of the mind (*animus*), not as he experiences them directly, but as he remembers them. Without being joyful, he can remember past joys; and without being sad, he can remember past sadness. However, the contrary also happens. Sometimes when he is joyous, he remembers sadness; and when he is sad, he recalls joy (10.14.21). These episodes differ from remembering that he remembers; for in these cases, the content of what he remembers contradicts the content of his present experience.

This phenomenon does not puzzle Augustine when he remembers past bodily pain with joy; for in one of the strongest dualistic statements in the *Confessions*, he says that the mind is one thing and that the body is another (10.14.21). This distinction between the mind (*animus*) and the body (*corpus*) keeps the two "parts" a human being in separate metaphysical compartments, where the dualism involved seems to support a Neoplatonic reading of Augustine's philosophical enterprise. However, the dualism implied by this distinction does not undermine Augustine's unrelenting quest for ontological unity. Though it is true that pain arises from a modification of the body, the feeling of pain is not a physiological phenomenon, but a psychological reality with which we must often contend. In saying that he is not puzzled by remembering past bodily pain with joy, perhaps Augustine means that when present joy and past pain coexist in the same mind, pain can be referred to the body, while joy can be referred to the soul (*animus*). If this is the case, the apparent contradiction of having the experience of present joy and the memory of past pain in the same mind and at the same time can be resolved.

Yet a problem still arises in those cases when we remember past sorrow with joy, or when we remember past joy with sorrow. In these cases, joy and sorrow are present in the mind (*animus*) at the same time, and neither of them can be referred to the body in contrast with the mind. It is also important to notice that as Augustine understands the terms in question, the mind (*animus*) is virtually identical with the memory (*memoria*).[42] As he formulates the point,

> when we order that a thing be committed to memory, we say, "See that you keep this in mind," and when we forget something, we say, "It was not in my mind," and "It slipped out of my mind." Thus we give the name of mind to memory itself. (10.14.21)

This means that the joy that I sometimes experience and the sorrow that I sometimes remember cannot be parceled out to the mind and the memory respectively, since the mind and the memory are identical. Yet in this case, two contradictory states of consciousness exist side by side in the same mind. Is it possible that despite the earlier identification of memory with the mind, memory does not belong to the mind after all? If so, Augustine could escape the contradiction that has arisen by assigning its terms to separate regions. Yet he responds to the suggestion that the mind and the memory are not connected closely by asking, "Who would admit such a thing?" (10.14.21).

The purpose of this section of the text is to prepare the way for Augustine's later discussion of our memory of the happy life (10.20.29), where the life we remember is not the same as the life we experience from day to day. In that context, it is essential for Augustine to claim that the happy life is in our memory, even though none of us are completely happy in our present situation. Thus, it is important for him to resolve the problem that arises when he says that both joy and sorrow can be present simultaneously in the same mind (*animus*).

Augustine tries to avoid this problem by using a bodily metaphor. In one of his richest and most puzzling uses of language, he tells us that the memory is "the belly of the mind" (10.14.21). He develops this metaphor by comparing joy and sadness with sweet and bitter food, suggesting that memories pass into the "stomach" where we store but no longer "taste" them. Augustine knows that this analogy might seem to be ridiculous, but he also insists that the body and its stomach and the mind and its memory have something in common (10.14.21). Thus, he reinforces his puzzling metaphor by insisting on the positive comparison between ingesting food and storing memories in the soul.

In the case of remembering past desire, joy, sadness, or fear, which are the four affections of the soul that the Stoics distinguish,[43] Augustine is disturbed by none of them simply by calling them to mind. This leads to the suggestion that just as "food is brought up from the stomach by rumination, so such things are brought up from memory by recollection" (10.14.22). Yet if we insist on the positive analogy between rumination and recollection, we might wonder why the affections we remember do not retain something of the "taste" of the original when they pass into the mind? Perhaps the explanation is that this is the respect in which the terms of the analogy, "which are not completely alike, really differ" (10.14.22).

Augustine continues to distinguish between affections that we remember and affections that we experience directly by contrasting a concept (*notio*) with a present experiential state. Though the soul experiences its own affections, there is a radical distinction between these affections and the concepts corresponding to them that we also store in our memory. This distinction is important, for it helps explain how we can think about our affections without feeling them. As Augustine formulates the point,

> Which of us would willingly speak of such matters if, whenever we name sadness or fear, we would be constrained to be sad or fearful? Yet we could not speak of this unless we found within our memory not only the sounds of their names, in keeping with the images impressed by bodily senses, but also conceptions (*notio*) of the things themselves, which we did not receive through any fleshly door. The mind itself, perceiving them by experience of its own passions, committed them to memory, or memory itself retained them for itself, even though they had not been committed to it. (10.14.22)

The distinction between affections that we experience and the concepts corresponding to them parallels the positive intent of Augustine's earlier metaphor for memory, where affections and concepts are kept apart in different compartments. Again, this distinction makes it possible for us to speak about the affections of the mind without experiencing them directly.

Despite the value of the distinction between images and concepts as a way of keeping contradictory cognitive contents in separate compartments, it is still uncertain whether we commit our conceptions to memory by means of images or not. For example, when we mention a stone or remember the sun, having concepts of them presupposes having their corresponding images in our memories (10.15.23). Otherwise, we would not be able to understand what the concepts corresponding to them mean (10.15.23). This does not imply that Augustine is confusing concepts (*notio*) with images (*imago*),[44] but expresses his conviction that understanding objects by means of concepts presupposes the presence of images in our memories. Images stand in between the real order and our capacity to make conceptual access to it, though Augustine also tells us that we know numbers directly without using images and that we know images directly rather than through other images that mediate our access to them (10.15.23).

These examples are important because they lead to a question about how we gain access to the nature of memory in contrast with particular memories that it makes accessible. When we speak about memory and recognize what we say, we recognize it in our memories; but we might wonder whether it is present to itself through its image or "present to itself through itself" (10.15.23). This is a rhetorical question; for Augustine tells us in the next paragraph that when he remembers memory, memory is present to itself directly rather than by means of an image (10.16.24).

Some commentators claim that Augustine is confused when he speaks about remembering his own memory.[45] The alleged confusion consists in a failure to distinguish between memory in general and particular acts of remembering that give us access to it. If we make this distinction, it would seem that an act of remembering could give us access to the nature of memory without being identical with it. Yet even if we draw a distinction between particular acts of remembering and memory itself, we draw this distinction with reference to our own memories. As a consequence, it is impossible to avoid Augustine's conclusion that in remembering the nature of memory, memory is present to itself directly. In this special case, what is remembered and the act of remembering are two aspects of memory understood as a self-transcendent context.

Perhaps the crucial point will become clear if we focus our attention on the paradoxical character of self-consciousness. Unlike the affections about which we can think without feeling them, the act of remembering the nature of memory contains itself as a content. Yet in addition to containing itself, memory also transcends itself in the act of recollection. In the first case, memory is present to itself as a content; in the second, it is self-transcendent in the act of remembering. As a consequence, the problem of presence and absence arises in the structure of consciousness that makes this situation different from the one in which we conceive our affections without experiencing them.

When memory remembers itself, it is both present and absent at the same time. Memory is present as a content because it "contains" itself, but it also transcends itself as an act of remembering. In this case, the content remembered and the act of remembering are dimensions of the same complex; and as a consequence, presence and absence are present together. Critics who claim that Augustine does not distinguish between acts of remembering and the nature of memory fail to pay sufficient attention to the self-transcendent character of memory that motivates his inquiry. Self-transcendence in the context of self-knowledge is a condition that makes Augustine's journey toward God possible, and it points to the (finite-infinite) structure of memory that mirrors the journey itself.

At this juncture, Augustine moves beyond the problem of memory to the problem of forgetfulness, suggesting that when we say the word "forgetfulness" and understand what it signifies, we recognize the reality to which it points by remembering it. Indeed, if we had forgotten this reality, we would not be able to recognize what the word in question means. In addition, he claims that when we remember memory, memory is "present to itself through itself" and that when we remember forgetfulness, "both memory and forgetfulness are present: memory by which I remember and forgetfulness which I remember" (10.16.24).

In saying that memory is present to itself through itself, Augustine is pointing to the phenomenon of self-transcendence that we have considered already. Unlike *Nous*, memory is not a closed circle, but a self-transcendent structure in which an act of remembering always transcends the content remembered. Since the nature of memory involves both act and content, and since the act transcends the content when these two sides of the nature of memory are held together, memory is a self-transcendent pathway that can bring about a positive relation between God and the soul. As we have noticed already, this pathway is not only a condition that makes Augustine's journey toward God possible, but also a reflection of this journey at the distinctively reflective level.

Augustine deepens his analysis of the nature of memory by claiming that when we remember forgetfulness, memory and forgetfulness are present together (10.16.24). However, he holds memory and forgetfulness apart within the context of memory by suggesting that memory is the act by which we remember and that forgetfulness is the content toward which this act is directed. However, this not only implies that memory is present and absent because it is self-transcendent, but also that presence and absence can be driven into the content of memory when what we remember is forgetfulness. This becomes especially clear when our memory of forgetfulness is brought into relation with our memory and forgetfulness of God.

When we remember forgetfulness, a fissure opens up within the content of memory that makes our capacity to return to God problematic. Yet as we shall soon discover, Augustine does not believe that for those who inquire about the nature of forgetfulness, forgetfulness in general and forgetfulness of God are ever absolute. As a consequence, he suggests that both forgetfulness itself and forgetfulness of God are present and absent in the structure of forgetfulness itself.

In his discussion of the happy life, Augustine claims that all of us remember God, at least in the minimal sense that we remember that we have forgotten him (10.20.29). In this way, he uses the phenomenon of forgetfulness to advance his discussion of the nature of memory as a pathway to God. On the other hand, he believes that our forgetfulness of

God and our consequent separation from him are so serious that more than a memory of God is required to overcome the chasm that separates us from him (10.16.25). As his analysis of the nature of memory moves toward its conclusion, Augustine indicates how its structure not only permits us to transcend ourselves in our journey toward God, but also how the fissure of forgetfulness can become a "window" through which God manifests himself to the one who has forgotten him.[46]

Since memory encompasses both memory and forgetfulness, and since our forgetfulness of God is never complete as long as we remember that we have forgotten him, we remember God, at least in a minimal sense. Yet the most important point to notice is that the fissure of forgetfulness at the heart of memory makes it possible for us to know God in a more full-bodied sense of the term. The same forgetfulness that presupposes that we have not forgotten God makes it possible for God to manifest himself (10.16.25), where this self-manifestation is the ground for the philosophical conversion in which Augustine has participated already (7.17.23). The relation between memory and forgetfulness is the condition that makes it possible for Augustine to undertake a journey toward God, and the structure of memory that includes forgetfulness is a reflective image of the relation between God and the soul that the mystical experiences of Books VII and IX presuppose (7.10.16; 9.10.24).[47]

Before we pursue these issues in more detail, several other problems about the relation between memory and forgetfulness need to be considered. The first of these issues emerges when Augustine asks the rhetorical question, "What is forgetfulness, unless it be privation of memory?" Yet having pointed to the relative nonbeing of forgetfulness by asking this question, Augustine also asks how forgetfulness can be present so that he can remember it. More than one commentator has suggested that Augustine's answers to these questions are inconsistent and that the status of forgetfulness understood as a privation precludes its presence as a content that we are able to remember. These commentators claim that Augustine should have analyzed forgetfulness in the same way that he analyses darkness and silence, where all three are privations about which it would be inappropriate to ask about their presence as contents of consciousness.[48]

When we notice the rhetorical character of Augustine's question about whether forgetfulness is nothing more than a privation of memory, we should be prepared for a negative answer; and we should not be misled into believing that Augustine has fallen into contradiction by giving us one. In fact, in discussing the status of forgetfulness, he moves beyond the kind of analysis he gives in the case of darkness and silence (10.17.26) in a deliberate and forceful way. Assuming that forgetfulness is more than a privation of memory, Augustine says that forgetfulness is retained in our memories. The reason that he gives for drawing this conclusion is that we retain what we remember, and that unless we remember forgetfulness, when we hear the word we would be unable to recognize what is signified by it (10.16.25). Formulated in a somewhat different way, to understand what "forgetfulness" means is to remember forgetfulness; and to remember forgetfulness is to retain it in our memories.

When we move in this direction, we encounter a paradox: forgetfulness is present so that we are not forgetful of it; but when it is present, we are actually forgetful (10.16.25). However, Augustine is no more confused in claiming that the forgetfulness we remember causes us to forget than he is in suggesting that when memory is present to itself, it is both present and absent at the same time. In both cases, he is speaking about the nature of memory within which the distinctions among memory, forgetfulness, and particular acts of remembering and forgetting arise. By its very nature, memory is self-transcendent when it is present to itself in an act of remembering; and in a similar way, it negates itself when it becomes aware of its own forgetfulness as a phenomenon that presents itself directly to consciousness. In this second case, forgetfulness transforms acts of remembering into acts of forgetting; and it transforms memory itself into forgetfulness as a pervasive condition. The forgetfulness that Augustine remembers is not simply the meaning of a word, but an existential and reflective predicament that causes him to forget God; and it is forgetfulness of this kind that he is most concerned to confront.

Augustine tries to avoid the paradox generated by the problem of forgetfulness by suggesting that when we remember forgetfulness, it might not be present in itself, but simply through its image (10.16.24). He moves in this direction to avoid the conclusion that if forgetfulness were present in itself, it would cause us to forget rather than to remember. Yet the most important dimension of his remarks emerges in the questions that he asks and in the confession that he makes at this critical juncture. Augustine says,

> What man will search this out? Who can comprehend how it is? Lord, I truly labor at this task, and I labor upon myself. I have become for myself a soil hard to work and demanding much sweat. (10.16.24)

The anguish that these questions express and the confession to which they lead reminds us of Adam's exile from the Garden of Eden,[49] and it reminds us as well of the existential wasteland into which Augustine wanders as a result of stealing forbidden fruit from his neighbor's vineyard (2.10.18). When God casts Adam out of the Garden, he condemns him to till the land and to labor with the sweat of his brow.[50] Having identified himself with Adam at the end of the pear-stealing episode (2.4.9), and having experienced the existential anguish that sin always produces, Augustine now extends the range of this anguish by identifying himself with the land upon which Adam labors, and by identifying the sweat of his brow with philosophical reflection (10.16.25).

If we take this comparison between Augustine and Adam seriously, several aspects of our earlier discussion of the problem of forgetfulness begin to fall into place. First, in suggesting that forgetfulness is more than a privation, Augustine is pointing to the fact that our forgetfulness of God is a reflection of the fall in which we have participated experientially. Second, forgetfulness of God is the condition that makes the fall possible, where the analysis of forgetfulness as a philosophical problem indicates that we continue to participate in it, even when we move to the reflective level. Finally, forgetfulness is like the fall because it involves a negative act of turning away from God. The ultimate reason that Augustine cannot analyze forgetfulness in the same way that he analyzes darkness and silence is that forgetfulness involves a volitional component that orients us away from the creative ground of our existence.

Augustine continues to express his amazement about the phenomenon of forgetfulness by comparing the problem of self-knowledge with the problem of knowing other things. In dealing with this phenomenon, we are not exploring the regions of the sky, measuring the distance of the stars from the earth, or attempting to measure the weight of the earth. Rather, we are focusing on ourselves, or more accurately, on our souls (*animus*) with which we identify ourselves for the purpose of reflective inquiry (10.16.25). As he focuses his attention upon himself, Augustine exclaims

It is no matter for wonder that what I am not is far distant from me; but what is closer to me than I myself? Consider: I do not understand the power of my own memory, and yet apart from it I cannot even name myself. What shall I say when it is certain to me that I have remembered forgetfulness? Am I to assert that what I remember is not in my memory? Am I to say that forgetfulness is in my memory to the end that I do not forget? Both answers are most absurd. What third answer is there? How can

> I say that the image of forgetfulness is retained in my memory,
> but not forgetfulness itself, when I remember it? (10.16.25)

When Augustine considers the possibility that what he remembers is
not in his memory and that forgetfulness is there so he will not forget, he
thinks about them only to lay them aside. And even when he moves
beyond both options to the possibility that the image of forgetfulness is
retained in our memories and not forgetfulness itself, he rejects this option as well. Since an image cannot be present to the mind without the
prior presence of the original from which it is derived, the image of
forgetfulness that is inscribed upon the mind presupposes the prior presence of forgetfulness itself. However, this leads to a puzzling question
about how forgetfulness inscribes its image on the memory, since the
presence of forgetfulness wipes away what is inscribed there.

It is tempting to assume that Augustine's problem about the memory
of forgetfulness rests upon an equivocation. In his formulation of this
problem, he distinguishes the word "forgetfulness" from what it signifies;
but it seems to be equally clear that he conflates the meaning of the word
with its referent. If we distinguish between the word, its meaning, and its
referent, we might wonder whether the paradox in question vanishes.

As a way of asking whether this is so, let us consider the following
possibility. When we understand the word "forgetfulness," we grasp its
meaning; but we are also able to distinguish the meaning of the word
from the thing itself. Thus, to remember either memory or forgetfulness
is not to have them present to consciousness, but to understand what the
words that signify them mean. Surely our awareness of what "forgetfulness" means does not cause us to forget it by implying the presence of
forgetfulness.

There is clearly something to this semantical objection to Augustine's
intentions; for at a number of places in which he develops his theory of
meaning, he conflates the meaning and the referent of a word.[51] However,
the problem of forgetfulness does not express a semantical confusion, but
points to the mysterious character of the phenomenon before us. When
Augustine speaks about forgetting something, he is referring to forgetfulness itself,[52] where this problem is analogous to the problem of nonbeing
(2.10.18). This fact prompts some philosophers to transform nonbeing
and forgetfulness into a relative form.[53] In the first case, nonbeing becomes difference or otherness; and in the second case, forgetfulness becomes partial and fragmentary rather than complete. Augustine himself
sometimes proposes a solution of this kind; and at a later stage of our

analysis, it will be important to consider his reasons for doing so. However, on this occasion he says,

> In some manner, although this manner is *incomprehensible* and *inexplicable*, I am certain that I have remembered forgetfulness itself, whereby what we remember is *destroyed*. (10.16.25, my emphasis)

In this passage, Augustine points once more to a comparison between the pear-stealing episode in which he falls away from God (2.10.18) and the phenomenon of forgetfulness in which the fall is recapitulated in reflective terms. In both cases, he suggests that a dimension of the phenomena in question is incomprehensible and inexplicable and that they cannot be given a place within a rational account of the human situation.[54] However, Augustine also acknowledges the truth about our fallen condition and about the forgetfulness of God that makes it possible, even though he is unable to understand it. In doing so, he suggests that truth is prior to meaning even though he is unable to understand the truth to which he is committed in both cases. This is a philosophical correlate of *fides quaerens intellectum*; and as we shall soon discover, Augustine will move from faith to understanding and from truth to meaning when forgetfulness becomes a window through which he passes beyond his memory to God.

Forgetfulness is a crucial element in Augustine's account of the nature of memory; and one of its most important roles is to suggest that we stand in contrast with what we need to remember because of the structure of memory itself. The mind is not a foundational principle that contains its own ground; and the forgetfulness that we often experience reflects this fact. In recognizing that the mind not only transcends itself, but also forgets, Augustine explodes the concept of the mind as a self-contained context. What first presents itself as a container that encircles its contents and that encircles itself opens out to a content that lies beyond itself. In the process, forgetfulness points beyond memory to our need for a source of redemption that transcends our powers of recollection.[55] It is this journey beyond recollection that we must now undertake.

Augustine does not attempt to move beyond memory without acknowledging its infinite depths. This is one of the reasons that he is reluctant to turn away from it. If he had not faced the problem of forgetfulness so resolutely, he might have remained within the circle of memory as a self-contained activity. In this case, *Nous* would have been the highest intellectual principle; and Augustine would never have been able to transcend Neoplatonism.[56] Indeed, before he passes through the open space of forgetfulness, he celebrates such a view by marveling at the power of memory: "Great is the power of memory! An awesome thing, my God, deep and boundless and manifold in being" (10.17.26).

Having pointed to the infinite depths of memory, Augustine identifies it, first with his soul (*animus*), and then with himself (10.17.26). The first identification is not intended to displace the earlier definition of a man as a composite of a soul and a body. Rather, his initial definition is the backdrop against which Augustine identifies himself with his mind and his memory. For the purpose of seeking God, Augustine believes that the body is irrelevant. Thus, when he asks the questions that arise at this juncture, "What am I?" and "What is my nature?" he answers them by referring to the aspect of himself that has a bearing on the mind's journey toward God (10.17.26).

As a way of reviewing the earlier stages of his journey, Augustine answers these questions about his nature by claiming that he is

> varied and manifold and mightily surpassing measurement. Behold! in the fields and caves and caverns of my memory, innumerable and innumerably filled with all varieties of innumerable things, whether through images, as with all bodies, or by their presence, as with the arts, or by means of certain notions and notations, as with the passions of the mind—for these memory retains even when the mind does not experience them, although whatever is in the memory is also in the soul—through all these I run, I fly here and there, and I penetrate into them as far as I can, and there is no end to them. So great is the power of memory! So great is the power of life, even in man's mortal life. (10.17.26)

It is important to notice three things about this passage. First, in pointing to the infinite depths of memory, he is calling our attention once more to the infinite dimension of the soul that expresses the fact that we are made in the image of God. Self-transcendence at both the intellectual and volitional levels is possible because of this infinite dimension, and it is by exercising it along the vertical axis of experience that the restless soul can finally come to rest in God. Second, the fact that memory can be organized into dimensions that stand in contrast with one another and that contain contents that vary from one human being to another points to the finite aspect of our nature that distinguishes us from God and from one another. Acts of self-transcendence not only express the infinite dimension of our nature, but also presuppose the finite dimension of our consciousness that permits them to remain self-identical. Finally, when Augustine claims that memory retains its infinite power even in this mortal life, he is pointing to the fact that even after the fall, the image of God has not been effaced. This will be an important point to remember when we focus our attention on the extent to which the fallen soul both can and cannot remember God.

Augustine responds to his mortality by crying out to God: "What then shall I do, O you who are my true life, my God?" (10.17.26), but he responds to his own question by claiming that he will pass beyond the power of his memory to reach God (10.17.26). The one he seeks is the Light he sees in the mystical experience of Book VII (7.10.16) and the voice he hears in Book VIII (8.12.29); and in seeking them again, he is attempting to trace out the pathway of the soul to God within the context of the soul itself. As he formulates the point,

> Behold, going up through my mind to you, who dwells above me,
> I will pass beyond even this power of mine which is called memory,
> desiring to reach you where you may be reached, and to cling to
> you there where you can be clung to. (10.17.26)

The reason Augustine gives for passing beyond memory in his journey toward God is that even animals have memory though they do not have a knowledge of God (10.17.26). He has used this argument before, pointing to the fact that since animals that do not know God have souls that adhere to their bodies, and since they are capable of sensation, we must pass beyond both of these powers in our search for God. Now he claims that since animals possess memory, and since God has set us apart from them, we must pass beyond memory to what is distinctively human (10.17.26). As he has indicated since the first page of the text, what is distinctive about ourselves is the fact that we stand in a cognitive and volitional relation to God, where this relation will finally allow us to come to rest in God (10.17.26).

The argument that Augustine uses at this juncture is more rhetorical than substantive, for it would be possible to distinguish humans from animals by contrasting higher with lower forms of memory. For example, though animals can remember the way home, and though they can acquire habits of action based on experience, they are not able to remember truths from the study of the liberal arts, the truths of mathematics, or either memory or forgetfulness that would give them access to the phenomenon of self-transcendence. Why then does Augustine not rest content with the claim that we differ from animals only with respect to the relative abstractness and sophistication of the level of memory that we are able to attain?

The reason that he does not do this is that in addition to speaking about our memory of God, Augustine wants to point beyond memory to another important aspect of the relation between God and the soul. This other aspect of the relation not only transcends the kind of memory that animals possess, but also transcends memory altogether. Augustine indicates what he has in mind by saying,

> Even beyond memory will I pass, so that I may find you—where?
> O truly good and certain delight, so that I may find you where?
> If I find you apart from memory, I am unmindful of you. How
> then shall I find you if I do not remember you? (10.17.26)

In this passage, the author of the *Confessions* makes it clear that he intends to pass beyond his memory to reach God, but he also implies that he will not be able to do this unless he remembers God. How are these two sides of the mind's journey toward God to be reconciled?

The problem that arises here is that Augustine must transcend memory to find God, but he cannot recognize what he finds without remembering him.[57] Memory must become self-transcendent if Augustine is to find what he seeks, but there are two sides of self-transcendence that it is important to distinguish. On the one hand, memory transcends itself as it moves toward the dimension of God that stands over against us. On the other hand, it must remember the one it seeks if it is to recognize God when it encounters him.

Two sides of the nature of God correspond to the two sides of self-transcendence that give us access to him. Our memory of God that has not been effaced by the fall gives us access to his immanent side, while illumination gives us access to the transcendent side of God in virtue of which he exists beyond the mind (10.17.26). It follows from these considerations that Augustine both remembers and does not remember God. He remembers God because he stands in a created relationship with him that is not obliterated by the fall; but he does not remember God because he has fallen away from him into an abyss. Our primary task in the following paragraphs will be to understand this complex ontological, epistemic, and volitional situation.

Augustine's first steps in moving toward the dimension of God that transcends the mind refocus our attention on the problem of forgetfulness. However, these steps seem to retreat from his earlier suggestion that forgetfulness is absolute. Forgetfulness breaks open the circle of Neoplatonic recollection to give him access to what lies beyond the mind; but at this stage of his reflections, Augustine analyzes forgetfulness as if it were only partial rather than complete. Yet this should not be surprising; for in moving toward the radical suggestion that he can find the side of God that lies beyond the mind, Augustine is taking initial steps about the nature of forgetfulness that are easily accessible to the philosophical consciousness.

Augustine takes the first of these steps by turning to the first two levels of the divided line[58] and by reminding us of the biblical story of the woman who loses a small coin.[59] She searches for it and finds it because she remembers it; for she could not recognize it as the coin that she loses unless she remembers it. Augustine concludes that this is the way that we always find objects that we misplace; and he claims that in cases of this kind, images play a crucial role in the process of recollection. When we lose an object, we retain its image in our memories; and when we find it, we recognize it through the image that remains within us (10.18.27). Is it possible that we find God because of images that he impresses on our memories?

This scarcely seems likely, since God transcends the images that we construct of him. Augustine has known this since his repudiation of Manichaeism (4.16.29), and it is impossible for him to return to a position that he has abandoned fifteen years earlier. However, this first step leads to a second that appears to be more plausible. Augustine takes this next step by considering what happens when memory itself loses something (10.19.28). When we forget something and try to remember it, we search for it in our memories; and we reject whatever is offered to us until what we are looking for presents itself. However, this fact puzzles Augustine, leading him to write, "We would not say this unless we recognized it, and we would not recognize it unless we remembered it. Yet surely we had forgotten it" (10.18.27).

Augustine tries to resolve this paradox by retreating once more from absolute to relative forgetfulness. In doing so, he introduces the distinction between part and whole and suggests that we retain part of what we forget and that we use it to remember the rest. For example, when we try to remember someone's name, traits of the human being that we normally associate with her are helpful clues; and when one of these identifying traits comes to mind, we often remember the name we had forgotten (10.19.28).[60] Recollection of this kind comes from our own memories, even when someone else gives us the clue we need. Yet if we had forgotten the name completely, we could not recall it even when another person reminds us of it. This fact leads Augustine to the following conclusion:

"We have not as yet completely forgotten what we still remember to have forgotten. Therefore, what we have completely forgotten we cannot even look for if it is lost" (10.19.28). The question that remains is whether we can apply this kind of analysis to our memory of God.

Augustine's preliminary answer to this question is that when we seek God, we seek the happy life that we have not forgotten completely (10.20.29). *On the Happy Life* is one of the first two dialogues that Augustine writes at Cassiciacum;[61] and by returning to this theme, he incorporates an earlier stage of his philosophical development into his present reflections. Augustine never wavers from the conviction that the happy life is the goal of philosophy, and he remains oriented toward it from the time he reads the book of Cicero that exhorts him to embrace the love of wisdom (3.4.8). However, he wonders how he seeks the happy life; and he responds to his own question by saying,

> Here I ought to tell how I seek it, whether through remembrance, as if I had forgotten it but still held to the fact that I had forgotten it, or out of desire to learn a thing unknown, whether one I never knew or one I had forgotten so completely that I did not remember that I had forgotten it. (10.20.29)

Two of the possibilities that Augustine considers presuppose a radical discontinuity between himself and the happy life, while the other presupposes that an initial continuity between himself and what he seeks has not been obliterated. In the first two cases, we are cut off from the happy life so completely that it would be impossible for us to remember it. In the third case, we remember the happy life sufficiently to reach for it by remembering the fact that we have forgotten it.

Augustine explores this third possibility by suggesting that the happy life is what everyone desires and that no one is free from this desire altogether (10.23.33). However, this raises a question about where we have known the happy life that makes us long to possess it. It also leads Augustine to ask about where we have seen the happy life that makes it possible for us to love it. Without answering these questions at this stage, he concludes that we possess the happy life, though he does not know how (10.20.29).

Augustine never abandons his agnosticism about how we know the happy life, and it is important for those who are inclined to attribute a particular theory to him about this issue not to forget this fact.[62] Yet he circumscribes the issue before us by distinguishing three kinds of happiness, where the third kind is the one about which he wants to inquire.

Augustine tells us that some people are happy because they possess the happy life, that others are happy because of hope, and that still others are happy in neither hope nor reality. Those who are happy in hope possess happiness to a lower degree than those who are happy in reality, but to be happy in hope is better than to be happy in neither hope nor reality. However, even to be happy in this third way is to be happy to some extent; for we would not desire to be happy unless we had possessed happiness already. Augustine concludes that everyone who desires to be happy has known happiness in some fashion, though he does not understand how, or understand the kind of knowledge with which we possess it (10.20.29).

Augustine is perplexed about whether our knowledge of happiness is in our memories. He writes,

> If it is there, then all of us have already been happy at some period, either each of us individually, or all of us together in that man who first sinned, in whom we all died, and from whom we are all born in misery. Of this last I do not now inquire, but I inquire whether the happy life is in the memory. (10.20.29)

Without reaching a definitive conclusion about the question of preexistence, Augustine brings this stage of his reflections to completion in the following way. First, he claims that we could not love the happy life unless we know it. Then he says that since we desire to possess it, we know it. Finally, he tells us that we could not know the happy life unless it were in our memories already (10.20.29). Augustine is committed to the view that to have the concept of the happy life is to remember it, where having a concept and remembering its content are identical.

Before we turn to Augustine's formulation of what he remembers when he recalls the happy life, let us return to his claim that if the happy life is in our memories, we have been happy before, either individually or in Adam. Having established the fact that the happy life is in the memory, it would seem to be necessary for Augustine to embrace one of these conceptions of human existence prior to the fall. However, it is interesting to notice that he does not do this, choosing instead to remain open to multiple possibilities about the issue in question.

In his book about the freedom of the will, Augustine considers four theories about the origin of the soul. According to the first, we receive our souls from our parents, which explains the fact that all of us inherit original sin.[63] According to the second, the soul is created at birth, which allows for the fact that all of us display original innocence prior to original sin.[64] According to the third, the soul is sent to rule and animate the body, to participate in mortality, and to redeem the body from corruption.[65] And according to the fourth, the soul that has been created good falls into the body as a punishment for sin.[66] Augustine never makes a definitive choice among these theories,[67] but in the *Confessions*, he does embrace the view that if the happy life is in the memory, we have been happy before, either individually or in Adam (10.20.29). How are we to understand this claim?

The claim that we have been happy at some "previous" period does not invalidate Augustine's repeated assertions in Book I that he does not remember his origins (1.6.7). Having the concept of the happy life permits us to infer that we have been happy before, but it does not allow us to remember our own individual happiness or to decide which theory of origins we ought to adopt. In addition, all of these theories are compatible with the claim that our memory of the happy life presupposes that we have been happy "before." The last three theories make explicit reference to the fact that original innocence "precedes" original sin; and the first theory presupposes that we receive innocence as well as sin from our parents, just to the extent that the image of God has not been effaced, either in them or in us.[68]

The reference to a "previous" state of existence need not point to a temporal state, but to the ontological priority of original innocence to original sin. According to this way of approaching the issue, a memory of the happy life is not a memory of the past, but a memory of the present in which God and the soul stand in a positive relation to one another along the vertical axis of experience.[69] Memory of the present means that we remember realities that are not past, but that are present eternally. From a temporal point of view, we cannot remember what is present unless we have experienced it before; but from the point of view of eternity, our past and present modes of access to the eternal present coincide.

The final and the most important point to notice about Augustine's claim that we have been happy before, either individually or in Adam, is that happiness in Adam can be analyzed in such a way that it includes individual happiness and that it permits the reader to embrace any of the four theories of the soul that Augustine considers without deciding among them. Since Augustine is discussing original happiness rather than original sin, the Adam to whom he calls our attention here is the Adam in whom original innocence resides in contrast with the original sin into which he falls. Adam understood in this sense is (1) the original man who is created good before he falls away from God; (2) what it means to be a man, where the first word about humanity is original innocence rather than original sin; and (3) the distributive collection of all men who display original innocence as a more primordial condition than original sin.[70]

The third clause of this analysis enables us to capture the concept of individual happiness prior to the fall, and the three clauses taken together permit us to state each of the four theories of the origin of the soul among which Augustine never chooses. The view that we inherit our souls from our parents is the logical product of the original innocence of the first man and a principle of genetic succession that permits original innocence to characterize all of Adam's descendents. The other three views are variations on the view that every individual displays original innocence as more fundamental than original sin. Finally, all four views presuppose the priority of original innocence to original sin as a way of giving us access to what it means to be human.

This analysis of the possibility of happiness prior to the fall displays hermeneutical charity to different theories about the origin of the soul, and it is a way of stating many different truths in one utterance. As we shall discover in our analysis of Book XII, both hermeneutical charity and this particular form of the relation between the one and the many are characteristic of the way in which Augustine proceeds in relation to his critics (12.15.18-12.15.22). We should proceed in the same way in relation to views about the origin of the soul that differ from our own, even though a decision to do this does not cancel our obligation to state our own views about the issue in question.

As I have indicated already, I embrace Gilson's suggestion that Augustine's memories of God are memories of the present rather than recollections of a previous mode of existence. This implies that the primary relation between God and the soul is ontological rather than temporal and that our original created condition has not been effaced by the fall. Within this context, Augustine moves from creation to the fall, from the fall to conversion, and from conversion to fulfillment.

Augustine's transitions from the first of these stages to the others permit us to graft the (finite-infinite) analysis of the human being that we have developed at earlier stages of our argument onto what participation in Adam means. Insofar as I participate in original innocence, I display a (finite$\overset{\uparrow}{-}$infinite) structure that brings me into a positive relation with God; and insofar as I participate in original sin, I exhibit a (finite$_{\mathrm{T}}$ infinite) structure that separates me from God. Against this background, the memory of God can be understood as the cognitive condition that makes it possible for me to overcome forgetfulness and to return to God as a (finite-infinite) being who comes back to itself. This (finite-infinite), being can then press on toward fulfillment by uncovering more and more of the richness of God that it has forgotten.[71] Thus, the memory of God is the ontological condition that makes conversion and fulfillment possible; and the overcoming of forgetfulness in both its cognitive and volitional forms is the reflection of what conversion and fulfillment mean at the distinctively reflective level.

Augustine pursues his analysis of our memory of the happy life by asking whether it involves the same kind of recollection as our memory of something that we have perceived, and he concludes that it does not because happiness is not a physical object visible to the eye. Then he wonders whether memory of the happy life is the same kind of memory as our recollection of numbers; and he replies once more that it is not. When we understand numbers, we do not keep striving for a state that will correspond to what we know; but when we remember the happy life, our striving for it continues (10.21.30). This is a crucial step in Augustine's account of the mind's way to God, and a proper understanding of it will allow us to distinguish between the cognitive and the volitional dimensions of his journey.

Augustine's conception of happiness distinguishes it from both physical objects and numbers, where this indicates that he is moving up the divided line and beyond it.[72] The important point to notice is that happiness displays two dimensions that require memory to transcend itself. Happiness is both in the memory and beyond it; and as a consequence, it is present and absent at the same time. When he focuses on the transcendent dimension of happiness, Augustine knows that it transcends consciousness; but when he considers its immanent dimension, he also knows that it is present as a cognitive content. His most serious problem is to place himself between these two dimensions and to follow the pathway that leads beyond himself to God. This pathway is the condition that makes Augustine's journey toward God possible and is the image of the journey at the distinctively reflective level.

Augustine begins to do this by comparing our memory of the happy life with our recollection of joy. The two are comparable because we can remember joy when we are sad, just as we remember the happy life when we are unhappy. Both joy and happiness are not physical objects, but affections of the mind; and both of these affections are positive or negative, depending upon whether the objects toward which they are oriented are good or evil (10.21.30). For example, when Augustine remembers past joys that are evil, he remembers them with sadness; and when he remembers past joys that are good, he remembers them with longing. In addition, when the good things that he desires are no longer present, he remembers them with sadness (10.21.30). In this case, his recollection of the happy life points to a separation between himself and the object of his deepest desire.

The fact that he can remember the happy life leads Augustine to ask, "Where, then, and when did I have experience of my happy life, so that I remember it, and love it, and long for it?" (10.21.31). And in order to place this question within the broadest possible context, he says,

> It is not merely myself along with a few others, but all of us without exception desire to be happy. Unless we knew this with sure knowledge, we would not want it with so sure a will. (10.21.31)

Once more Augustine suggests that we know what "happiness" means and that we desire to be happy because all of us have experienced it. However, in not telling us where or when our "earlier" experience of happiness occurs, he leaves open the possibility that this experience might have occurred "in Adam" and that any of the four theories of the origin of the soul that he considers might be correct.

Instead of dwelling on the Neoplatonic point that knowing what "happiness" means presupposes an earlier experience of the happy life, Augustine embraces the equally familiar Aristotelian claim that even when we pursue different ways of life, all of us want to be happy.[73] For example, if two individuals are asked whether they want to be soldiers, one of them might reply that he does and the other that he does not. However, both of them want to be happy; and both want to pursue different vocations in order to be happy. Thus, one finds joy in one way of living; and the other finds it by pursing a different path (10.21.31). However, all of us agree that we want to be joyful, where the joy we long to embrace is called "the happy life." Although one of us seeks it in one way and the other seeks it in a different way, all of us strive to have joy. This leads Augustine to conclude from this fact that joy is in the memory and that it is "recognized when the words 'happy life' are heard" (10.21.31).

Though Augustine believes that all of us remember the happy life, he does not believe that all of us are happy (10.22.32). The recollection of the happy life is the epistemic framework within which we can ask about the relation between God and the soul; and without this framework, we would be unable to undertake the journey toward the God that we have forgotten. Yet Augustine insists that the joy we seek is not granted to the wicked, but only to those who worship God for his own sake and for whom God himself is joy. Thus he tells us,

> This is the happy life, to rejoice over you, to you, and because of you: this it is, and there is no other. Those who think that there is another such life pursue another joy and it is not true joy. Yet their will is not turned away from a certain image of joy. (10.22.32)

Augustine is committed to the view that whatever joy we pursue, it stands in an imagistic relation with joy as the highest level of the ontological continuum that our search for God presupposes. However, he also calls our attention to a transcendent dimension of joy that manifests the grace of God. Though Augustine's recollection of joy generates the epistemic framework within which his thought develops, he experiences the transcendent side of joy only when God addresses him directly (10.21.31). God has granted him joy of this kind in Milan and Ostia, and he describes his relation to joy in a fashion that reflects these earlier experiences (10.22.32). Thus he says, "This is the happy life, to rejoice over you, to you, and because of you: this it is, and there is no other" (10.22.32).

By moving in this direction, Augustine does not forget about the semantical and the epistemic frameworks within which he works. The immanent side of joy and happiness are accessible within this context, and he is able to climb toward it by using a Neoplatonic ladder. However, the transcendent dimension of these same experiences requires a divine interjection (7.10.16; 7.14.23; 10.22.32). As a consequence, Augustine distinguishes between true and false joy, not only by distinguishing joy from a certain image of it, but also by contrasting followers of God from those who turn away from him (10.22.32). The Neoplatonic orientation toward the happy life is a matter of the intellect, while the Christian response to it depends upon an orientation of the will. Augustine discovers this experientially in the garden in Milan (8.12.29), and he expresses it reflectively by distinguishing between those who embrace the happy life from those who merely seek an image of it (10.23.33). In this way, his discussion of the nature of memory becomes once more a reflective image of his earlier experience.

At this juncture, Augustine must face the problem of binding the immanent and transcendent dimensions of his analysis together. In beginning to do so, he suggests that our recollection of happiness is a function of the intellect, while our commitment to it is an expression of the will. As a way of developing this point, Augustine asks,

> Is it uncertain, then, that all men desire to be happy, seeing that they do not truly desire the happy life, who do not desire to have joy in you, which is the only happy life? Or do all men indeed desire this? But, since "the flesh lusts against the spirit, and the spirit against the flesh," so that they do not do what they wish, do they fall down to what they are able to take, and are satisfied with this? (10.23.33)

Augustine responds to these questions by taking four steps that lead beyond his memory toward the transcendent side of God. The first step broadens his definition of happiness and places this richer conception of it within the context of both the will and the intellect. The second deals with the problem of why we turn away from God in spite of our vague awareness of God's existence. The third focuses on how we come to know the one from whom we have turned away experientially. And the fourth considers the question of how God makes this knowledge possible by speaking to us directly. In discussing these issues, Augustine not only completes his account of the nature of memory as a condition that makes the knowledge of God possible; but also constructs a reflective image of his earlier experience.

Augustine broadens his definition of happiness by connecting joy with Truth. He asks whether we would rather rejoice in Truth than falsehood, and he replies that we would no more hesitate to say this than that we would hesitate to say that we desire to be happy. On this basis, he defines the happy life as "joy in the truth." (10.23.33). Thus he exclaims: "This happy life all men desire; this life which alone is happy all men desire; all men desire joy in the truth" (10.23.33).[74]

Augustine has known many men who want to deceive others, but none who wants to be deceived (10.23.33). Yet this leads him to ask, "Where then have they known this happy life, except where they knew truth as well?" (10.23.33). Augustine responds that when a human being loves the happy life, he loves the truth and that her or she would not love the truth unless there was some knowledge of it in their memories (10.23.33). Once more, Augustine points to a "prior" awareness of the happy life, which he now identifies with truth; and he does this without defending a particular theory about the origin of the soul and without overriding his earlier suggestion that we are happy in Adam, in whom the image of God has not been effaced.

If those who want to deceive others presuppose knowledge of the truth, why do they not rejoice in the truth; and why are they unhappy? Augustine tells us that unhappiness results when a man turns away from God and turns toward finite things instead (10.20.29; 10.23.33). Yet why do we turn away from God who can be identified with the Truth that we can remember? Augustine says:

> It is because [we] are more strongly taken up with other things, which have more power to make [us] wretched, than has that which [we] remember so faintly to make [us] happy. Yet a little while there is light among men. Let [us] walk, let [us] walk, lest the darkness overtake [us]. (10.23.33)

In this passage, Augustine brings the cognitive and the volitional dimensions of his argument together by suggesting that our faint recollection of the happy life is not sufficient to overcome our infinite desire for finite things.

After the fall, this infinite desire displaces our longing for God (10.24.35); and it leads to a forgetfulness of God that manifests itself on two levels. From an epistemic point of view, the fallen soul retains only a faint memory of God; and from a volitional perspective, it turns away from God to embrace a world of its own. In the first case, we have forgotten God intellectually; in the second, we have forgotten him volitionally. Though both kinds of forgetfulness presuppose that we remember God in the sense that we remember that we have forgotten him, Augustine insists that this memory is faint, on the one hand, and that it is misdirected on the other.

The first kind of forgetfulness is privative, which points to the truth of the claim that Augustine should have given an account of the nature of forgetfulness as a privation of memory. However, the second kind of forgetfulness is performative, which suggests that the forgetfulness of God involves a volitional orientation away from him, first toward finite things, and then toward the *nihil* out of which these things are created. Thus, forgetfulness is not only a privation of memory, but also a window through which we fall toward nothingness (2.10.18; 10.23.34). Yet when conversion occurs at both the intellectual and the volitional levels, it also becomes a window through which we can return to God. In order to point to this window, Augustine reminds those who have turned away from God that there will be light in the world for a little while, and that they need to walk in it so darkness will not overtake them.[75]

Augustine continues to call our attention to the volitional side of forgetfulness by asking why truth begets hatred, and he also asks why the one who preaches the truth has become an enemy to those who remember the happy life. The reason is that those who love something other than the truth want what they love to be the truth; and because they do not want to be deceived, they refuse to admit that they have been deceived about the nature of truth (10.23.34). Augustine elaborates this point by claiming,

> they sometimes hate the truth for the sake of what they love instead of truth. They love the truth because it brings light to them; they hate it in as much as it reproves them. Because they do not wish to be deceived but wish to deceive, they love it when it shows itself to them, and they hate it when it shows them to themselves. (10.23.34)

The problem at this stage of the argument is existential rather than theoretical. Those who do not want to be exposed by the truth are often made manifest against their will, while Truth itself is not made manifest to them. The fallen soul desires to remain hidden behind the fig leaves that cover its sin,[76] but it does not desire that anything remain hidden from it. However, judgment is rendered against the soul that attempts to hide from God; and the cognitive import of this judgment is that though it is not hidden from the Truth, the Truth is hidden from it. On the other hand, the fact remains that even in its fallen condition, the soul prefers to have joy in what is true rather than in what is false. Thus, Augustine points beyond creation and the fall to conversion and fulfillment by claiming, "Happy, therefore, will it be, when there is no obstacle in between and it shall find joy in that sole truth by which all things are true" (10.23.34).

In the third stage of his argument, Augustine turns to the question of how we come to know God experientially. In one of the classic passages of the *Confessions*, he exclaims:

> Behold, how far within my memory have I traveled in search of you, Lord, and beyond it I have not found you! Nor have I found anything concerning you except what I have kept in memory since I first learned of you. For since I learned of you, I have not forgotten you. Wheresoever I found truth, there I found my God,

truth itself, and since I first learned the truth I have not forgotten it. Therefore, ever since I learned about you, you abide in my memory, and I find you there when I recall you to mind and take delight in you. (10.24.35)

At the earlier stages of his analysis of the nature of memory, Augustine says that all of us remember God in the sense that we remember that we have forgotten him (10.24.35). This implies that we have a faint recollection of God because we have been created in God's image and because the created relation between God and the soul has not been effaced by the fall. Yet now Augustine moves beyond these minimal claims about his knowledge of God in four ways. First, he says that what he knows about God has been kept in his memory since he first learns of him. Second, he claims that since he learns of God, he has not forgotten him. Third, he tells us that wherever he finds Truth, he finds God, and that since he first learns the Truth he has not forgotten it. Finally, he says that ever since he learns about God, God abides in his memory and that he finds him there when he calls him to mind.

There is a sense in which Augustine knows about God simply because he is a human being in whom the image of God has not been effaced, and there is another sense in which he knows about God since he first learns about him in childhood (10.24.35). However, Augustine's claims about his knowledge of God point beyond the doctrine of recollection and beyond the early stages of his religious education to the episodic moments in which he learns about God in the mystical experiences that he recounts in Book VII (7.10.16). In those experiences, Augustine does not learn about God by gathering and collecting what has been scattered and neglected, or by reflecting upon what his mother and others within the Christian community have taught him (7.10.16), but by turning to his own experience. In the final analysis, learning about God requires divine illumination, where illumination outstrips recollection, performs an important soteriological function, and allows God to abide within the soul to which he manifests himself (10.25.36).

Memory gives Augustine access to the immanent side of God, and illumination gives him access to God's transcendent side. In the first case, he remembers a nonfallen relation to God that allows him to have a faint recollection of God (7.17.23); in the second, he encounters God as the standard of Truth that makes his intellectual conversion possible (7.10.16). There is also a voluntaristic dimension at this stage of the argument that reflects Augustine's Christian conversion. In the garden in Milan, Augus-

tine finds God by responding to a voice that addresses him from beyond
a garden wall (8.12.29). Now speaking and hearing come to the center of
our attention once more when Augustine says,

> Where then did I find you, so that I might learn to know you?
> You were not in my memory before I learned to know you. Where
> then have I found you, if not in yourself and above me? There is
> no place, both backward do we go and forward, and there is no
> place. Everywhere, O Truth, you give hearing to all who consult
> you, and at one and the same time you make answer to them all,
> even as they ask about varied things. You answer clearly, but all
> men do not hear you clearly. All men ask counsel about what
> they wish, but they do not all hear what they wish. Your best
> servant is he who looks not so much to hear what he wants to
> hear, but rather to want what he hears from you. (10.26.37)

The voice of God rather than Neoplatonic recollection is the focus of
Augustine's reflections at this juncture. Though he remembers the immanent side of God as a condition that makes it possible for him to look for
the one he has forgotten (10.26.37), forgetfulness becomes a window
through which the transcendent side of God manifests itself, not only as
Truth, but also as the omnipresent voice that speaks to his heart (10.26.37).
Yet Augustine is also careful to say that God transcends the distinction
between the immanent and the transcendent sides of his nature and that
there is no place within which he can be confined. As a consequence,
language about God must be stretched to the breaking point if we are to
speak about him adequately,

The God who transcends the mind in Books VII, VIII, and IX
(7.10.16; 8.12.29; 9.10.24) is the experiential correlate of the transcendent
side of God to which Augustine refers in Book X (10.26.37), and his
relation to God's transcendent dimension is a condition for and an image
of the experiences he recounts in those earlier contexts. Though he can
remember God's immanent side through recollection, illumination by the
light of truth and transformation by the voice of the divine teacher are
necessary if the intellectual and the volitional conversions that Augustine
recounts in these earlier contexts are to be possible.[77] An encounter with
the God beyond the mind must also be repeatable if Augustine is to move
beyond a faint image of God, and beyond the experiential episodes in
Milan and Ostia, to the kind of intellectual and volitional relationship
with God to which he is calling our attention in the reflective books of

the *Confessions*. In these last four Books of the text, Augustine enacts what he describes in Book VII–IX, pointing to the permanent possibility of an intellectual and a volitional relationship with the ground of his existence.

Having moved from the nature of memory to a faint recollection of the happy life, from the memory of the happy life to a recollection of God's immanent side, and from a memory of the immanent side of God to an encounter with the God beyond the mind, Augustine admits that he has loved God belatedly (10.21.38). Though God is "within," Augustine is outside himself; and as a consequence, he looks for God among the things that God has created. Augustine's willful preoccupation with finite things has caused him to "rush headlong" toward finite things, where he forgets God by falling away from him. Augustine is not a character in a Platonic recollection myth who forgets what he once knows, but a protagonist in a Christian drama who chooses to turn away from the ground of his existence. Yet there is a remedy for Augustine's fragmented condition, and he reminds us of it by remembering his intellectual conversion in Milan (7.10.16) and his Christian conversion in the garden soon afterwards (8.12.29). He writes,

> You have called to me, and have cried out, and have shattered my deafness. You have blazed forth with light, and have shone upon me, and you have put my blindness to flight! You have sent forth fragrance, and I have drawn in my breath, and I pant after you. I have tasted you, and I hunger and thirst after you. You have touched me, and I burn for your peace. (10.27.38)

If Augustine is to overcome forgetfulness, something other than recollection is necessary. Indeed, he must apprehend God as the standard of truth; and he must hear the voice of God directly. What happens to Augustine in Milan (7.10.16) are not isolated episodes, but autobiographical reflections of the structure of consciousness. Memory is the ontological condition for the possibility of Augustine's intellectual and moral conversions, but it is also a reflective image of the phenomenon that occurs when Augustine sees the light of truth and responds to the voice of God that addresses him directly. Memory and forgetfulness are both the ground and the reflection of Augustine's earlier experience; and in his analysis of them, he brings experience and reflection together as images of one another. Thus, he forges a unity between the experiential and the reflective dimensions that the text before us exemplifies.

AUGUSTINE'S SPIRITUAL CONDITION (10.28.39–10.41.66)

At the end of his account of the nature of memory, Augustine returns to the experiential dimension of his journey by focusing his attention on his spiritual condition when he writes the *Confessions*. Thirteen years have passed since the death of his mother in Ostia (9.11.27), and he has now become a Bishop of the Catholic Church in North Africa.[78] Yet even though he has moved toward fulfillment by participating in the mystical experience in Ostia (9.10.24) and by beginning to serve the Christian community of which he becomes a part at the end of Book IX, Augustine has still not reached the end of his journey.[79] Furthermore, he suggests that he will not be able to do so until he cleaves to God with the whole of his being. In the meantime, he is a burden to himself, and the chasm between himself and God remains so wide that he is in doubt about the final victory (10.28.39).

Thirteen years after his conversion, Augustine remains a convalescent who must depend completely on God's cleansing power. God is the Physician; he is the sick man. God is merciful; Augustine needs mercy. And however embarrassing this fact may be to Neoplatonists, the one who has participated in more than one mystical experience is floundering in a sea of adversities that makes "shipwreck of endurance." As Augustine says more than once, "The life of man upon the earth is a trial" (10.28.39). The author of the *Confessions* is preparing us for the account of his present spiritual condition; and he does not wish to conceal the struggles with which he must still contend, which are unavoidable, ever changing, and the ceaselessly recurring background of life. Augustine's only hope rests in God; and this leads him to say, "Give what you command and command what you will" (10.29.40). What God commands is continence, but no one is capable of exercising it unless God makes it possible for him to do so (10.29.40).

The concept of continence is broader than the concept of chastity, and it points to the need for self-control in every dimension of human existence. Continence binds up the fragments of Augustine's fragmented existence and brings him back to unity with God. In doing so, continence is a consequence of the moment of conversion in which the (finite-infinite) being that has attempted to become infinite in its own right returns to itself to embrace its finitude (10.30.41).[80] Having been created, having fallen, and having been converted, Augustine longs for fulfillment that expresses itself in an increasing degree of self-control that God makes possible.

Even though Augustine makes progress as he moves from conversion to fulfillment, progress is possible only because he continues to struggle with the sins that remain even after sin as a fundamental condition has been overcome in the garden in Milan (8.12.29). Augustine's orientation toward God has changed as a result of his conversion, but the habits of a lifetime constitute a problem that he must continue to confront. The transition from conversion to fulfillment begins in Book IX, continues experientially in Book X, and expresses itself reflectively in Books X–XIII. It is the account of Augustine's sins, of his longing for fulfillment, and of his progress toward self-control to which we now turn and about which Augustine says, "Give what you command, and command what you will."

Augustine follows a customary outline in discussing his spiritual condition, confessing his sins under three headings. First, he considers the lust of the flesh (10.30.40–10.33.50); then he focuses on the lust of the eyes (10.34.51–10.35.57); and finally, he calls our attention to the pride of life (10.36.58–59).[81] These phrases point to a hierarchy of levels, the second and third of which are more serious than the first. Moving up the ladder that these distinctions presuppose, Augustine begins with the body, turns toward the mind, and finally focuses his attention on the will. The order in which he proceeds makes it clear that his most serious problem is neither bodily nor mental, and that willfulness remains the central issue in his account of the relation between God and the soul.

Touching, tasting, smelling, hearing, and seeing are the five categories under which Augustine discusses the lust of the flesh. These categories reflect the activity of the five senses, where Augustine begins with touching and with the problem of fornication in which it can express itself. From the time of his conversion, Augustine not only abstains from fornication, but refrains from committing himself to marriage as well. Yet he emphasizes the fact that the life of chastity that he embraces is a divine gift rather than a human achievement. By accepting this gift, he is not following a Neoplatonic dictum to reject the body, but using his body to express the grace of God (10.30.41).

Despite the fact that he turns away from it, Augustine does not minimize the temptations that sexuality poses. Old habits do not vanish immediately; and in Augustine's case, they continue to plague him thirteen years after his conversion. Intellectual and volitional transformations do not cancel suppressed physiological needs, and the images of past sexual acts persist in Augustine's memory with lasting consequences. These images surge into his mind when he is awake and asleep; and though they have no power over him when he is attentive, he admits that in sleep they bring him pleasure, arousing "consent and something very like the deed itself" (10.30.41). In cases of this kind, images have so much power over his soul and his flesh that they persuade him to do in sleep what he would never do when he is awake. Thus he asks, "At such times am I not myself, O Lord my God?"

There is a great difference in Augustine between times when he is awake and times when he sleeps. When he is awake, reason makes it possible for him to resist temptations; but when he is asleep, reason seems to be just as asleep as he is. On the other hand, Augustine wonders why he can sometimes resist temptations even when he is asleep; for this suggests that reason is present in his sleeping state after all. This is not the only place where presence and absence emerge as dominant themes in the *Confessions*. In an earlier context, Augustine is perplexed about whether what we have learned is in our memory; and he moves from claiming that it is, to suggesting that it is not, to claiming that it both is and is not. At this third level, what we have forgotten poses the task of uncovering scattered memories from the caverns in which they are hidden (10.18.27).

In the case before us, Augustine claims that there is such a great difference between the strength of reason when he is awake and when he is asleep that when he succumbs to temptation in sleep, he returns to wakefulness with a clear conscience. In fact, he concludes that what happens to him in sleep is not something that he does, but something done in him over which he has only limited control, but over which he grieves (10.30.41). The sins he has in mind are sexual; and they have left their marks on his soul because of his previous behavior. This is the reason that the sexual habits of Augustine's past become operative when he is asleep. However, when Augustine acts in accord with them, the acts in question are not direct expressions of his will, but expressions of patterns of action to which he has become accustomed. It is for this reason that he claims that what happens while he is asleep is not what he does, but something done to him, however much me may grieve over them.[82]

Augustine believes that God can heal the diseases of his soul even when they express themselves only in sleep. He also believes that God can do this, not only in this life, but also at the very moment in which he is writing about the issue in question (10.30.42). Yet it is important to notice that in making these claims, Augustine not only subordinates the body to the soul, but also subordinates both the soul and the body to himself. In praising God for what he can accomplish with respect to the problem of sexuality, he asks that his soul be permitted to follow himself as he reaches for God; and he concludes his remarks about the problem before us by claiming,

> . . . Make perfect in me your mercies, even unto the fullness of peace, which my inward and outward members will have with you, when "death is swallowed up in victory." (10.30.42)

In this repetition of his earlier request that God make perfect what he has already begun in him, Augustine does not identify himself exclusively with his soul, but anticipates the resurrection in which both the inward and the outward dimensions of his being will participate in the perfection of God.

Having dealt with the problem of sexuality, Augustine now turns to the sense of taste and to the problems of eating and drinking that pertain to it. He tells us that these problems will continue to confront him until God gives him an incorruptible body that will last forever. Yet for the moment, his habits press in upon him; and he responds to them by carrying on what he calls a "daily warfare by fastings" (10.31.43). God has taught Augustine to regard food as medicine, where even the food that he eats becomes a symbol for what brings healing to the soul. Nevertheless, a problem arises about his relation to eating and drinking that Augustine cannot resolve. When he passes from being empty to being full, this transition brings pleasure, where bodily health is the end that eating and drinking are supposed to satisfy. However, the process of moving toward health brings pleasure and often takes precedence over the goal it is intended to reach (10.31.44).

Here Augustine faces a problem that reminds us of the pear-stealing episode (2.4.9), where this problem can be understood as a condition that makes the earlier problem possible and that reflects its structure at the distinctively reflective level. In the orchard of his neighbor, Augustine loves the act of stealing rather than its object (2.4.9); but now he discovers that this act presupposes the passage from emptiness to self-accentuation. The food necessary for health is not sufficient for pleasure, but it is often unclear whether we continue to eat from necessity or for its own sake (10.31.44). This fact makes the passage from emptiness to fullness ambiguous: on the one hand, it can be an appropriate culmination of a natural human desire; on the other hand, it can be an illegitimate transition from will to willfulness.

Both the pear-stealing episode in which Augustine and his friends both steal and taste the pears and the problem of eating in general reflect the fragmented structure of the human situation, and there is no straightforwardly rational solution for either problem. Augustine sees the analogy between the two cases, but he is uncertain about how to respond to it. Thus, it is not surprising that he says,

> The unhappy soul finds cheer in this uncertainty, and in it prepares an excuse and a self-defense. It rejoices that what suffices to maintain health is not evident, so that under pretense of health it may disguise a pursuit of pleasure. (10.31.44)

Adam and Eve look for an excuse for eating forbidden fruit (2.6.12), and Augustine tries to shift the blame for the pear-stealing episode by saying seven times, "I would have never done it alone (2.8.16)." Yet neither fig leafs nor excuses can conceal the fundamental flaw in human nature. This flaw often deflects us from the goal of our natural and spiritual intentions to a preoccupation with the means for achieving it.

When Adam and Eve hide from God, he demands that they abandon their fig leaves. In Augustine's case, and in words that reflect the biblical passage that he reads in the garden in Milan, God's voice demands that Augustine put off "surfeiting and drunkenness" (8.12.29). Augustine says that drunkenness does not trouble him but that overabundance of food sometimes does. Nevertheless, he responds with confidence that God will be merciful so that this problem "may be put far from me" (10.31.45). In the Garden in Milan, Augustine puts on a new garment, and this new garment not only reverses the relation between the finite and the infinite dimensions of his soul, but also allows him to embrace continence for the first time (8.12.29).[83] Thirteen years later, he tells us that continence is a gift from God; and as he longs to receive this gift again, he continues to hear God speaking in the words of the Bible: "Do not go after your lusts, but turn away from your own will."[84] As a different biblical text also assures him, "For neither if we eat shall we have the more, nor if we do not eat shall we have the less."[85]

These biblical passages put the problem that occupies Augustine in perspective. The fundamental issue with which he is confronted is the lust of the flesh rather than the food he eats or refrains from eating. Yet Augustine also hears another voice that generalizes these earlier admonitions. This time it comes from the Epistle to the Philippians, where Paul says,

> For I have learned in whatever state I am to be constant therein . . . and I have known how both to abound and how to suffer need . . . I can do all things in him who strengthens me.[86]

From a cosmological point of view, both Paul and Augustine have been made from dust; and from a soteriological point of view, they have become dust by turning away from God. In the first case, they can do nothing apart from the one who has brought them into existence; in the second case, God redeems them from the dust into which they have fallen. And as they both continue to depend upon God, they can do all things through the one who strengthens them.[87] In this passage, the transitions from creation to the fall, from the fall to conversion, and from conversion to fulfillment are recapitulated as the pivotal themes around which Augustine's reflections turn.

In bringing his discussion of the problem of eating and drinking to a conclusion, Augustine's use of allegorical discourse that he learns from Ambrose serves him well. He tells us that he does not fear the uncleanness of meat, but only the corruption of an incontinent appetite. The desire for food is not a problem considered in itself, but becomes a problem only when it turns us away from God (10.31.46). Augustine's attitude about this question is typical of his appraisal of nature: Nature is good in itself, but it is a source of temptation when it ceases to point beyond itself toward its creator.

Augustine cannot deal with the problem of consumption as decisively as with the issue of fornication. He can abandon fornication once for all, but eating and drinking pose problems that require constant attention. As he says himself, "The bridle put upon the throat must be held with both moderate looseness and moderate firmness" (10.31.47). Augustine's conversion in the garden transforms him completely, and this crucial act requires no repetition (8.12.29). Yet the price he pays for being Adam's descendent is a daily struggle with temptation. Augustine places himself in the space between God and the soul by embracing this conflict; and he does so, even though he can never settle the problems it raises once for all (10.31.47).

When Augustine turns away from the problem of eating and drinking to the sense of smell, he claims at the outset that the appeal of odors does not trouble him much. In this case, presence and absence do not pose a problem. Augustine says, "When they are absent, I do not seek them, and when they are present, I do not reject them, but I am prepared to do entirely without them" (10.32.48). Yet Augustine also tells us that he does not trust his assessment of this problem altogether; and a certain skepticism surfaces when he admits that he might fall prey to deception in this case. He formulates the problem of deception with which he is confronted here with stark simplicity: Darkness conceals our capacities from us; our powers lie hidden unless experience brings them to light; and no one should feel secure as he faces the ambiguities of life (10.32.48). Augustine concludes that life places us in the middle ground between becoming better and becoming worse and that as we stand there, the mercy of God is our only consolation.

Having displayed psychological insight by pointing to the possibility that he might be deceived in what he says about himself, Augustine confesses that the delights of the ear once had a powerful effect upon him. However, he tells us that God has already set him free from them (10.33.49). Augustine responds to a trained voice as it sings the Word of God, but he also tries not to cling to the melodies he hears. In fact, he always attempts to free himself from singing whenever he wishes; and he insists that the words are more important than the music. In this way, he places the Word of God at a higher level than its musical expression (10.33.49). Augustine admits that music inflames him to embrace God more readily than words by themselves; but when the kinetic element in music outstrips the words and appeals to him because he is an embodied being, it inverts the proper order of his affections. In this case, he sins unknowingly by attending to the form rather than the content of what it expresses (10.33.49).

When Augustine tries to avoid this kind of deception, he errs in the direction of austerity, sometimes believing that the Church should banish the songs it has adopted. When this mood overtakes him, he embraces the suggestion of Athanasius that the inflection of voices ought to be more like speaking than singing (10.33.50). Nevertheless, Augustine remembers what the songs of the Church can mean to one who has returned to God; for immediately after his conversion, he sheds tears when he hears the hymns that celebrate the glory of God (10.33.50). Now the words move him more than the music; but on those earlier occasions, music is essential in giving him emotional access to their significance. Thus, Augustine acknowledges the utility of the custom of singing in the Church (10.33.50).

When Augustine listens to music, he vacillates ". . . between the danger of sensual expression and wholesome experience." Yet he concludes, "I am inclined . . . to approve the practice of singing in church . . . so that through the pleasure afforded the ears the weaker mind may rise to feelings of devotion" (10.33.50). Lest we believe that this remark expresses condescension, we should remember that Augustine includes himself within the group of weaker minds at an earlier stage of his development. The author of the *Confessions* never places the aesthetic dimension of experience on the same level as the religious dimension to which it points. Yet he is sensitive to the value of music, and he speaks abruptly to those who do not understand the problem with which he is struggling. Augustine addresses people of this kind by claiming:

> See how I stand! Weep with me, and weep for me, you who in this matter bring about within yourselves some good from which like deeds issue. For you who do not do this, these problems do not affect you. (10.33.50)

Finally, Augustine turns away from his readers toward God, asks God to listen, and begs him to have mercy upon him. In doing so, he also implores him to heal him because he has become an enigma to himself.

Augustine concludes his discussion of the sins of the flesh by focusing on "the pleasure of the eyes." He writes:

> The eyes love fair and varied forms and bright and beauteous colors. Let not such a thing possess my soul: may God who made these things good, yea, very good, may he possess it. He is my good, not they. Each day they affect me all the while I am awake. No rest from them is granted to me. . . . For this queen of colors, this light which bathes all the things we look upon, drops down in many ways wherever I may be throughout the day, and beguiles me while engaged in some other task and not even observing it. So strongly does it entwine itself about me, that if it is suddenly withdrawn, it is sought with longing, and if it is long absent, it causes mental depression. (10.34.51)

The auditory dimension of experience is the most important element in Augustine's *Confessions*; for it is only by speaking and hearing that he is able to make his confession to God. Nevertheless, the passage before us is a forceful expression of the centrality of vision in human experience.

The light Augustine values most is accessible only when he closes his eyes. In fact, this might lead us to believe that only a blind man can see it. In this connection, Augustine mentions Tobit,[88] Isaac,[89] and Jacob,[90] all of whom saw the Light in their blindness (10.34.52). There are two kinds of blindness that can afflict every individual. One is blindness to God, and the other is blindness to the world. Those who seek God long for an inner vision, while those who turn away from him are "blind lovers" of a merely corporeal light (10.34.52).

Even though the two kinds of light can be distinguished, Augustine does not wish to keep them in separate compartments; and he uses the auditory dimension of experience to mediate the contrast between them. In doing so, he says that those who praise God for the light that permits them to see the world can take it up into a hymn that gives them access to the Light that flows from God. Singing makes it possible for us to resist the seduction of the eyes; and it also allows us to raise our "eyes" to God, who is the source of our salvation (10.34.52).

In his discussion of the sins of the eyes, Augustine mentions artifacts that sometimes attract our attention. Clothes, shoes, vessels, pictures, and statues imitate the forms of nature; and when our eyes copy them to please ourselves, we often forsake God. In doing so, we sometimes destroy what the maker of the objects intends them to be. Yet Augustine tries to redeem the situation once more by using an auditory metaphor, raising a hymn to God for all the artifacts that the artisan makes. He also tells us that he offers a sacrifice of praise for the beautiful forms these objects reflect. The forms in question pass through the medium of the soul into the artist's hands, but they come from a higher form of beauty that exists above the mind (10.34.53).

Craftsmen discover the norm by which they judge the beauty of things in Beauty itself, but they often fail to derive a "norm for use" from this same source (10.34.53). In the first case, the problem the craftsman faces is a problem of the intellect; but in the second case, it is a problem of the will. Though Augustine understands the distinction between these two kinds of norm, he often fails to resist the entanglements of finite beauty in which he becomes enmeshed (10.34.53). Yet when his weakness captivates him, God rescues him; and he sometimes does so even when Augustine does not know it. On other occasions, Augustine admits that God's intervention is painful because finite things continue to dominate his attention (10.34.53).

Augustine's examination of the lust of the flesh begins with the problem of fornication and ends with the pleasure of the eyes. In between, he considers taste, smell, and sound as sources of temptation. Yet now Augustine turns to a level of sin that is much more complex than the one he has been considering. Sins of the flesh seek to gratify the senses, but we sometimes strive for a vain and curious desire for knowledge. In this case, we do not seek pleasure in the flesh, but attempt "to acquire new experiences through the flesh" (10.35.54). This desire is "rooted in the appetite for knowledge"; and since the eyes are the primary sense when the quest for knowledge is involved, it is called "the lust of the eyes" (10.35.54). Once more, we find that Augustine binds the soul and the body together by using metaphors, and that he moves from the first level of sins to the second by relying on metaphorical connections.

While the lust of the flesh focuses on pleasure, the lust of the eyes pursues curiosity. The desire for pleasure seeks things that are "beautiful, melodious, fragrant, tasty, and soft"; but in seeking new experiences, curiosity often seeks the contrary (10.35.55). The curious man often pursues the objects toward which his attention is oriented because he has a passion for novelty. For example, we might take pleasure in a lacerated corpse that makes us shudder. In normal circumstances, we would avoid such a sight; but when curiosity becomes our chief motivation, we flock to see it as if beauty had drawn us there (10.35.55).

At the beginning of Book X, Augustine condemns people who are curious about his spiritual condition, and he responds to them as if they had transformed him into a corpse (10.3.3). He also objects to the adolescent curiosity that he displays in visiting the theater, for the false images that he finds there turn him away from images that could have led him toward God (3.2.3; 10.35.55–10.35.57). Finally, he says that curiosity motivates us to learn about the powers of nature that have no bearing on our destiny. In doing so, they lead us away from the creator to the creature by severing the connection between them (10.35.57).

When Augustine writes the *Confessions*, science is not what it becomes in the later Middle Ages. In fact, he often associates it with astrology, on the one hand, and with soothsaying on the other (4.3.4; 4.3.5; 7.6.8; 7.6.10). Yet if Augustine could have foreseen the scientific revolution, he would have approved of it. The doctrine of creation *ex nihilo* makes it clear that creatures are not gods, as the Greek philosophical tradition claimed; and this fact opens up the possibility that the finite order can be investigated in its own right. However, there is another strand in Augustine's approach to the natural order that we must also take into account. Augustine is committed to the view that nature is a domain of symbols that points beyond itself, where this way of dealing with what has been created shifts our attention away from nature taken in itself to nature as an expression of God. Indeed, as Augustine expresses the point in (10.6.9), it is the beauty of nature that makes is possible for us to rise toward God.

When he writes Book X of the *Confessions*, Augustine is free from some of the curiosity that had captivated him at an earlier stage of his life. The theater no longer attracts him; he has no interest in astrology; and he has never sought advice from spirits or taken sacrilegious oaths

(10.35.56). Yet he still succumbs to a longing for knowledge that he does not need. For example, the anxiety with which Augustine struggles sometimes overpowers him; and it prompts him to demand signs from God as validations of God's power to sustain human existence (10.35.56).

Minute things also provoke Augustine's curiosity. Sometimes he begins by tolerating idle tales about others, but often ends by listening attentively (10.35.57). Augustine no longer goes to the circus to see a dog chasing a rabbit, but a race in the fields that occurs easily distracts him. This fact leads him to exclaim:

> When I am sitting at home and a lizard is catching flies or a spider is trapping them as they blunder into its web, how often does this catch my attention! Is the activity any different, merely because the animals are small? (10.35.57)

In these cases, Augustine moves quickly from looking at the creature to praising the creator; but he admits that it is not God who first attracts his attention. Indeed, he claims that his life is filled with trivial incidents that cause him to turn away from God; and he says that his only hope is to be found in God's infinite mercy (10.35.57).

With hope in God in the background, Augustine shifts his attention to the third level of the sins that beset him. In doing so, he focuses on the pride of life, where the problem he faces is neither bodily nor mental, but volitional. The distortion of the will is the central problem that Augustine confronts from the beginning of his life to the end, and his insistent attempts to deal with it take him beyond Plotinus to what is distinctively Christian in his thinking.[91] The problem of pride can be divided into two parts: first, Augustine considers his desire for self-vindication; then he deals with his longing for praise.

Augustine says that God has already healed him from pride of the first kind. In the garden in Milan, he has transformed him from a (finite-infinite) center of self-accentuation to a (finite-infinite) center of self-acceptance (8.12.28–8.12.30).[92] The desire for self-vindication is a particular form of the desire for self-accentuation, and Augustine rejoices that he has abandoned it for the "easy yoke" that Christ has placed around his neck. Christ himself says that his yoke is easy and that his burden is light, but Augustine discovers that this is so only when he accepts the grace of God (10.36.58).

Augustine's freedom from the desire for self-vindication points to the aspect of his moral conversion that he need never repeat. However, he still craves the love of other men and the praise it generates. Augustine knows that God resists the proud and gives grace to the humble, but he also knows that his office as a bishop complicates this problem considerably. The society in which Augustine lives requires his subordinates to love and fear him as an officeholder, and this fact leads Augustine to take pleasure in the devoted responses of his followers. Here Augustine imitates Satan and is tempted to become his comrade; for Satan's sin is not only rebellion against God, but also a desire for worship from men (10.36.59).

The language of this part of the text takes us back to the Garden of Eden,[93] and it also returns us to the vineyard where Augustine steals forbidden fruit (2.4.9). In both cases, finite beings not only try to become gods, but also crave the praise of their companions. Eve wants the approval of Satan;[94] Adam wants the approval of his wife;[95] and Augustine wants the approval of his friends (2.8.16). Pride is both a vertical and a social phenomenon; and its tragic expression not only seeks to displace God, but also tries to steal the praise that only God should receive. The theft Augustine commits in the vineyard of his neighbor requires companions (2.8.16), and the displacement of God is complete only when he secures the praise of the companions who join him in committing it.

When Augustine and his friends say, "Let's go, let's do it," (2.9.17), the performative language they use to initiate their action expresses the fact that they are companions of Adam and Eve in turning away from God. In addition, the voice that speaks through them is the voice of Satan, tricking them into believing that if they invert the order of creation, they will become gods.[96] Augustine understands the problem that the pear-stealing episode raises; and in the account of his conversion in the garden, he participates in the divine reversal of the words of Satan by putting on a new garment called, "Jesus, the Christ" (8.12.29). In this way, the words of Satan that tell us that we can become gods become the Word of God that tells us that we must become human.

Since his conversion in Milan, Augustine moves through stages in which God continues to change him, not only pointing beyond fallenness to conversion, but also pointing beyond conversion to fulfillment. Yet as he moves along this pathway, he faces a series of problems with which he continues to struggle after he has become a Christian. One of these problems manifests itself in the fact that when someone praises him for a gift that God has given him, the praise sometimes pleases him more than the gift (10.36.59). In such cases, the parishioner is superior to the bishop; for though the gift that God has bestowed upon Augustine pleases his followers, their leader sometimes derives more pleasure from the gift of praise than from the gift of God (10.36.59).

The pride that the longing for praise expresses comes to focus in an auditory metaphor when Augustine tells us that his "daily furnace is the human tongue" (10.37.60). In this way, he reasserts the primacy of speaking and hearing as the fundamental dimension of the *Confessions*. Augustine is confident that he can hold the lust of the flesh and the lust of the eyes in check by acts of the will, and he is free from the desire for riches that makes sin on all three levels possible (10.37.60). Yet he wonders how to put his resistance to the praise of others to the test. Must he lead a life that will make his followers detest him to find out whether he can live without it? This is ridiculous; for Augustine knows that he should never use the method of difference[97] to decide the issue in question. However, unless praise is absent, it is hard to know whether he is free from dependence upon it (10.37.60).

Augustine's provisional solution to this problem is to admit that praise delights him, but that the Truth delights him more. He wishes that the approval of others would not add anything to his joy about his goodness, but admits that praise increases and blame diminishes it (10.37.61). Indeed, he even has an excuse for the fact that his joy increases when the praise of other people is added to his goodness. God not only demands continence, but also righteousness; and as a consequence, God balances what he asks us to reject with what he wants us to affirm. The shift from continence to righteousness allows Augustine to focus on his neighbor and to claim that the neighbor is more important than the goodness that he praises in Augustine (10.37.61).

Augustine sees that he ought to value the truth of his neighbor's opinion more than its agreement with his own, but he is uncertain about whether he ever does this. On this matter, he knows less about himself than God does; and as a consequence, he prays, "I beseech you, my God, show me to myself, so that to my brothers, who will pray for me, I may confess what wounds I find in me" (10.37.62).[98] Once more, Augustine makes it clear that the community to which he is addressing himself at this stage of the *Confessions* is the community of Christians with whom he begins to participate in the events recorded at the end of Book IX. Yet Augustine does not stop with a prayer and with an expression of confidence that his fellow Christians will pray for him. Instead, he turns inward once more to uncover the truth about the relation between himself and others.

The impetus to do this derives from the shift in his attention from continence to righteousness. Continence tells him what he ought not to love, while righteousness tells him what he ought to love in other people (10.37.61). If we are to love our neighbors as ourselves, we must learn to balance their appraisals of us with our evaluation of ourselves. Augustine tries to do this by raising a question about the proper relation between himself and others. In doing so, he asks why unjust blame directed at another man moves him less than when the same thing happens to him (10.37.62). At this juncture, he has not succeeded in shifting from continence to righteousness and in obeying one of the two great commandments to love his neighbor as himself.[99]

Augustine does not try to solve this problem by continuing to reflect on the relation between himself and others. Rather, he deals with this problem by turning toward the relation between God and the soul that has motivated his confessions from the outset. It is within this vertical context that he must fight the battle with himself that has implications for his relation with others. At this juncture, Augustine confesses that he is poor and needy; but it is also important to notice that his condition begins to be transformed when he seeks the mercy of God (10.38.63). When he isolates himself within the vertical relation between God and the soul, he finds the kind of peace that a proud man can never understand (10.38.63).

Despite this fact, Augustine cannot escape the temptation that arises from what other people say about his conduct. This temptation arises from his love of praise, which leads him to beg for and to collect marks of approval (10.38.63). Even when he reproves himself for allowing this temptation to move him, this reproof often expresses the pride from which he is attempting to escape. Augustine tries to turn away from pride by turning inward; but when he congratulates himself for his contempt of glory, he often derives an even emptier glory (10.38.63). In this case, the egocentric predicament from which Augustine is unable to escape expresses itself in the fact that he does not glory in contempt of glory, but glories over his contempt of it.[100]

Augustine mentions another problem that is similar to the problem of false humility. In this case, he is tempted to be complacent with himself, neither pleasing nor displeasing others (10.39.64). Yet by pleasing himself in this way, Augustine knows that he is displeasing God. He does this by taking pleasure in what God gives him as if it were his own or by assuming that God gives it to him because of his own merit (10.39.64). Finally, even when he admits that the gifts of God are expressions of grace, he is often envious because the grace of God expresses itself in gifts to other people (10.39.64). Pride in the opinions of others drives Augustine back into himself to confess his sins; but when he turns inward, he finds the same pride that separates him from God. Pride in the gift of grace then drives Augustine back toward others, but it transforms the pride produced by what they say about him into envy that they have received the grace of God as well. This circular interaction between himself and others generates an abiding agitation within Augustine's soul, and only the grace of God can cure him of it.

Augustine continues to focus on grace as he summarizes the stages of his journey toward God. First he asks, "When is it that you have not walked with me, O Truth, teaching me what to shun and what to seek" (10.40.65). Then he turns toward the external world and toward the senses that give him access to it. The senses bridge the chasm between Augustine and the world that stands over against him, and they also give him access to his body and his senses (10.40.65). Then Augustine turns inward toward the recesses of his memory; and he finds that it contains a wealth of riches. Yet when he reflects on the infinite richness of memory, he becomes afraid, claiming that he can understand none of these things without God, and that God himself is not identical with any of them (10.40.65).

Augustine labors within the measureless halls of memory, distinguishing and evaluating what he finds there. He also enumerates the senses that allow him to acquire basic information; and within the measureless hall of memory, he investigates certain things, deposits others, and takes out still others (10.40.65). Yet Augustine insists that God is not identical with the ability that makes it possible for him to conduct this investigation, claiming instead that God is the abiding light that allows him to see the pathway along which he has been moving (10.40.65).

As he turns inward, Augustine not only sees the light of truth, but also hears God teaching and commanding him (10.40.65). Both visual and auditory metaphors connect God and the soul; and at this stage of his account, Augustine emphasizes the auditory dimension. As he moves up the ladder from the soul to God, Augustine can hear God speaking; and he takes pleasure in listening to the voice of God as often as he can. The voice that first speaks to him in Milan (8.12.29) now points to a Place where Augustine can find rest; and as God gathers his fragmented life together, he gives him a foretaste of peace (10.40.65).

The moments of "indescribable sweetness" to which God gives Augustine access at this juncture (10.40.65) stand in the same relation to his search for inner happiness as the vision in Milan stands in relation to the knowledge of God (8.12.29) and as the vision with Monica stands in relation to his search for the Christian community in the world (9.10.24). In all these cases, Augustine apprehends God momentarily. Yet in the first case, he calls away from God through the weight of his sin; and in the third, he falls back into ordinary things, drawn by his weight and swallowed up again and again by his usual ways of being. These matters are the temptations about which he is speaking, which are conditions in which he is not willing to be, but which stand in contrast with an abiding relationship with God that he has not been able to attain.[101]

CHRIST, THE MEDIATOR (10.42.67–10.43.70)

At the end of Book VII, Augustine realizes that he needs a mediator if he is to find the pathway to God (7.19.25); and in Book VIII, he finds him when he puts on a new garment called "Jesus, the Christ" (8.12.29). The mediator that he seeks in Milan is both God and man; and as a consequence, he is able to unite the temporal and the eternal, even though we must always keep them apart from a conceptual point of view. The unity of God and man in the mediator permits Augustine to reject the Phontian, Arian, and Plotinian view that he is incompetent because he is only human (10.43.68).[102] In the second half of Book X, Augustine's aim is not to prove the existence of God from the side of the world or to find the way to him, but starting from there, to discover how the world can conform to the demands of God as revealed in Christ (9.13.34–37). In his first discussion of our need for a mediator (7.19.25), the question is whether the mediator is God; the question here is whether he is human (10.42.67).[103]

As Augustine brings Book X to a conclusion, and as he looks once more for a mediator who is both divine and human, he asks, "Whom should I find to reconcile me to you? Was I to turn to angels? By what prayers? By what rites?" (10.42.67). Then he replies,

> Many men who strive to return to you, and are unable to do so by their own strength, have tried such things, so I have heard, and have fallen victim to desire for curious visions, and have been accounted fit for delusions. Lifted aloft, they have sought you by pride of learning, thrusting out their chests rather than smiting their breasts. By similarity of heart, they have attracted to themselves fellow conspirators and partners in their pride, "the powers of the air," by whose potent magic they have been deceived. For

they were seeking a mediator by whom they might be cleansed,
and none such was there. (10.42.67)

Augustine rejects this way of returning to God because it exhibits the
pride of the philosophers. Pride in their learning makes philosophers
susceptible to a "desire for curious visions" that leads to delusions and
make them subject to "powers of the air" whose "potent magic" deceives
them (10.42.67). Following an exclusively intellectual pathway also leads
these men to embrace a deceptive mediator. Pride seeks a mediator who
will cleanse it from unrighteousness, but the mediator it finds is Satan
rather than Christ (10.42.67). The devil disguises himself as an angel of
light,[104] and he becomes a counterfeit version of the Light of Truth that
Augustine encounters in Milan (8.12.29), and that he sees again when he
moves beyond his memory to the God beyond the mind (10.17.26). The
devil who identifies himself with counterfeit light is able to lure those
who are proud because he imitates God by not having a body (10.42.67);
and since the typical Neoplatonist wants to escape from the body, it is
natural that the mediator they seek does not have one.[105]

The Neoplatonic way of returning to God imitates the pathway that
Augustine follows; and like all imitations, it contains a grain of truth. The
Neoplatonist realizes that a "'mediator between God and man' must have
something like to God and something like to men" (10.42.67). If he were
only like man, he would be too far from God; and if he were only like
God, he would be too far from us. Yet the Neoplatonists only find a
mediator that reflects their pride. The only thing that he has in common
with man is his sin, and the only thing he has in common with God is
not having a body. This allows Satan to boast that he is immortal; but
because of his rebellion, he shares condemnation with his followers
(10.42.67). In this case, as in every other, the root of sin is an act the will;
and it leads to condemnation, whether the one who commits it is embodied or not.

In the garden in Milan, Augustine finds a mediator, who stands in
between our sin and the righteousness of God (8.12.29). Now he indicates how mediation is possible by formulating the conditions that allow
the mediator to play his mediating role. He writes,

The true mediator . . . appeared between mortal sinners and the
immortal just one, mortal with men, just with God. Because the
wages of justice is life and peace, he thus appeared that, being
joined through justice to God, he might make void the death of

> sinners now justified. . . . For as man, he is mediator, but as the
> Word, he is in no middle place, since he is equal to God, and
> God with God, and together one God. (10.43.68)

Insofar as Christ is to be identified with the Word of God, he is identical with God; and insofar as he is a man, he can serve as the mediator between God and man. At this stage of his inquiry, Augustine needs an embodied mediator to make it possible for him to deal with the temptations with which he is confronted.[106]

Augustine can put on Jesus, the Christ (8.12.29) because he is both victor and victim, where the crucial transaction has both analogical and dialectical dimensions. The dialectical dimension emerges when Christ becomes the victor because he is the victim, and it sustains itself when he stands before God as a priest because he first stands before us as a sacrifice (10.43.69). These dialectical transitions, which combine the ransom theory with the atonement theory of the crucifixion, make conversion possible; and when we think about them, our thought becomes a reflective image of the experience in the garden to which they point.

We are able to participate in these transitions because we can stand in an analogical relation, first with the mediator, and then with Augustine in the moment of redemption. When Augustine puts on a new garment, the transition within his soul reflects the dialectic of redemption; for in victimizing his pride, and in embracing his finitude, Augustine is reestablished as a victor made in the image of God.[107] On this occasion, Augustine's experience reflects the death and the resurrection of Christ; and his attempt to trace out the structure that makes this experience possible permits him to become an image of it at the distinctively reflective level.

Augustine tells us that without the incarnation, he would have despaired. He also says that the medicine of God brings healing to his soul because Christianity contains something that Neoplatonism lacks. When Augustine remembers the words from the preface to the Gospel of John, he finds the key to the kind of mediation that overcomes the separation between God and the soul. Unlike the devil who sins, Jesus takes our sins upon himself; and unlike the devil who is unembodied, and is thus unable to help us deal with our temptations, Christ is embodied to make salvation and fulfillment possible (10.43.69).[108]

Before Augustine appropriates the incarnation as the ground and as the reflection of his earlier experience in the garden, the burden of his sins almost drives him into the wilderness, where he can continue to carry on the inward struggle with his sins. Yet the voice that has spoken to him before speaks again, forbidding him to go and comforting him by saying, "Therefore Christ died for all: that they who live may now live not to themselves but to him who died for them" (10.43.70).[109] Just as the final paragraph of Book IX leads to his attempt to conform to the commands of Christ, so the final paragraph of Book X leads him to embrace the task that is to be distinctive of his life as a Bishop.

Augustine finally casts all his cares upon God; and by beginning to reflect on the new life that he will live, he tells us that he wants to contemplate God's Law, moving in this way from the knowledge of the incarnated Christ to his divinity (10.43.70).[110] Proceeding in this way involves coming to know the hidden treasures of the Scriptures (10.43.70). In this way, the great rhetorician is preparing us for the exposition of Scripture that he will undertake in the last three Books of the text.

Yet having pointed to the intellectual task that he is about to undertake, elaborated the conditions that make his quest for transformation possible, Augustine remains at the existential level by celebrating the Eucharist in the final sentence of Book X.[111] First he tells us that Christ has redeemed him by his blood; and then he says,

> Let not the proud calumniate me, for I think upon my ransom, and I eat and drink, and share it with others, and as a pauper I desire to be filled from him among those who eat and are filled. . . . (10.43.70)

Earlier Augustine says that even though he catches a glimpse of God, he is unable to be filled with him (7.17.23). Now he says that he wants to be filled by participating in the sacraments of the Church and by interpreting Scripture (10.43.70). Finally, he returns to the first chapter of Book I by quoting the words, "And they shall praise the Lord that seek him" (10.43.70). In this way, he brings the analysis of memory and the confession of his sins to a conclusion and brings them both into a positive relation with his experiential journey.

2

The Problem of Time (Book XI)

Augustine's discussion of the nature of time calls our attention to the contrast between time and eternity and places it within a context in which both issues are crucial themes. In addition, Augustine's analysis of the nature of time is usually considered in abstraction from the larger context in which he embeds it.[1] However, the difficulty with approaching Augustine's conception of time in this way is that he develops it not only by discussing the contrast between time and eternity, but also by engaging in an act of confession that binds time and eternity together. If we are to understand his reasons for calling our attention to the paradoxes of time, we must approach it as part of a comprehensive way of dealing with the relations between time and eternity and between God and the soul.

In the last three Books of the *Confessions*, Augustine turns his attention to the exposition of Scripture, where the first themes that he considers are creation *ex nihilo* and the speaking Word that makes creation possible. Divine creation is one of the central themes of the *Confessions*, and the speaking Word is the generative power that brings the temporal order into existence from absolute nonbeing. The mystery of eternity and the intelligibility of the world are brought together by the power of creation that expresses itself in an act of speaking. Yet this creative act also leads to a philosophical problem with a mysterious dimension of its own. Having claimed that God creates the world *ex nihilo* and that a radical contrast obtains between time and eternity, Augustine asks and responds to a question that continues to perplex the philosophical consciousness: "What then is time? If no one asks me, I know"; but if I wish "to explain it to someone who . . . [asks] me, I do not know" (11.14.17). The remainder of Book XI is devoted to showing why this problem is so intractable, not only theoretically, but also existentially, and to point the way to a resolution of it.

Augustine's discussion of the nature of time displays spatial, temporal, and eternal dimensions, all of which must be taken into account if we are to understand the problem before us. When he distinguishes the past, the present, and the future and takes up the question of how time can be measured, Augustine spatializes the temporal continuum (11.11.13; 11.16.21).[2] When he asserts that the modes of time are aspects of the soul that express themselves in memory, apprehension, and expectation, he temporalizes his earlier spatialization to give it human significance.[3] And when he speaks about himself as stretched out, gathered up, and stretching forth toward God, he eternalizes time as the existential and reflective medium in which he seeks to understand the ground of his existence.[4] Taken together, these ways of understanding the nature of time constitute a place that grounds and reflects the stages of Augustine's journey toward God and of his encounters with him.

The spatialization of time involves a transition from the past to which Augustine gives us access in the experiential parts of the book to the framework of the past, the present, and the future in which it has its proper place. From this point of view, Books I–IX point to the past; Book X focuses on the present; and Books XI–XIII evoke the future. The temporalization of time is a different way of generalizing the earlier discussion, moving from memory as a mode of temporality to remembering, apprehending, and expecting as the wider context of which memory is a part. If memory is both an ontological condition that makes acts of remembering possible and an imagistic reflection of them, time is the condition for and image of the entire range of Augustine's experience. Finally, the eternalization of time points to the past in which Augustine is fragmented, to the present in which he is unified, and to the future in which he longs to participate. Here Augustine brings the structure of his experience and the nature of time together by developing the distinctions between being stretched out as a fallen creature, being gathered together in conversion, and stretching forth toward God as a member of a transformed community.

Augustine's analysis of the nature of time begins with a prereflective understanding of it (11.11.13) that expresses his participation in the order of creation and that points to the fact that the image of God has not been effaced. However, the paradoxes into which he is led in developing this analysis express the distention and distraction into which he falls as he reflects upon the temporal flux in which he is embedded. Against this background, the concept of time that Augustine elaborates brings the temporal flux, the distention of the soul, and a positive orientation toward God together (11.26.33) in a reflective conversion that mirrors the existential conversion of his will and his intellect. Finally, time is fulfilled by providing the matrix in which Augustine stretches forth toward God, not as distended or distracted, but extended intently toward the contemplation of God (11.29.39).

Augustine's discussion of the nature of time falls naturally into three parts: temporality is first understood as a cosmological flux of spatialized modalities; it is then interpreted as an ecstatic domain in which memory, apprehension, and expectation manifest themselves; and it is finally characterized as a window to eternity[5] in which the soul seeks contact with the One who creates and sustains it. The existential, the ecstatic, and the reflective movement from one of these stages to another propels Augustine toward God, where the presence and the absence of the Word of God enable him to interpret the biblical account of the relations between time and eternity, on the one hand, and between God and the soul on the other.

MOTIVES FOR CONFESSION (11.1.1–11.2.4)

At the beginning of Book XI, Augustine focuses our attention on his reasons for continuing the *Confessions* by asking two rhetorical questions: first, he wonders whether God is ignorant of what he says in time; and then he asks whether the creator of heaven and earth sees what is done in time only at a certain time. Though the answer to both questions is "No," they provide the context in which Augustine asks a different question about why he sets out an account of so many deeds before God. The answer to this question is that he is not attempting to teach God something that God does not know already (11.1.1), but is trying to arouse his own affections, and the affections of his readers (11.1.1), so that all of us may say what the author says in the first sentence of the book, "Great is the Lord and greatly to be praised" (11.1.1). Finally, Augustine completes his initial attempt to orient our thinking by exclaiming, "I have already said this, and I will say it again: for love of your love I perform this task" (11.1.1).

By referring to the beginning of the book, and by calling our attention to what he has said already about his reasons for writing the *Confessions*, Augustine is connecting the last three Books of the text with the first nine. As we have discovered already, he does not regard the text as a bifurcated document, but as a unified attempt to move from faith to understanding. Books I–VI describe his journey toward God; Books VII–IX indicate how he finds what he seeks; and Books X–XIII are attempts to understand what he has found. Yet it is also important to notice that by seeking to arouse his own affections and the affections of his readers toward God, Augustine is still addressing the universal audience to which he speaks in the first nine Books of the text. In Books I–IX, he attempts to lead his readers into a positive relationship with God by giving an account of his experiential journey; and in the passage before us, he gives his readers a final opportunity to embrace the standpoint of faith by attempting to arouse our affections toward the ground of our existence.[6]

Augustine moves beyond this universal audience to those who have embraced the standpoint of faith by pointing to a second motive for participating in the act of confession. Those who have undertaken the journey toward God and have found what they seek must lay bare their condition before God so that he might set them free altogether. Augustine believes that God has begun to do this already by permitting us to move beyond our fallen predicament to the conversion of our wills and our intellects, and he anticipates the day in which both dimensions of our nature are fulfilled. God makes it possible for us to accomplish the experiential dimension of this task through the seven sanctifying operations of the Holy Spirit.[7] As the Sermon on the Mount expresses the point, Christ calls us to be poor in spirit, meek, mourners, hungry and thirsty for justice, merciful, clean of heart, and peacemakers.[8] By contrast, he suggests that the intellectual dimension of the enterprise both has and is being undertaken in the analysis of memory, the problem of time, and the hermeneutics of creation. Augustine's quest for fulfillment expresses itself both experientially and intellectually, and our task in analyzing the last four Books of the text is to indicate how this is so.[9]

As we have discovered already, there is a ten to thirteen year chasm between Books IX and X of the text; but Augustine does not explain why this chasm exists until the second paragraph of Book XI (11.2.2). In this paragraph, he says that even if he had been able to fill the chasm by confessing all the considerations that have led him to preach and to dispense the sacraments to God's people, the "drops of time" are precious to him, and that he has wanted to meditate upon God's Law for a long time, confessing what he knows and what he does not know about it (11.2.2). Augustine now has a new task, and it consists in focusing his attention on the exposition of Scripture rather than on the external events of his life in this ten to thirteen year period.[10]

The fruit of Augustine's decision not to go into the desert, which he mentions at the end of Book X (10.43.70), is the exposition of the Scriptures to which he commits himself at this juncture. In addition to participating in the external events of his life after the death of his mother, Augustine has been studying the Bible;[11] and he wants to make the results of these reflections available to his readers rather than continuing to focus on the external details of his experience. The fact that Augustine proceeds in this way suggests that his intellectual conversion in Milan (7.17.23), the conversion of his will in the garden (8.12.29), and the shared mystical experience with his mother (9.10.23) are the crowning existential moments of his life and that nothing that occurs afterwards, with the exception of his present sins in Book X (10.2.2; 10.43.70) is significant enough to warrant autobiographical treatment in the episodic sense of the term.[12] As a consequence, Augustine turns away from experience to reflection, attempting to use what he has learned about the Scriptures as a way of moving from faith to understanding.

Augustine knows that he must replenish his body and his mental powers, attend to the service he owes to other men, and attend as well to what he does not owe but renders. The first two are necessary for making inquiry possible, the third is necessary for life in society, and the fourth is necessary for the humility that comes from the confession of the inner life to other Christians.[13] Against this background, Augustine says that his motive for engaging in the exposition of Scripture is that it might advance the cause of "fraternal charity" (11.2.3). At the beginning of Book X, he begins to address himself to fellow Christians (10.1.1); and he continues to do so here by turning his attention toward the Bible. In Book X, Augustine also points to the connection between the community of love to which he speaks and the problem of how to decide whether he is telling the truth in making his confessions (10.3.3; 10.41.66). Now he brings this community of love and the hermeneutics of charity that corresponds to it into relation with eternity by praying that he will not lie, and that he will neither fall into error in the exposition of Scripture or mislead other people by misusing it (11.2.3).

In speaking about his desire to turn away from the external events of his life to the exegesis of Scripture, Augustine says that he wants the free hours that flow away (*diffluere*) to be spent on nothing else but the exegesis of Scripture. He also says that at God's command, "the minutes fly away (*transvolare*)"; and he prays that from them, God will bestow upon him a time (*spatium*) for meditation on the hidden things of the Law (11.2.3). Finally, he prays that God will not close up the Books of the Law from those who knock upon it (11.2.3).

The first thing to notice about Augustine's request for a time for meditation is that the hours that flow away and the minutes that God commands are created rather than fallen. Formulated in the language of our earlier analysis, the cosmological flux with which Augustine begins his reflections about the nature of time is a (finite-infinite) matrix[14] in which every moment comes to be and passes away *ad infinitum*. This matrix is a product of God's creative act, and it must not be confused with the fallen temporality from which Augustine needs to be redeemed. Finitude considered in itself is not a negative condition, and there is no need for a finite creature to wish for liberation from it.

The second important factor about Augustine's request for a time for meditation is that it can be carved out from the cosmological flux only by the grace of God. Even though the flux is created (finite-infinite) rather than fallen (finite-infinite),[15] Augustine will be able to meditate upon the Law only if the flux is stabilized (stabililty$_1$) sufficiently so that he will be able to focus his attention on the Word of God. One of the purposes of Augustine's theory of time is to indicate how stabilization of this kind is possible, where the theory that is grounded in God's grace[16] establishes the reflective framework within which meditation can occur.

The third point to notice is that a time for meditation must be distinguished from a time of dissolution. Meditation on the Law presupposes a positive orientation toward God, while a time of dissolution results from a negative orientation toward the cosmological flux. Though the flux is created (finite-infinite) rather than fallen (finite-infinite), we fall away from God when we turn toward it and lose ourselves in it.[17] The request for a time for meditation expresses Augustine's desire to focus his attention on God and to turn away from an exclusive preoccupation with the temporal order. In this way, he attempts to move from faith to understanding, where what he wants to understand is the Word of God as it expresses itself in the Bible.

Finally, in asking that the hidden things of the Law be opened to him when he knocks, Augustine connects the final stage of his inquiry with the earlier Books of the text. First, his reference to the hidden things of the Law points to a distinction between the surface and the center of the Bible and to the biblical text as a mystery cavern that we must bend over

to enter (3.5.9). Having remained on the surface of the text when he first
attempts to read the Bible (3.5.9), and having begun to move from the
surface to the center of the text by learning how to give an allegorical
interpretation of it, Augustine asks that what might otherwise remain
hidden from him will be opened when he knocks (11.2.3). This reference
to knocking is the second way in which Augustine connects this part of
the *Confessions* with the earlier stages of his inquiry. In Book I, he says
that those who seek God shall find him (1.1.1); and in Books XII and
XIII, he reiterates this chain by placing seeking and knocking within the
biblical context that they presuppose. In this second context, we find the
promise that undergirds the journey from faith to understanding:

> Ask, and you shall receive; seek, and you shall find; knock, and
> it shall be opened to you. For everyone who asks receives, and he
> who seeks finds, and to him who knocks it shall be opened.
> (12.1.1)

The secrets of the Law about which Augustine knocks are written on
many pages, and Augustine prays that these pages will be opened to him
(11.2.3). It might seem that Augustine's expository focus is the whole
Bible, where he wants to begin with the creation of heaven and earth and
end with the eternal kingdom and the holy city (11.2.3).[18] However, in
the last three Books of the *Confessions*, he gives an interpretation of the
first chapter of Genesis rather than an exposition of the Bible as a whole.
He does this because he believes that the opening chapter of the Genesis
is a microcosmic expression of the Bible as a whole that begins with
creation and that points to a final consummation.[19]

By praying that he be permitted to undertake this task, Augustine
approaches God through the same mediator who makes it possible for
him to be converted in the garden in Milan (8.12.29). First, he tells us
that the mediator is the Word of God through whom the world is created
(11.2.4). Then he claims that this same mediator is the one who calls us
to adoption as children of God, seeking us when we do not seek him and
seeking us so that it might be possible for us to seek him (11.2.4). Third,
he says that having made adoption possible, the mediator makes interces-
sion for us as he sits on God's right hand (11.2.4). Finally, he tells us that
the mediator gives us access to the knowledge and the wisdom that are
hidden in him by making what is concealed in Scripture available to us
(11.2.4). The drama of Augustine's life is reflected in these stages, and his
exegesis of the first chapter of Genesis leads us from the moment of

creation with which this drama begins to the moment of fulfillment with which it ends. Yet as this drama begins to move toward fulfillment, why does Augustine want a time for reflection on the hidden things of the Law? The reason for this is that the Scriptures tells us many things that we could not know by ourselves.[20] Though some things in Scripture are obvious, others are not, and one of these difficult passages is the first chapter of Genesis to which Augustine turns in Books XI–XIII.[21]

It is difficult to understand the inner workings of God in the creation of the world as they are revealed in the Scriptures. Before Augustine writes the *Confessions*, Platonists had been able to know the nature and existence of God and had distinguished God from the world; but they had assumed falsely that they know the inner working of the divine mind, which they insist is subject to the same limitations as theirs. This shows itself in their rejection of the incarnation, where even though the two sides of it must be distinguished, there is no reason to believe that they cannot be united. It is also evident in the desire of the Platonists to seem wise about how things come from God and about how God values them. Yet their knowledge of God contains none of this. Augustine, by contrast, turns away from what the Platonists claim to know by setting forth the hidden things of Scripture.[22]

Yet a question arises at this point about why there are hidden things in Scripture. At least one answer is that the Scriptures are not only about the Son of God in his humanity, but also about him in his deity (11.4.4). More precisely, the difficult points about God pertain to the divine nature and the inner workings of the Godhead. The human domain involves a familiar logic, while the divine domain involves a logic that holds together what we must consider separately. Yet if we understand the hidden things of Scripture, Augustine suggests that we will come as close as possible to the perfected life of the saints (11.2.3). Peaceful satisfaction as opposed to endless inquiry is the goal of the *Confessions* (11.2.3), and Augustine points to this goal by calling our attention to the Sabbath rest (13.36.51–13.38.53), which we can reach in this life, only through the contemplation of difficult passages of Scripture.[23] Finally, it is important to notice that the praise of God to which contemplation leads (11.2.3) takes us back to the beginning of the text, fulfilling the task of praise set out in the opening lines of Book I (1.1.1).

The final stage in our discussion of Augustine's motives for confessions is to ask, what is the content of the difficult text to which we are about to turn our attention in Books XI–XIII? As we shall discover, it contains God's own account of how and why he creates the world from the beginning[24] to the emergence of the Heavenly City.[25] This account is a gift of the Holy Spirit in which God explains his relation to the world, and it differs from what we can know about God through philosophy or natural theology. It also differs from what Christ teaches us about the conditions that we must fulfill to enter God's Kingdom.[26] Instead, it is about God's relation to the world as it is revealed in Scripture and it is to be understood from the text of Genesis.[27]

CREATION AND THE SPEAKING WORD (11.3.5–11.13.16)

Plotinus once asked, "Why does the One unfold?"[28] Though we can follow the trail of creation back to God, and though Plotinus says that creation occurs because God emanates the other two hypotheses,[29] natural reason does not make is possible for us to understand why God has created time, space, multiplicity, and change. In responding to this problem, Augustine works through the first three clauses of Genesis, where he finds an account of how God creates the world through the Word out of nothing, which the Spirit perfects by turning it toward God (11.3.5). Plotinus had recognized a similar order of descent,[30] but Augustine is responding to the problem by working from an entirely new trinitarian view of creation.[31]

Augustine begins to develop this view by moving to the first page of the Bible, asking that he might "hear and understand (*intellegere*)" how in the beginning, God creates heaven and earth (11.3.5). By proceeding in this way, he suggests that speaking and hearing are more fundamental than writing and reading and that the written words of the Bible are the context in which he wishes to hear God speaking. This way of proceeding also suggests that Augustine is moving from faith to understanding and that he wants to understand the meaning of what he hears when he reads the Bible.

These suggestions are confirmed by Augustine's remarks about the author of the text upon which he is focusing his attention. Augustine assumes that Moses wrote Genesis; but since he is no longer alive, Augustine knows that he is not available to explain what he means. This problem is compounded by the fact that Augustine would understand what Moses says only if he had spoken Latin rather than Hebrew (11.3.5). In both cases, Augustine wants what he cannot have—a verbal encounter with Moses in the absence of which he seems to be cut off from the meaning of the text.

There are two levels of interpretation that should be distinguished here. First, Augustine needs to make access to the language in which the author of Genesis speaks to him; second, he wants to ask the author what he means by what he says. The first condition cannot be satisfied because Moses speaks Hebrew rather than Latin, and the second cannot be fulfilled because Moses is no longer alive to explain what he means. Yet even if both conditions could be met and he could speak with Moses face to face, how would Augustine know whether what Moses says is true? Augustine says that he would know this, not from Moses, but from Truth itself, speaking neither in Hebrew, Greek, or Latin, but in a fashion that transcends determinate languages altogether. In this case, the voice of Truth would say, "He speaks the truth"; and only on this basis could Augustine know that the author of the first sentence of Genesis is speaking the truth (11.3.5).

In his earlier discussion of the nature of memory, Augustine suggests that he comes to know the truths of the liberal arts through recollection, where recollection can be understood as a process of collecting and gathering (10.11.18). Augustine also claims that illumination plays a crucial role in that context by permitting him to apprehend what he has collected and gathered (10.11.18). As he moves away from the Liberal Arts to the knowledge of God, illumination becomes even more important as a way of giving Augustine access to the dimension of God that transcends the ontological continuum. In this case, God cries out to him and shatters his deafness, making it possible for him to undertake an existential journey that begins with creation and leads toward fulfillment. In the present context, illumination continues to occur because the divine teacher tells Augustine that the words of Moses are true;[32] but since he cannot question Moses about the meaning of the words of Genesis, Augustine also asks God to extend the range of illumination to make it possible for him to understand (*intellegere*) them (11.3.5).

The understanding that Augustine seeks presupposes that the words of Moses are true; and with this presupposition in the background, he takes up a twofold task. First, he tries to understand how he knows that the words of Moses are true; and then he attempts to understand what they mean. The first issue occupies him for a single paragraph and requires him to enrich the concept of divine illumination (11.3.5). The second problem stretches over eleven paragraphs and permits him to develop a detailed account of the distinction between God and his creatures (11.4.6–11.13.16).

Augustine begins his discussion of the first statement in Genesis by standing at the point of intersection between time and eternity and by drawing a distinction between heaven and earth, on the one hand, and the one who brings them into existence on the other. The primary indication that heaven and earth are created is that they are subject to change and variation. Whatever has not been created, but exists, "has nothing in it which was not previously there, whereas to have what once was not is to change and vary" (11.4.6). Things that are subject to change and variation "cry out" that they do not make themselves; for before they come to be, they may not create themselves (11.4.6).

We must not forget that change and variation, and the cosmological flux that is constituted by them, do not imply fallenness. This should be especially clear in the present context, where things that change and vary are products of God's creative act (11.4.6). Unless God is to be blamed for the fall, it is of the utmost significance that we distinguish the created condition of the cosmological flux (finite-infinite) from the fallen condition that results when we turn away from God (finite-infinite).[33] With this distinction in mind, we can distinguish between the goodness of the created order in which things change and vary and the fallen condition that results from seeking ultimate satisfaction in creatures rather than in the creator. This is a theme with which Augustine has been occupied from the beginning of his inquiry, suggesting that a radical distinction must be drawn between what should be used (*uti*) and what should be enjoyed (*frui*). In the context before us, things that change and vary are good because we can use them to give us access to God; and they participate in our fallen condition only when we misuse them for purposes of our own.

In focusing our attention on the difference between the creator and created things that change and vary, Augustine says that self-evidence is the voice with which these things speak to us (11.4.6). Earlier he claims that God speaks to him and says that the words of Moses are true, pointing to the crucial role of divine illumination in giving him access to the truth of the Book of Genesis. Now he says that created things have a voice of their own, and that the voice with which they speak is to be identified with the self-evidence of what they say (11.4.6). Unless we are to be led astray by too many voices, it is important to understand that in Augustine's epistemology, self-evidence is another name for divine illumination.[34] The voice that tells Augustine that God makes heaven and earth is the same voice that tells him that things that change and vary are created, and that they do not create themselves. In both cases, God speaks to Augustine by making truths about God, truths about creatures, and truths about the relation between them self-evident.

As we have noticed on previous occasions, Augustine does not give arguments about the existence of God, about the relation between God and the world, and about the world itself, but calls our attention instead to a set of immediate inferences that we make about the issues in question (7.4.6). First, it is immediately evident that things exist. Second, it is equally evident that they have been created, since they are subject to change and variation. Third, it is self-evident that whatever has not been created, but exists, never changes and varies. Fourth, it is evident that to display characteristics that once did not exist is to change and vary. Fifth, it is obvious that things that change and vary do not make themselves; for before they come to be, they do not exist. Finally, it is apparent that God, who never changes, creates things that change and vary. Otherwise, there would be no explanation for the fact that finite things come into existence.

Augustine concludes his discussion of self-evidence as a way of knowing that what Moses says is true by connecting the creator with the creatures that he brings into existence. Since created things are beautiful, good, and existent, Augustine claims that they reflect the beauty, the goodness, and the existence of God (11.4.6). Otherwise, there would be no explanation for the fact that these qualities emerge from the cosmological flux that God brings into existence. Another way to state this point is to say that God stabilizes (stability$_1$) the flux by forming it, where the formation in question allows things to come into existence as discernible entities in their own right. However, Augustine is careful to distinguish creatures from the creator by pointing to the chasm that separates them. He says,

> Yet they are not so good, nor are they so beautiful as you, nor do they even be in such wise as you, their creator. Compared to you, they are neither good, nor beautiful, or real. (11.4.6)

Finally, he places all these points within the context of divine illumination by claiming that we know what he has said about God, the world, and the relation between them because of God, even though our knowledge compared with his is ignorance (11.4.6).

Having established the fact that God creates the world by appealing to self-evidence, Augustine turns to the second problem that the words of Moses raise by asking how God makes heaven and earth. In the first two paragraphs of Book I, the author of the *Confessions* tells us that we call upon God in order to know him; and on this basis, he takes up the task of explaining how it is possible for us to do so. In the paragraph before us, he follows this same pattern, first claiming that God creates the world, and then turning to the question of how he does so (11.4.6).

Augustine begins to answer this question by claiming that God does not work in the same way as a human artist, who transforms one body into another by imprinting forms upon it. He also tells us that the artist imprints a form on something that exists already and that already displays the power to be. By contrast, God creates the artist's mind, his body, the intellect by which he controls his creative imagination, and the antecedently existing material out of which he fashions other things. Yet these remarks lead Augustine to repeat his earlier question about how God creates heaven and earth and to answer it by claiming that there is no larger context within which God brings heaven and earth into existence (11.5.7).

Heaven and earth do not provide this context, for they do not exist before God creates them. The air, the waters, the world as a whole, and the material from which they are made also fail to constitute the context in question; for all of them are products of God's creative act rather than the framework within which this act occurs. This leads Augustine to claim that nothing exists apart from the existence of God, and it also leads to the conclusion that he will elaborate in the next four paragraphs. In formulating this conclusion, Augustine says, "You spoke, therefore, and these things were made, and in your Word you made them" (11.5.7).

At the outset, Augustine's conclusion about how God creates the world raises more questions than it answers, leading him to focus his attention on how God speaks, on how we know this, and on what the first verse of Genesis means when it speaks about the Word of God. The most important thing to notice about how God speaks is that the voice of God does not begin and cease to speak in time in the same way that the voice from the clouds at the baptism of Jesus says, "This is my beloved Son" (11.6.8).[35] On that occasion, the voice begins and ceases, sounds forth and passes away, where each syllable follows the one that precedes it until the last one sounds and there is silence. In the case in question, it is clear that a creature's movement, that is to say, a temporal movement, utters these syllables in obedience to God's eternal will (11.6.8). By contrast, the Word of God is different from temporal words that "flee and pass away"; and we know this by listening to the eternal Word of God, by comparing it with words sounding in time, and by noticing the difference between them (11.6.8). What we find when we do this is that when God says, "Let heaven and earth be made," he does not speak in time, but speaks from eternity.

Yet what is the Word that is spoken eternally and in which all finite beings are created? Augustine answers this question by claiming that instead of speaking words in sequence, the Word of God speaks "once and forever" (11.7.9). Otherwise, there would be time and change at the heart of eternity. We know that God speaks in the way that Augustine indicates by listening to the voice of Truth, where hearing what it teaches involves a direct apprehension of self-evident truths about the relation between time and eternity. Things in time come to be and pass away; but the Word of God is eternal. Augustine concludes that God says "once and forever" all that he says by his Word, who is coeternal with him, and that whatever he says shall be made is made by a voice that speaks from eternity (11.7.9).

In developing the contrast between time and eternity, Augustine claims that temporal things "do not exist, because they flee and pass away" (11.6.8). Formulated in a somewhat different way, he tells us that

> In so far as anything which once was now no longer is, and anything which once was not now is, to that extent such a thing dies and takes rise. (11.7.9)

These claims are important, not only because they point to a contrast between God and the creatures that he brings into existence, but also because they call our attention to a concept of nonbeing that characterizes the created order prior to the fall.

The nonexistence of things that come to be and pass away is an instance of what might be called relative as opposed to absolute nonbeing. In Greek, the contrast in question is reflected in the distinction between *me on* and *ouk on*; and in Latin, it is expressed in the distinction between *non esse* and *nihil*. Yet as the terms in all three languages suggest, relative nonbeing is less radical than nothingness without qualification, where a created being displays nonbeing in the first sense in so far as it is this and not that, here and not there, not yet, not now, and no longer.

In his discussion of the pear-stealing episode at the end of Book II, Augustine claims that he and his adolescence companions engage in an act that is oriented toward absolute nonbeing (*nihil*), and that the companionship they share in doing so is nothing (*nihil*) as well (2.8.16). By contrast, the passage before us suggests that beings that have been created do not exist (*non esse*) simply because they are not eternal.[36] It will be important to keep the distinction between these two forms of nonbeing in mind when we discuss the problem of time, for Augustine will say again and again that time as we usually understand the term does not exist. When he does this, he is not implying that time is to be identified with absolute nonbeing, claiming that time is evil, or suggesting that God ought to be blamed for creating it, but simply pointing to the natural consequences of cosmological passage.

When Augustine says that words that are uttered in time do not exist because they flee and pass away, he claims that the words in question are far beneath him, just as God is far above him (11.6.8). In making this assertion, he is placing himself in the middle ground between God and the world within which the journey toward God, encounters with God, and the quest of faith for understanding can unfold. When it is considered in itself, the natural order is good; and it is important not to overlook the fact that it has a proper place on the ontological continuum that God brings into existence. Yet Augustine also claims that this domain does not exist because it comes to be and passes away, even though the relative nonexistence of the temporal order is to be distinguished from the absolute *nihil* toward which we plunge when we turn away from God to seek fulfillment in creatures rather than in the creator.

Another way to express this point is to distinguish the natural birth and death of nonhuman creatures from the spiritual birth and death presupposed by the doctrines of creation and the fall. Augustine believes that animals that are beneath us on the chain of being are not only subject to change, but are also subject to generation and corruption (4.10.15). By contrast, he believes that though human beings change and develop, we are not subject to the law of birth and death that characterizes the natural order. Even though we are temporal creatures, we come to be and pass away, not because of the cosmological flux, but because of the creative act that brings us into existence and because of our failure to orient ourselves toward God (4.11.17). As we shall see in our subsequent discussion of the nature of time, this implies that we must draw careful distinctions among cosmological time that does not exist (*non esse*), time that is relevant to creation (finite↑infinite), fall (finite↑infinite), and fulfillment (finite–infinite)↓, and time that characterizes our fallen (finite↑infinite) condition.[37]

Before we turn to these issues, let us return to Augustine's attempt to deal with the relation between time and eternity by reiterating the point that in the act of creation, God speaks once for all through the Word that is coeternal with him. When we return to this point, it is important to notice that Augustine adds this crucial qualification:

Whatever you say shall be made, then it is made. But while you do not make anything otherwise than by speaking, yet not all things which you make by speaking are made simultaneously and eternally. (11.7.9)

In this respect, Augustine differs from Plotinus, who believes that the world is generated eternally through an eternal act of God.[38] One of the most important consequences of this difference is that since neither time nor created things are eternal, the endless cycle of birth, death, and rebirth is destroyed. This implies that the created order is on a more positive footing in relation to God than it is in antiquity, and it points to the biblical claim that the world that God creates is good.[39]

Yet what does it mean to say that God speaks eternally and that what he says is spoken once and forever, but that he does not make all things simultaneously and eternally? The answer Augustine gives is that what begins and ceases to be, begins and ceases when it is known in God's eternal reason that it will begin and cease, even though nothing begins and ceases in this eternal context (11.8.10). In this answer, Augustine presupposes a distinction among three ways in which temporal properties can be assigned. First, things in time have these properties directly. Second, when finite knowers know things of this kind, temporal properties qualify both the knower and the known. Finally, though God knows things in time, in this special case, time qualifies only the known and not the knower. As Augustine formulates the point, God knows when finite things will begin and cease to be, even though God himself is eternal rather than temporal. In this case, there is a correspondence between nontemporal ideas in the mind of God and their temporal instantiation in the world.

The distinction among these ways of assigning temporal properties is important for two reasons. First, it provides a way of bringing time and eternity together without compromising the eternity of God. As a consequence, God can know what is happening in time without being subject to the flow of time. Second, it allows for an act of creation in which things in time are spoken eternally without implying that the things in question are cotemporal. This means that finite things can be indexed temporally so that one succeeds another without implying that God is temporal rather than eternal.

Augustine begins to elaborate the conception of God's eternal reason by identifying it with the Word that speaks at the "beginning" of creation (11.6.10). Earlier Augustine gives his reasons for believing that God creates the world and tells us that creation is the act though which everything comes into existence. He also says that it follows from these claims that creation is an act of speaking and that in God's Word, all things are made. It is possible to understand this implication if we equate the divine Word with God's eternal reason, on the one hand, and with the beginning in which this Word is uttered on the other. Creation begins with the ratio of God, which makes the act of creation intelligible by analogy with the rational dimension of the soul that guides the creative imagination of the artist. Creation also occurs "in the beginning," for everything that exists presupposes the "prior" existence of God as its source. When we identify the Word of God with this preexistent source and with the ratio that manifests itself in the beginning, it follows that the Word of God creates the world "from the beginning" (11.8.10). This is Augustine's initial answer to the question he raises earlier about how God creates heaven and earth.

In addition to identifying the Word of God with the principle that brings the world into existence, Augustine identifies it with the beginning in which God speaks to us. In this way, he transforms an exclusively cosmological account of the act of creation into an account that has soteriological implications. The Word of God to which Augustine is calling our attention is not only the creative source of the world, but also the ground of the Gospel; and within this context, God speaks to us in the flesh. Yet the one who speaks in this way is also identical with the divine teacher who speaks to us. With respect to the Word of God that speaks within, Augustine says,

> There, O Lord, I hear your voice speaking to me, since he who teaches us speaks to us. But a man who does not teach us, even though he speaks, does not speak to us. Who teaches us now, unless it be stable Truth? Even when we are admonished by a changeable creature, we are led to stable Truth, where we truly learn "while we stand and hear him" and "rejoice with joy because of the bridegroom's voice" restoring us to him from whom we are. (11.8.10)

Augustine summarizes his conclusions about how God creates the world by glossing the first verse of Genesis which says that in the beginning, God creates heaven and earth. He does this by claiming that "in the beginning" means "in your Word," "in your Son," "in your Power," "in your Wisdom," and "in your Truth, speaking . . . and working in a wondrous way" (11.9.11). In this way, he connects the cosmological beginning in which the act of creation occurs with the soteriological beginning in which God speaks directly to us, and upon which our existential transformation and our quest for understanding depend.

Augustine knows that it is impossible to understand all the implications of the first verse of Genesis that points to the beginning of creation,
on the one hand, and the beginning of salvation on the other. However,
he never loses sight of the fact that he stands in between God and the
nothingness from which he has been created and that he is a creature
made in the image of God. This leads him to say that he both shudders
and glows with passion: he shudders in so far as he is unlike the one from
whom he comes, and he glows with passion in so far as he is like him
(11.9.11). Formulated in terms of our earlier distinctions, Augustine is a
(finite-infinite) being made in the image of God. In so far as he is finite,
he is unlike God; and in so far as he is infinite, he is like the one from
whom he comes. When these two dimensions are held together, Augustine's
soul vibrates with awe and infinite longing; and his restless heart continues to search for the ground of its existence until it finds rest.

There is a sense in which Augustine finds the rest he seeks in the
garden in Milan, for he tells us at the end of his conversion narrative that
he is at peace (8.12.29). However, the confession of his spiritual condition
in Book X makes it clear that his conversion must be distinguished, not
only from his fallen condition, but also from fulfillment (10.16.25;
10.20.29). After his conversion, in which the consequences of the fall are
dealt with decisively, and after the confession of his present sins in the
second part of Book X, Augustine turns his attention to the quest for
fulfillment, both intellectually and volitionally. At this stage of his journey,
he speaks to the intellectual dimension of his predicament by telling us
that Wisdom shines through him and cuts through the clouds that cover
him over because of his sin (11.9.11). He also speaks about the volitional
aspect of his quest for fulfillment, claiming that he will be unable to
reclaim his original goodness until God heals all his diseases (11.9.11).
Yet as his future is being weighed in the balance, he expresses confidence
that God will "redeem [his] life from corruption," "crown him with mercy
and compassion," and "satisfy his desire with good things" (11.9.11). Finally, he points toward the future by claiming that we are saved by hope
as we wait in patience for God's promises to be fulfilled (11.9.11).

Augustine's final remarks about the Word of God address his audience directly, asking us to hear God speaking to us as God is speaking to
him. In this way, he points to the fact that the words of the text are
written with passion to speak to that portion of his audience that is able
to understand what he says. To make this possible, Augustine says that he
will "cry out boldly" with words from the Bible, saying, "How great are
your works, O Lord; you have made all things in Wisdom" (11.9.11). This

leads, in turn, to Wisdom that exists in the beginning and through which God creates heaven and earth. The Wisdom in question is the ground of creation, but it is also the cognitive content that Augustine is attempting to understand as he brings his reflective journey to completion.

The final stage of Augustine's account of how God brings the world into existence takes up a skeptical objection to what he has said in the previous paragraphs, and what he says about it is presumably intended for part of the Christian audience that he has been addressing since the beginning of Book X (10.1.1).[40] The skeptical objection begins with the question, "What was God doing before he made heaven and earth?" and it is expressed in the form of a trilemma:

1. If God does nothing before creation, why does he not continue in this way forever, just as he previously refrains from working?
2. If any new motion arises in God, or a new will is formed in him to create the world, how would God be eternal? For if anything appears in God's substance that is not there previously, his substance is not eternal.
3. If it is God's eternal will for the creature to exist, why is the creature not eternal also? (11.10.12)

If we take the prongs of this trilemma together, it follows that either nothing is created, or God is not eternal, or the created order is itself eternal (11.10.12). All of these consequences are unacceptable to the orthodox Christian.

Augustine does not reply initially to this objection by considering each of its prongs one by one. Instead, he says that people who say such things do not understand God and do not understand how God creates the world. Though they attempt to grasp eternal things, their hearts "flutter among the changing things of past and future" and are vain (11.11.13). Thus Augustine asks the crucial question about the relation between the fluttering heart and the contrast between time and eternity:

Who will catch hold of it, and make it fast, so that it stands firm for a little while, and for a little while seize the splendor of that ever present eternity, and see that it is incomparable to them . . . ? (11.11.13)

A number of important points about the relation between time and eternity emerge when we consider this question and focus our attention on the predicament to which it is addressed. First, "the changing things of past and future" that never stand fast are created rather than fallen; and though they participate in relative nonbeing, they are good because they are created expressions of the goodness of God. Second, if we orient ourselves toward time rather than eternity, we fall away from God; and we share the predicament of those whose fluttering hearts lead them to ask foolish questions about the relation between time and eternity. Finally, failing to stand fast has two distinguishable senses: on the one hand, the cosmological flux is unstable because it involves temporal passage as a definitive element; on the other hand, a negative orientation toward God is unstable because it leads our fluttering hearts to occupy themselves with the changing things of past and future.

There are two corresponding senses of stability that ought to be distinguished: stability (stability$_1$) the first sense involves the stabilization of the cosmological flux, and stability (stability$_2$) in the second sense involves the stabilization of the fluttering heart. Augustine's theory of time will show us how stabilization of the first kind can be achieved, but only the grace of God makes it possible for stabilization of the second kind to occur. Augustine's discussion of the nature of time and of its relation to eternity involves a complex interplay between these two kinds of stabilization, where time is brought to a standstill in both cases.

Augustine continues to characterize the nature of time by claiming that a "long time cannot become long except out of many passing movements, which cannot be extended together . . ." (11.11.13). Then he claims that in eternity "the whole is present" and "nothing can pass away," where by contrast, "no time is wholly present." Finally, he asks the question,

> Who will see that all past time is driven back by the future, that all the future is consequent on the past, and all past and future are created and take their course from that which is ever present? (11.11.13)

When this question and the preceding remarks about the relation between time and eternity are taken together, several important points about Augustine's concept of time emerge that are often neglected. First, time has a dynamic dimension because many passing movements constitute it (11.11.13).[41] Second, these passing movements cannot be extended together because no time is wholly present.[42] Third, from the standpoint of eternity, the whole is present; but from the standpoint of time, this is not the case.[43] Fourth, the past, the present, and the future are related to one another as a dynamic sequence of elements; for the past is driven back by the future, just as the future is consequent upon the past (11.11.13). Finally, time takes its course from what is ever present, suggesting that temporal passage is contained somehow in eternity (1.6.10).[44]

In the meantime, Augustine asks the crucial question about the relation between time and eternity: "Who will hold the heart of man, so that it may stand still and see how steadfast eternity, neither future nor past, decrees times future and those past?" (11.11.13). In answering this question, he suggests that even though the stabilization (stability$_2$) of the fluttering heart is what is at stake, stabilization of this kind could not occur apart from the stabilization (stability$_1$) of the cosmological flux. Augustine's theory of time spells out the conditions for stabilizing the flux, where stabilization in this case involves what Augustine refers to later as conversion to form (12.12.15).

This kind of stabilization corresponds to the goodness of creation, where time in its created condition expresses the experiential stability of the soul at the theoretical level. However, when we fall away from God and when our fluttering hearts are bound to changing things of past and future, conversion of a second kind is required to bring us back to the one from whom we have turned away. One of Augustine's most important tasks will be to undercover a concept of time that reflects the conversion of the soul at the theoretical level and that makes his existential conversion possible.

Before he turns to these issues, Augustine tells us that he does not answer the one who asks what God is doing prior to the creation of the world with the frivolous reply that he is preparing hell for those who pry too deeply into subjects that are beyond their reflective capacity. Instead, he says that if by heaven and earth all creation is understood, before God makes heaven and earth, he does not make anything. Whatever God makes is a creature, and Augustine is certain that God does not make any creature before he makes all creatures taken as a whole (11.12.14).

Against this background, Augustine attacks the prongs of the trilemma posed to him by individuals who are still held captive by the kind of dichotomous thinking from which he has escaped. Their flighty minds wander among mental pictures (*imago*) of past times, and they wonder why it takes God so long to create the world. However, Augustine claims that individuals of this kind wonder at falsities (*falsa*); and in attacking the first prong of the trilemma that raises a question about what God is doing prior to the creation of the world, he says that since God is the creator of all the ages, no time exists before God makes it. More specifically, if there were a time before God makes heaven and earth, he does not rest, but makes it; and if there were no time before creation, the objectors should not ask what God does then (11.13.15).

Time is one of the things that God creates, for its instability (instability$_1$) points to its creation as a (finite-infinite) matrix.[45] This implies that God is not only the ground of temporal episodes, but also the creator of the temporal framework within which these episodes occur. These facts serve to undermine the first prong of the skeptical objection to Augustine's account of the nature of creation. However, we should also notice that fluttering hearts express themselves in flighty minds. The fluttering heart manifests itself existentially in a negative orientation toward God, and the flighty mind displays this negative orientation theoretically in inadequate conceptions of time and its relation to eternity. Augustine's conversion in the garden in Milan remedies the first problem (8.12.29); and as we shall discover in subsequent sections of this chapter, the theoretical conversion made possible by his theory of time remedies the second.

In bringing his discussion of the skeptical objection to a conclusion, Augustine focuses his attention on the second and the third prongs of the trilemma that has been formulated in response to his account of the relation between time and eternity. The second prong asks how Augustine can avoid attributing a new will to God that expresses itself in the act of creation, and the third asks how he can avoid claiming that the creation of the world from eternity implies that the world is as eternal as its source. Augustine responds to both prongs by indicating that they rest on a misunderstanding of the nature of God (11.13.15).

Augustine tells us that God does not precede time by existing in time; for if this were not the case, God would not precede all times. Instead, he precedes all times in his "ever present eternity," and he surpasses all future times, since they are to come and will soon be past (11.13.16).[46] This relation between time and eternity is grounded in the fact that God's "years neither come nor go," in contrast with ours. Augustine points to God as the source of existential stability by claiming that God's years "stand all at once, because they are steadfast. . . ." Our years "shall all be, when they shall be no more," but God's years are "today," which "does not give way to tomorrow, nor does it succeed yesterday." In God's case, "today" is "eternity"; and we reach it by stretching out along the vertical axis of experience that connects time with eternity. When we do this, we make access to the one who creates time, turn our gaze to the one who is before all times, and begin to understand the fact that not at any time does time not exist (11.13.16).

Augustine's response to the second and third prongs of the trilemma point to the fact that since God is eternal, it is impossible for a new will to arise in him at the "moment" of creation (11.13.16). This moment has meaning only within the finite order in contrast with the internal life of God that brings it into existence. On the other hand, the fact that the world is created from eternity does not imply that the created order is just as eternal as its source. In this special case, the product of a nontemporal act has temporal properties by virtue of which the creator and the creature stand in radical contrast with one another (11.13.16).

Even though Augustine insists that creation is not a temporal relation, he is equally emphatic in emphasizing the fact that time opens out to its creative source in the same way that memory opens out toward the transcendent dimension of God beyond the mind (11.13.16). In the central existential Books of the *Confessions*, Augustine gives us access to the ways in which his existential journey reaches its culmination in both intellectual and volitional encounters between God and the soul. In the remainder of this chapter, we will consider the ways in which Augustine's concept of time makes these experiential relations possible and will point to ways in which his account of temporality reflects his earlier experience at the distinctively reflective level.

WHAT IS TIME? (11.14.17–11.20.26)

Augustine summarizes the results of the previous section by claiming that it is never the case that God does nothing, since he is the creator of time. He also says that time is not coeternal with God, since God is permanent, and time is not. Finally, he tells us that impermanence is a defining trait of temporality; for without it, time would not be what it is (11.14.17). As a consequence, the essential nature of the cosmological flux expresses itself in coming to be and passing away, where time is one of the things that God creates and declares to be good. The transience of the temporal flux is not a negative condition from which Augustine wants to escape, but the framework about which he raises the familiar philosophical question that is often associated with his name.

At this pivotal stage of his inquiry, Augustine asks the question, "What is time?" In responding to it, he intends to comprehend, express, and explain what is presupposed when we talk about time in ordinary conversation. Augustine would have agreed with G. E. Moore that no difficulties arise about the concept of time if we confine ourselves to ordinary language.[47] However, he also wants to ask a question about the nature of time by placing himself within the Platonic tradition, where questions of this kind are familiar aspects of the philosophical procedure of Socrates.

Yet the question that Augustine is raising here is more difficult than the analogous questions that we find in the Platonic dialogues. When Socrates asks, "What is piety?"[48] "What is friendship?"[49] "What is courage?"[50] or "What is justice?"[51] he assumes that the forms about which he is inquiring are stable and that one of the most important tasks of philosophical reflection is to bring the unstable character of our knowledge into a stable relation with them. By contrast, Augustine's question about the nature of time presupposes that time and our knowledge of it are unstable and that both of them need to be stabilized (stability$_1$) through a process of what Augustine later calls a conversion to form (12.12.15).

Augustine moves in this direction when he asks for the second time, "What then *is* time?" One way to understand this repetition of the original question is to assume that the emphasis falls on the *is*, where the knowledge that Augustine wants to achieve points beyond the flux to a stable mode of temporal existence. When he asks his famous question, Augustine is not asking what time is and is not (*esse et non-esse*), for he knows already that the temporal flux is to be understood in terms of coming to be and passing away. Rather, he is asking what will serve to bring the temporal flow to rest so that he can have a time for meditation on God's Law. In asking the question, "What is time?" Augustine is attempting to stabilize the flux to prevent himself from going astray in it. This is the existential significance of his philosophical inquiry about the nature of time.

Another way to relate the experiential and the theoretical dimensions of Augustine's enterprise is to notice that his question, "What is time?" corresponds to his earlier question, "Who am I?" (9.1.1). In both cases, Augustine is looking for stability, where the relation between God and the soul can provide a stable framework within which his temporal existence unfolds. Augustine writes ten Books of the *Confessions* in which he attempts to answer the question, "Who am I?" When he asks the analogous question, "What is time?" he hopes to bring time to a standstill in order to contemplate the one he has been seeking during his experiential journey.

Before we turn to Augustine's discussion of the nature of time, it is important to emphasize the distinction we have drawn between two kinds of temporal stability, both of which Augustine will be pursuing as the discussion unfolds. The first kind of stability (stability$_1$) gives us access to the "form" that time displays and to the conditions that make it possible for us to participate in a positive orientation toward God. In this case, conversion to form manifests itself as conversion to comprehension, which Augustine's theory of time makes possible. By contrast, the second kind of stability (stalility$_2$) presupposes that we have fallen away from God and that we need to be restored through a theoretical conversion that is analogous to Augustine's existential conversion in garden in Milan. In this second case, we need to move from the distraction of a fluttering heart to the meditation of a steadfast mind that the grace of God makes possible.

When Augustine asks the question, "What, then, is time?" he gives the well-known answer, "If no one asks me, I know; if I want to explain it to someone who . . . [asks] me, I do not know" (11.14.17). Yet in the midst of uncertainty about how to proceed, he says that he is confident about this:

> If nothing were passing away, there would be no past time, and if nothing were coming, there would be no future time, and if nothing existed, there would be no future time. (11.14.17)

This is the phenomenological starting point of Augustine's investigation, and it stands in between what he knows and what he does not know. On the one hand, he knows what the word "time" means; on the other hand, he does not know how to give a philosophical analysis of the concept corresponding to it.[52] In trying to move from one pole to the other, he stands in the middle ground where he can express relative confidence about the possibility of success and where he can begin to discuss a problematic issue.

Augustine makes it clear from the outset that the existence of time presupposes the existence of changing things; and as a consequence, time can be understood initially as a function of things that come to be and pass away (11.14.17). This is the cosmological flux to which Augustine calls our attention when he speaks about the impermanence of time as its defining trait. On the other hand, when he asks the question, "What is time?" Augustine makes it clear that he wants to move beyond the cosmological context of generation and corruption to a time that abides.

As a way of pointing to the instability of time in which the soul can become disoriented and distracted, Augustine leads his readers through a cluster of paradoxes about the nature of time.[53] Thus he tells us that the past no longer is, the future is not yet, and the present is not always present. In all three cases, time does exist (*non-esse*) in the canonical sense of the term. Though this is less clearly true of the present than of the past or the future, Augustine insists that since the present passes into the past, it does not exist because the cause of its being is the fact that it will cease to be. Indeed, the present can be a mode of time rather than eternity only because it tends toward nonbeing (11.14.17).

Augustine is not claiming that the future does not exist because what is in the future is not occurring in the present, nor is he claiming that the past does not exist because what is in the past has occurred already.[54] Rather, he is claiming that the past, the present, and the future do not exist as standpoints in which he can engage in the contemplation of the Word of God. This is so because the three temporal modes are shot through with negation, making it impossible for Augustine to find a place of rest in any of them.

Another way to express the belief that time does not exist is to say that the future "is" only because it is *not yet*, the past "is" only to the extent that it is *no longer*, and the present "is" only because it *was not* and *will be no longer* (11.15.18). This way of formulating the issues makes it clear that time is not only fleeting and evanescent, but that it is also impossible to capture it conceptually when the future, the past, and the present are placed side by side. As McTaggart has attempted to demonstrate, and as we have indicated already, a contradiction arises when the same event is said to be both past, present, and future.[55] However, Augustine's point is not that a temporal episode involves a contradiction, whether we view it from a timeless or a temporal point of view,[56] both of which Augustine embraces at a later stage of his argument (11.21.27).[57] What concerns him instead is that the cosmological flux is unstable and that this instability manifests itself in the fact that the past, the present, and the future exemplify relative nonbeing (*non esse*). This leads quite naturally to a question about how time can be understood as the matrix in which the autobiography of Augustine has been constructed.

An account of Augustine's conception of time can be formulated only if we understand from the outset that the temporal flux that he is attempting to bring to rest has both static and dynamic dimensions (11.16.21).[58] Augustine's life involves an interplay between these two dimensions, and it is only by taking these elements into account that we can frame a concept of time that is adequate to his experience. It is equally important to notice that both the static and the dynamic dimensions of time are objective rather than subjective in the ordinary sense of these much abused terms and that this continues to be the case, even when Augustine claims that the temporal modes are modifications of the soul

(11.26.33). In contrast with the ancient thinkers, time exists only *for* the created intelligence, as Starnes has suggested,[59] even though it is important to point out that it also exists *in* the soul. This implies that temporal passage and temporal relations are to be located both in the real and the logical orders, even though they are reflections of the relative nonbeing that Augustine is attempting to bring to a standstill.

At this stage of his analysis, Augustine attempts to turn away from the problem of the relative nonbeing of time by moving in a predicational direction. In doing so, he suggests that the past and the future can be long or short, since there can be a long or a short temporal interval from one temporal moment to another (11.15.18–20).[60] Yet this suggestion collapses when we notice that something nonexistent can be neither long nor short. Perhaps as McTaggart, Broad, and Sellars suggest, instead of saying that the past or the future is long we should say that it was or will be long.[61] Yet once again we encounter insuperable difficulties: the past was not long when it was past because it did not exist then, and the future will not be long when it is still in the future because the future is not yet. Again, Augustine is not saying that the future and the past do not exist because they are not occurring.[62] Rather he is claiming that they do not exist because nonbeing (*non esse*) is inherent in their definition. Having moved from the cosmological flux to the relative nonbeing of time, and from relative nonbeing to a temporal interval that is said to be long or short, we find that time within this predicational context is infected with the same kind of nonbeing that makes time itself so intractable (11.15.18).

Perhaps the period of time in question either was or will be long when it was or will be present so that in both cases it would be appropriate to say that it exits. However, this suggestion presupposes that the present can be long; and typical reflections on the pattern of Zeno ought to convince us that this is not the case. A period of a hundred years cannot be present all at once, for it is constituted by a set of fleeting moments that succeed one another. The same thing can be said of a day, an hour, a minute, and a second so that only a point of time that cannot be divided into more minute parts can be called "the present." However, this specious present flies away so quickly from the future into the past that it cannot be extended (*extendere*), and that as a consequence, the present has no space (*spatium*) that can be long (11.15.20).

There are, of course, analyses of the specious present according to which it has a certain "length."[63] Indeed, this is part of what we mean when we speak about the specious present. However, these analyses all pertain to the way in which the present appears to consciousness and to which the mathematical analysis of Zeno is irrelevant.[64] Simply because the specious present cannot be divided either indefinitely or infinitely does not cancel the fact that it can be a mode of consciousness and that it can appear to the soul as extended in an analogical sense of the term. Indeed, at a later stage of our reflections, we will find that Augustine develops an analysis of this kind that has bearing on the characterization of time (11.28.37).

At the moment, Augustine returns to the speed with which the present moves from the future into the past and in claiming that the present is not extended in space, he makes two important points. First, he points to the cosmological "now" in virtue of which things in time come to be and pass away. He has suggested already that time has a cosmological dimension because it is a function of *changing things*. Now he deepens this aspect of his analysis by claiming that as the present moves from the future into the past, it constitutes the ontological ground of change and development. The only difficulty with this conclusion is that the cosmological "now" that changing things presuppose does not exist (*non-esse*). This leads to Augustine's second point that the non-existent present has no space (*spatium*) in which to unfold (11.15.20). This is clearly true if space is understood as a three-dimensional framework in which changing things can be located. Yet perhaps the present has a "space" in an extended sense of the term that will permit it to serve as the ontological ground of changing things in time. It is the quest for such a space where the "now" both moves and grounds the movement of things that leads Augustine to struggle with the problem of the stabilization of time.

In dealing with this problem, Augustine turns to the relation between time, on the one hand, and the measurement of time on the other. He tells us that he perceives intervals of time and compares them with one another, saying that "some are longer and some shorter" (11.16.21). In doing so, he focuses his attention on these temporal intervals as they are present to consciousness. He also measures how much longer or shorter one time may be than another, and we do this by perceiving and measuring times as they pass by. Presumably, Augustine believes that he is able to sense the difference between a long and a short period of time. Thus he combines the static, the dynamic, and the psychological dimensions of time by claiming that he can measure periods of time as they pass by.[65] However, Augustine insists once more that we cannot measure past times that exist no longer or future times that do not yet exist; for it is impossible for us to measure what is not (*non est*). Thus he concludes, "as long as time is passing by, it can be perceived and measured, but when it has passed by, it cannot be measured since it does not exist" (11.16.21). Again, Augustine is claiming that the past and the future do not exist, not because they are not occurring, but because relative nonbeing (*non esse*) is definitive of their nature.

Augustine now considers an objection that might be made to his claim that the past and the future do not exist. Perhaps when the present comes into existence from the future, it proceeds from "some hidden source," and when the past comes out of the present, it recedes into "some hidden place" (11.17.22). If this were not the case, how could prophets predict the future; or how could historians narrate past events that they cannot perceive? Augustine concludes, "If such things were nothing at all, they could not be perceived in any way. Therefore, both future and past times have being" (11.17.22).

In attempting to make progress with the problem of time, Augustine asks God not to allow him to be diverted from his fundamental intention (11.18.23). This prayer is important because it points to his need for temporal stability if he is to succeed in dealing with the problem before him. Yet the theoretical stability (stability$_1$) that Augustine seeks cannot be found apart from the stability (stability$_1$) of time. Thus he says that wherever the future and the past are, they must be there, not as a future and a past that do not exist, but as a present that exists as present (11.18.23). As we have suggested, and as we shall discover in detail, the present to which he is pointing has temporal, eternal, and psychological dimensions, combining the three aspects of the present that have dominated the discussion of the nature of time since McTaggart's famous attempt to prove that time is unreal.

One way to make access to the psychological of the present is to claim that the narration of past events is made possible by words drawn from images that are implanted in the soul by things as they pass before the senses. In such a case, we can apprehend an image *of* the past *in* the present because the image is *in* our memories (11.18.23). In an analogous way, the premeditation of future actions can be present even though the actions themselves do not exist. Augustine insists that only what exists in the present can be seen, where "seeing" future things is seeing their causes or signs, which exist already. As he formulates the point, "Those who predict the future fix their gaze upon things present with them" (11.18.24).

Having asked God to help him once more to focus his attention of the present moment (11.19.25), Augustine says that since the past and the future do not exist, it is not proper, strictly speaking,[66] to say that there are three times—the past, the present, and the future. Yet this does not preclude the possibility that there are three times that we can understand as functions of the present—"the present of things past, the present of things present, and the present of things future" (11.20.26).[67] In this formulation, the present has a privileged place; and this is so because the present exists, which the past and the future do not. Earlier Augustine says that even the present does not exist because the cause of its being will cease to be because it tends toward nonbeing (11.14.17). What accounts for the fact that he is now prepared to ascribe existence to the present?

As we shall discover, Augustine's reason for doing this is that the present is the standpoint from which he moves beyond the flux of changing things (11.21.27). As Augustine understands it, the present is not a subjective phenomenon, where the subject stands in contrast with the object. Instead, it is a soul that is higher on the continuum of changing things and higher than time in which these changes occur (11.21.27). This crucial fact about its status permits it not only to stabilize the flux (stability$_1$), but also to stabilize the flighty mind and the fluttering heart that turns away from God on the reflective level (stability$_2$). In a familiar passage, Augustine points to the conditions that make stability in both senses possible by claiming that the three temporal modes are in the soul and that the present (*praesens*) of things past is memory (*memoria*), the present (*praesens*) of things present is intuition (*contuitus*), and the present (*praesens*) of things future is expectation (*expectatio*) (11.20.26). In all three contexts, the present displays psychological, temporal, and eternal dimensions. It is psychological because it is a modification of the soul; it is temporal because it occurs in the present moment; and it is eternal because it points to God along the vertical axis of experience.[68] This is the beginning of Augustine's constructive analysis of the nature of time.

MEASURING TEMPORALITY (11.21.27–11.27.36)

Having encountered paradoxes in attempting to deal with the nature of time, Augustine now approaches the problem of time indirectly by focusing upon how we measure it. In doing so, he reiterates his earlier claim that we cannot measure what does not exist or what has no extension (*spatium*). As a result, Augustine concludes that the past, the present, and the future cannot be measured and that time itself can be measured only as it passes from what does not exist, by what lacks space, to what exists no longer (11.21.27). Yet Augustine also asks how temporal passage can be measured if what we measure is not in a certain space. In this case, the indefiniteness of the expression in question points to a concept of space in an extended sense of the term; and "space" becomes an exclusively temporal phenomenon.[69] This question leads him to turn away from his reflections momentarily and to turn to God, praying in the name of Christ that God will not prevent him from making the transition from belief to contemplation (11.22.28).

This moment of silent meditation is important because it points to the need for stability without which Augustine would be unable to complete his analysis of the nature of time. Time is a phenomenon that is both familiar and hidden, prompting Augustine to ask for light from God who illuminates him.[70] He has been converted in the garden by the mediator in the name of whom he prays (8.12.29); he has studied so he will be able to receive what he seeks; he has believed so he will be able to speak; and he wants to reflect on the mystery and the measurement of time as a way of contemplating God (11.22.28).

Augustine considers the possibility that time is the motion of the heavenly bodies, but he concludes that the time by which we measure their motion is more fundamental than the motion itself. The argument that leads him to this conclusion unfolds in the following way: if the light of the heavenly bodies ceases to exist, and a potter's wheel continues to move, time would still exist as the standard by which we could measure its motion. As a consequence, we could say that the rotations of the wheel move with equal speeds or that some turns are longer and some shorter, where in both cases, speed is a function of time. Augustine concludes that even though the concept of a day would have no application if the stars and lights of heaven cease to be, it would not follow from this fact that time does not exist (11.23.29).

Augustine continues his discussion of time, by which we measure the motion of bodies; and he does so by discussing the concept of a day. Placing aside the conventional concept of a day as the time that the sun spends over the earth, consider the following possibilities: (1) the movement of the sun from east to east constitutes a day; (2) the period in which this movement occurs is a day; and (3) a day is the movement and the period taken together. If we take these possibilities in turn, we find that paradoxes arise in all three cases. On the one hand, if the movement of the sun from east to east were a day, a day would be spent if the movement occurs in an hour. On the other hand, if the period in which the sun moves from east to east were a day, and if it were an hour in duration, the sun would have to go around twenty-four times to constitute a day. Finally, if a day were the movement of the sun and the period in which the movement occurs taken together, we would not have a day if the movement occurs in one hour, or if the sun stands still for twenty-four hours. In all three cases, we find that if time is equated with the movement of the heavenly bodies, paradoxes arise that undermine Augustine's attempts to answer his original question about the nature of time (11.23.30).

Augustine now turns away from the question about what constitutes a day and returns to the question, "What is time?" by which we measure the movement of the sun. When he does so, he says that if the sun moves from east to east in half the time it usually takes, the first takes a single period and the second a double period. This relation remains constant, even if the sun sometimes behaves in one way and some times in the other (11.23.30).

This thought experiment permits Augustine to deny that movements of the heavenly bodies constitute periods of time.[71] And when he considers the possibility that the sun might stand still while a battle occurs,[72] he realizes that time would continue to unfold, even under such circumstances (11.23.30). Thus he suggests that time is "a kind of distention" (*distentio*), or so it seems at this stage of the discussion (11.23.30).

Augustine's use of the term *distentio*, and his initial hesitation in doing so, are grounded in the meaning of the word itself. *Distentio* means something that is "stretched apart, expanded, and extended," often in different directions. The third meaning of the word is an ideal way of conveying the richness of what Augustine wants to communicate when he claims that the present can be measured only if it is extended in a certain space. The space he has in mind is an analogical extension of space in the usual sense; and insofar as it includes the past, the present, and the future as constituent elements, it is "extended" in different directions simultaneously.

Since time as he understands it is dynamic rather than static, it is also appropriate for Augustine to choose a term to characterize the nature of time that points to the expansive dimension of time as it passes from the future into the past. In this way, he captures the passage of time as well as its temporal extension in a single conception. On the other hand, the inseparable prefix, "dis," is inherently negative, where "being stretched apart" as a translation of *distentio* points in a negative direction. One commentator claims that Augustine uses the word *distentio* in an exclusively negative way and that he believes that temporal existence is essentially negative as well.[73] However, this conclusion is incompatible with the first two meanings of *distensio* that we have distinguished, and with the positive use to which he puts this concept in the analysis of time that he finally develops (11.27.36; 11.23.30). As we shall see, Augustine believes that distention is both a positive and a negative phenomenon, the first of which points to the original goodness of creation and to the new creation of conversion, and the second of which points to the fallen condition from which he wants to be redeemed.

At this juncture, Augustine reiterates his claim that the movement of a body is one thing and that time is another. Though a body never moves except in time, the movement of a body does not constitute time (11.24.31). It is also important to notice that when a body moves, we measure how long it moves from the time this movement begins to the time it ceases. We can do this only by perceiving these bodily movements as they pass by, and we can determine how long a movement is only by drawing a comparison, saying that this is as long as that, this is twice as long as that, "or something of the sort" (11.24.31). If we wish to be more precise, we can do so by marking off the places from which and to which a body moves; and by taking a period of time as a standard, we can say how long it takes for the movement to occur (11.21.34). Augustine finally brings this stage of his argument to a conclusion by extending the range of his remarks from bodies that move to bodies that remain at rest:

> If a body is sometimes moved in different ways and sometimes stands still, then we measure in time not only its movement but also its standing still. We say, "It stood still just as long as it was moved," or "It stood still twice or three times as long as it was moved," and whatever else our measurements either determine or reckon, more or less, as the saying goes. Time, therefore, is not the movement of a body. (11.24.31)

Though Augustine knows that time is not the movement of a body, he does not know what time is. Yet how does he know temporal facts about himself without knowing the nature of time? Perhaps he does not know how to express what he knows, or how to give a philosophical analysis of a concept that he has no difficulty using in ordinary conversation. However, this implies that Augustine does not even know what he does not know. In this respect, his situation is more acute than the conditions of many characters in the Platonic dialogues, who have forgotten what they know and who can recover their implicit knowledge through recollection.[74] As a consequence, Augustine moves beyond recollection by expressing his dependence on God for enlightenment. In a quotation from the Psalms, Augustine says: "You will light my lamp, O Lord, my God, you enlighten my darkness" (11.25.32).

Augustine knows that he measures tracts of time; but insofar as they are temporal, he does not know what he measures. He also knows that he measures the motion of bodies in time, but he wonders whether he does not also measure time itself. Indeed, he believes that it would be impossible for him to measure the movement of a body if he were unable to measure the time in which it cannot move. However, we cannot measure a longer by a shorter temporal interval in the same way that we measure the relative lengths of things in space. We can only measure times as they pass by in "space" in an extended sense of the term, and we must distinguish space as a three-dimensional framework in which things exist from the "space" in which the temporal modes are located (11.26.33). One consequence of this is that there is a difference between a long and a short syllable as they are written on a page and these same syllables as we pronounce them. In this second context, we can pronounce a syllable more slowly or more rapidly, where in this case, the rate of passage becomes an issue for the first time. In a spatial context, the length of a syllable remains constant; but in the context of time, it varies depending upon the rate at which it is uttered (11.26.33).

Augustine moves directly from the claim that the rate of an utterance can vary to a repetition of his suggestion that time is a distention. Earlier, he makes this suggestion because we must distinguish periods of time from the time that would continue to unfold, even if the sun stands still (11.23.30). Now he does so because the rate of passage of an utterance in which a short syllable may be "long" and a long syllable may be "short" must be distinguished from the spatial contrast between a long syllable and short one that we can measure on a page.

Against this background, Augustine also moves beyond the suggestion that time is a distention *simpliciter* by wondering whether it is a distention of the soul (*animus*) (11.26.33). One reason that he wonders about this might be that the context of recitation in which he is now framing the problem of time is linked essentially with the "extension" and the "expansion" of the soul (11.26.33). This reference to the distention of the soul is the first reference of its kind in the text, and it points to the fact that Augustine is taking an additional step in developing his conception of time. In the first step, he identifies the past, the present, and the future with the present of things past, the present of things present, and the present of things future; and on this basis, he identifies the second sequence with memory, intuition, and expectation (11.20.26). In the second step, he identifies time with movements in space that we can differentiate from the context in which movement of this kind occur (11.24.31).

Finally, he suggests that we can understand the distention of time as a distention of the soul, which will be a way of combining the distention of the soul, on the one hand, with the distention of memory, intuition, and expectation on the other (11.26.33).

Having drawn our attention to the relation between time and the distention of the soul, Augustine repeats the pivotal claim that we are able to measure time. However, he returns to the stage of the analysis before the distention of the soul comes into the picture by reminding us that we "do not measure the future, because it does not yet exist," that we "do not measure the present, because it is not extended in space," and that we "do not measure the past, because it no longer exists." Then he repeats his earlier claim that we measure "times that pass, but are not yet past" (11.26.33).

Before he elaborates the point that time is a distention of the soul, Augustine exclaims, "Be steadfast, O my mind, and attend firmly. Look to where the truth begins to dawn" (11.27.34). In urging himself to be steadfast and attentive, Augustine is pointing once again to the stability that is required to plumb the depths of the problem before him. In the existential Books of the *Confessions*, he moves from creation (1.6.7), to the fall (2.4.9), to conversion (8.12.29), to a foretaste of fulfillment in the mystical experience he shares with his mother in Ostia (9.10.24). Now he suggests that the stability (stability₁) that characterizes the soul in its original innocence and that is reappropriated in his conversion in the garden in Milan is a necessary condition for the conversion (stability₁) of time. As Augustine moves from faith to understanding, this conversion is occurring in and through his analysis of the nature of time, especially at the point where the truth begins to dawn.

Augustine begins to pursue the truth that he has glimpsed by returning to the problem about how temporal phenomena can be measured. He asks us to consider a case in which a voice begins to sound, does sound, and ceases to sound. Before it begins, it cannot be measured because it does not exist yet, and after it ceases, it cannot be measured because it exists no longer. Therefore, Augustine claims that we can measure it only while it is sounding; for at that time, it exists (*id est*) (11.27.34). Yet as the word *distentio* suggests, even when the sound exists and can be measured, it is not static, but is going on and going away into the past. While it is passing away, it is being extended over some tract of time (*spatium temporis*) where it could be measured; for the present has no space (*spatium*). As in an earlier case (11.14.17), Augustine does not say that the present does not exist, as he does with reference to the past and the future (11.27.34), but only that it is not extended. This is another indication that the present is the clue to his analysis of time.

In the case before us, what Augustine is measuring is a sound that is "moving" through time, where the context in which it is moving is neither an expanse of space, nor a "space" of time that is "extended" in the present, but a tract of time into which it is being extended as it passes away. In this case, Augustine is embracing the specious present as a tract of time that is generated by temporal passage and to which his theory of time gives us access (11.26.33). With respect to this theory, the most important question that arises is how he intends to show that the temporal movement that he is trying to measure is a *distentio*, that it is a distention of the soul (*distentio animi*), and that a distention in this sense makes a time of meditation possible because it is more stable than the temporal flux that does not exist (*non esse*).

The crucial step in Augustine's attempt to answer this question is to show that something cannot be measured unless it is bounded, as Augustine himself must be if he is to achieve reflective stability. In this connection, he says that a continuous sound can be measured only from its beginning to its end; and as a result, a voice that never stops sounding cannot be measured. However, if we wait for the voice to cease, it cannot be measured then because it exists no longer. Augustine is convinced that we measure tracts of time, but not those that are not yet, not those that are no longer, not those that are prolonged without any break, and not those that have no limits. This implies that we are not only unable to measure the future, the past, and the present, but also passing times that have no boundaries (11.27.34). This is a turning point in the discussion, apparently leading Augustine to turn away from his earlier statement that we measure times as they pass by, but are not yet passed (11.26.33).

The only way to reconcile the claim that we measure things that pass with the assertion that we cannot do so is to distinguish the flux of passing times that has no boundaries and that does not exist (*non esse*) from passing times that exist (*esse*) because they are bounded. As we shall see, temporal episodes become accessible on the basis of Augustine's theory of time, which combines temporal, psychological, and eternal dimensions, and which stabilizes time as a way of making a time for meditation possible. In the final analysis, Augustine believes that his theory of time, together with the one toward whom his meditations are directed give him the stability he seeks, both existentially and reflectively.

It is no accident that at this stage of his argument Augustine turns his attention to the hymn of Ambrose entitled, "*Deus creator omnium*" (11.27.35).

He has spoken about this hymn already in discussing the death of his mother, where he is finally able to weep and to find a resting place in relation to the One who makes it possible for him to love all things in God (9.12.32). Now he turns to this same context to find the stability he needs to measure temporality. Before he tries to show how to do this, Augustine suggests that in scanning the hymn in question, he measures a long syllable by a short one. Yet the following familiar difficulties arise with respect to this suggestion: (1) Augustine cannot measure a long syllable by a short one while it is passing, since it has no boundaries; (2) He cannot measure a long syllable before he completes the scanning of it, since it will not exist yet; and (3) He cannot measure a long syllable by a short one when both have passed away, since both exist no longer (11.27.35).[75]

In response to these familiar difficulties, and in answer to the question, "If a long syllable follows a short one, how do I retain the short syllable and how do I apply it to the long syllable when I measure it?," Augustine reaches a fundamental conclusion. He says, "I do not measure the syllables themselves, which no longer are, but something in my memory that remains fixed there" (11.27.35). This is Augustine's answer to the problems of the nonexistent past and the nonextended present (11.27.35) that we have struggled with already. Earlier we have wondered how Augustine intends to show that time is a distention and that more fundamentally, it is distention of the soul (*distentio animi*). Now we find him pointing to the answer by claiming that we measure the memory of a syllable, which is "extended" (*extentio*) in time, and which is a distention of the soul, where remembering and what we remember are an act and a content of the mind respectively.

Before he moves explicitly to the problem of the conversion of time, Augustine elaborates the conclusions he has reached by emphasizing the fact that he measures time in the mind. And as if to anticipate the objection that he is about to embrace a subjective conception of time, he asks us not to interrupt him by claiming that time exists and not to interrupt ourselves by giving way to our prejudices (11.27.36). His reason for moving in this direction is not to anticipate the Cartesian distinction between *res extensa* and *res cogitans*,[76] but to emphasize the contrast between what is (*esse*) and what is not (*non esse*). When Augustine asks, "What is time?" he is asking how time can *be* as opposed to being subject to the relative nonbeing of the past, the present, and the future. Now he begins to answer this question by turning inward, where traces that passing things have made upon him remain even after the things themselves have passed away (11.27.36).

I have emphasized on several occasions that Augustine draws conclusions about the nature of time from conclusions about how time is to be measured. Since we measure what we remember, and since memories are distentions of the soul, he claims that time itself is to be identified with the distentions in question. By contrast with the past, the present, and the future, which do not exist (*non esse*) in the strict sense of the term, a distention of the soul exists (*esse*) in the present all at once. This is what Augustine has been seeking, so it should not be surprising that he identifies time in the normative sense with it (11.26.33).

It might seem that to claim that the distention of the soul exists all at once is to say that it is eternal, where a claim of this sort would blur the distinction between time and eternity. In Book I, Augustine himself emphasizes this distinction by addressing God in the following way:

> You are supreme and you are not changed. Nor is this present day spent in you, for in you are all these times. Unless you contained them, they would have no way of passing on. And because your years do not fail, your years are this very day. No matter how many have already been our days and the days of our fathers, they have all passed through this single day of yours, and from it they have taken their measures and their manner of being. And others still shall also pass away and receive their measures and manner of being. (1.6.10)

Yet even though he draws a radical distinction between time and eternity, Augustine places time in God as the eternal context in which it exists. This implies that time and the distention of the soul with which he identifies it exist in God all at once, at least from the standpoint of the eternal present in which it participates. Though the distention of the soul is a certain "spread-out-ness," both it and all its constituents are related to God along the vertical axis of experience,[77] and this is what is meant by claiming in this context that the distention of the soul exists "all at once."

In the course of our analysis, we shall find that the distention of the soul exists all at once in two additional respects. Since we are made in the image of God, we can unify memory, apprehension, and expectation in the present moment (11.27.34), just as God unifies time within the context of eternity (1.6.10). In addition, memory, intuition, and expectation exist all at once in the present because they are traces of what has passed, is passing, and will pass through it (11.27.34). If we take the three dimensions of this account together, the eternal, psychological, and temporal dimensions of the distention of the soul exist "all at once" in the present in all three senses.

The identification of time with the distention of the soul makes it possible for Augustine to take another crucial step in his analysis. Earlier he seeks a time for meditation, asking God to bring stability to his soul so he may stand firm and listen to God's voice. Now he suggests that this can be done if we focus our attention on temporal episodes that do not simply come to be and pass away. The stability of memory will permit time to come to a standstill and will give Augustine access to God as the one toward whom faith seeking understanding is directed.

We might summarize the conclusions that Augustine has reached in the following way:

- Time has a cosmological dimension; and when it is identified with the flux that comes to be and passes away, it participates in relative nonbeing (*non esse*)
- Time can be stabilized (stability$_1$) by the mind, where the mind stands in contrast with what it stabilizes as something higher to something lower
- In measuring passing times, we measure our present mental states rather than things that come to be and pass away
- Time is identical with states of the soul that we measure rather than with the cosmological flux with which Augustine begins his reflections.

Augustine extends his conclusions about the measurement of time to periods of silence, claiming that they can be measured as if a voice were sounding during the periods in question. In this case, we "recite" the verses of a poem as if we were speaking aloud,[78] where the activity involved in doing so is part of what we mean by the nature of time. Augustine concludes that time is not only a content of consciousness that abides when things with the temporal flux pass away, but also an activity in virtue of which we move from one state of consciousness to the next (11.27.36). This implies that time is a mental state that is both *in* and *of* the soul simultaneously, where the temporal content within the soul comes to be there because of an activity in which the soul is engaged.

Augustine does not lose the flow of time by identifying it with a mode of the mind, and he expands the concept of time as a distention of the soul to include both the present and the future. He holds these two dimensions of his analysis together by claiming that present intention *transfers* the future into the past, where the past increases through a diminution of the future until the whole is past (11.27.36). We should not overlook the fact that the activity of transferring the future into the past is an intentional action in what Aquinas would call "the real order." Actions of this kind are to be distinguished from the intensionality of memory, intuition, and expectation that make these temporal contents present to consciousness.[79] Finally, the activity of transferring the future into the past is internal rather than external to awareness, where all the modes of awareness exist in the present (11.27.36). In the following section, we will explore the relation between acts of consciousness and activities that link one of these acts with another, where the relation between them is the key to Augustine's attempt to bring the temporal flux to a standstill.

MEMORY, APPREHENSION, AND EXPECTATION (11.28.37–11.28.38)

It is possible for the future, which is not yet, and the past, which is no longer, to diminish and increase respectively only because three modes of the soul are involved in these transitions. The soul looks forward, considers, and remembers, so that the reality toward which it looks passes through what it considers into what it remembers. As Augustine elaborates the point, future things do not exist yet, but there is an expectation *of* the future *in* the soul; past things exist no longer, but there is a memory *of* the past *in* the soul; and though the present that passes away in an instant lacks spatial extent (*spatium*), attention abides. It is through this abiding "space" that what "shall be present proceeds to become something absent" (11.28.37). These considerations lead Augustine to the unorthodox conclusion that the future and the past are not long, but that a "long future" is "a long expectation of the future," and that a "long past" is "a long memory of the past," both of which are modifications of the abiding present (11.28.37).

It is important to notice that we should not speak about an expectation of a long future or a memory of a long past because the contents of the acts in question do not exist (11.28.37). This leaves no other option than to understand a long future as a long expectation of the future and a long past as a long memory of the past, where extensive magnitudes that qualify existing things are transformed into intensive magnitudes that qualify acts and contents of consciousness. Once this has been done, the past, the present, and the future become a threefold distention of the soul, where expectation, attention, and memory are ways in which the soul can transcend the flux of what comes to be and passes away. We are able to transcend the flux because our expectations and memories exist in the present, where we make access to the intentional contents that these acts present to consciousness. As opposed to things within the cosmological flux that come to be and pass away, these acts and contents abide in the present; and it is this abiding quality that brings stability to the soul that orients itself toward them. However, we must not forget that Augustine attempts to preserve the flow of time as well as the stability he needs in order to bring the temporal flow to a standstill. He preserves this dynamic dimension by claiming that attention transfers expectation into memory and that the reality that we expect passes through what we consider into what we remember, where what shall be present proceeds to become something absent. The crucial question to be faced is how Augustine preserves the stable and the dynamic dimensions of time simultaneously.

Augustine understands memory, attention, and expectation as acts of the mind in which we remember, attend to, and expect the intentional contents toward which we orient our attention. The contents in question are located in what scholastic philosophers call the logical order, while acts of awareness that give us access to them are to be found in the real order as modifications of a present that abides. This abiding present is "extended" in an analogical sense of the term, and it permits acts of awareness to exist side by side in a "community" of temporal modes that would otherwise be subject to the relative nonbeing (*non esse*) of the cosmological flux. This community is analogous to the the community of parents and nurses with which Augustine begins (1.6.7–8), to the community of teachers and schoolmates to which he moves (1.12.19–1.19.30), to the community of adolescent companions with whom he steals the pears from his neighbors vineyard (2.4.9–2.10.18), to the community of Manichaeans with whom he lives for nine years (4.1.1; 5.3.3–5.7.13; 5.10.18–19; 5.14.25; 7.2.3), to the community of Neoplatonists that makes his intellectual conversion possible (7.9.13–7.17–23), to the Christian community that he enters (8.12.30) after his conversion in the garden in Milan (8.12.30), to the community that undergirds his mystical experience with his mother in (9.10.23–26) and to which he speaks in (10.1.1), and to the community of days in which Augustine seeks eternal rest (13.35.50–13.36.51). The community of temporal modes is a necessary condition, not only for finding the stability (stability$_2$) he needs to orient himself toward God and to bind the text before us together,[80] but also for finding a time for meditation on God's Law.[81] In displaying acts and contents of consciousness that exist as stable aspects of the present, the soul also engages in activities that transfer expectations into memories. As a consequence, we must not only bind acts and contents together in understanding Augustine's concept of time, but we must also understand how acts, contents, and actions that permit us to move from the future to the past are to be related to one another.

As a way of indicating how all these elements are related in Augustine's conception of time, let us turn to his own example of what is involved when he recites a Psalm that he has memorized. Before the recitation begins, his expectation extends over the whole Psalm; and after it has begun, his memory extends over that part of the Psalm that he has recited already. The life of this action is distended into memory and expectation by virtue of what he has said and is about to say. By contrast, his attention is present; and what is future is borne along by it in the present so that it becomes past. The more this is done, memory is lengthened and expectation is shortened until the entire expectation is exhausted (11.28.38).

What is the content, what is the act, what is the action, and how are these elements unified in the example before us? When Augustine says that his expectation extends over the whole Psalm, and when he claims that his memory extends over that part of the Psalm that he has just recited, the Psalm is a content of consciousness, understood as an intentional object, in contrast both with the acts of awareness that extend over it and the action involved in reciting it. Contents, acts, and actions are unified by the fact that the contents of which Augustine is aware, the acts by which he makes access to them, and the actions by which he moves from one to the other are dimensions of the soul that abide in the present.

There is a reciprocal relation between the Psalm that Augustine recites and his recitation of it in which its intentional content and the act of awareness of it depend on the recitation rather than the other way about. The Psalm in question is identified as the one that Augustine is about to recite and as the one that he has begun to recite already, where its content is assigned to the future or the past as a function of the recitation. This is what Augustine means when he says that the activity involved in the recitation transfers what it expects into what it remembers, where the activity in question passes through present attention that does not come to be or pass away.

What Augustine transfers from the future to the past are neither acts nor actions, but contents of consciousness through which he moves one step at a time, transferring expectation into memory until the content of his expectation is exhausted. The passage from expectation to memory is internal to an act of attention that abides in the present; and for this reason, Augustine is able to transcend the temporal flux with which his reflections begin. Memory, intuition, and expectation, and the transition from one to the other involve a movement from presence to absence within the context of consciousness. Within this context, Augustine moves from an expectation to memory by engaging in an action that lengthens the memory as it shortens the expectation.

Let me formulate the crucial points once more. First, present attention unifies present expectation and present memory, where what is in the present are acts of consciousness that have the properties of being long or short in an analogical sense of the terms. Second, to say that attention bears expectation along so that it becomes memory is to say that two modes of the present are connected by an action in the present that abides, where what we expect and what we remember are contents of acts of attention that come to be and pass away within the present. Finally, acts, contents, and actions are connected by the fact that actions transfer contents to which we make access through acts of awareness from the future to the past through the present. In response to the question, "What *is* time?" (11.14.17), Augustine begins with the relative nonbeing (*non esse*) of the cosmological flux; but he answers the question by developing a concept of the present in which acts, contents, and activities of the mind are bound together in a single context.

Augustine generalizes his concept of time by claiming that it not only undergirds his account of reciting the Psalm, but also applies to every syllable of which the Psalm is constructed. In addition, he says that he can give the saame analysis of the larger action of which reciting the Psalm is a part, of the whole of a human being's life in which this larger action is included,[82] and of the entire age of men of which one man is only a fragment. However, these generalizations raise two questions about Augustine's conception of time that force us to broaden our analysis. First, what kind of soul not only holds a syllable, a Psalm, and the whole of a life together in the present, but can hold the entire age of human beings together in the present as well? Whatever might be the case in the first three instances, the mind that can perform the fourth task would presumably be superhuman and might appear to be of doubtful relevance to Augustine's attempt to bring stability (stability$_1$) to the soul. Second, what is the relation between the stabilized (stability$_1$) concept of time toward which Augustine has led us and the cosmological concept of time with which he begins? It might seem that cosmological time is a more comprehensive concept than time as a distention of the soul, where the present is embedded in the cosmological flux as a subordinate element. How can we respond to these questions as a way of bringing our account of Augustine's concept of time to a conclusion?

STRETCHED OUT, GATHERED UP, STRETCHING FORTH (11.29.39–11.31.41)

We can begin to answer these questions by reflecting on created and fulfilled concepts of time with which a converted (stability$_2$) concept of time stands in contrast. After Augustine completes his analysis of time and shows how attention can bind expectation and memory together, he returns to the negative concept of distention according to which his life is a distortion and distraction (11.29.39). In doing so, he exploits the "dis" in *distentio*, pointing to ways in which he is pulled apart in opposite directions, and calling our attention to the contrast between distention in the negative sense and the kind of stability (stability$_1$ and stability$_2$) to be found in created and converted conceptions of temporality. In its created condition, time is stabilized (stability$_1$) by binding memory, attention, and expectation together in a present that abides; and when time is converted, the first kind of stabilization (stability$_1$) is reappropriated (stability$_2$) by turning away from the cosmological flux toward God. Preoccupation with the temporal flux without bringing it into relation with God is a theoretical expression of Augustine's fallen condition, and it reflects the distortion and distraction of his existential situation at the theoretical level.

Augustine says that he is dissipated in many things and in many ways, pointing to his fall away from God (11.29.39) that disrupts the existential stability (stability$_1$) that he has been created to express (11.29.39). When his stability (stability$_1$) has been lost, it should not be surprising that the concept of time that results poses such an intractable problem. On the other hand, Augustine says that the mediator has gathered him together (*colligere*) from his former ways, permitting him to forget what is behind, and not distended (*distentio*), but extended (*extentio*), to stretch forth toward God according to a positive intention (*intentio*) (11.29.39).[83] In this case, the gathering and collecting that has led to knowledge (10.11.18) and that expresses itself existentially in the Neoplatonic visions of Book VII (7.10.16; 7.17.23) point to transformation and fulfillment, where these existential conditions presuppose the temporal (stability$_1$) of original innocence (finite$^\uparrow$infinite) and express themselves in a concept of time that recovers the temporal stability (stability$_1$) that has been lost by the fall (finite⌐infinite).[84] By recovering this concept, Augustine moves toward a time for meditation, where faith becomes understanding, and where the journey from a fallen to a converted concept of time finally moves toward completion. Augustine points to a concept of time that makes fulfillment possible by speaking of the moment in which the soul flows into God, purged and melted by the fire of love (11.29.39).

Behind the concepts of fallen, converted, and fulfilled temporality there is a created conception of time that Augustine's analysis of the nature of time presupposes. At the conclusion of his analysis, he points to the conceptual possibility of a creature who knows the whole of the past and the future, just as he knows the Psalm that he has recited. Augustine says,

> Surely, if there were a mind possessed of such great knowledge and foreknowledge, so that to it are known all things past and future, just as I know one well-known psalm, then supremely marvelous is that mind and wondrous and fearsome. From it whatever there is of past ages and of ages to come is no more hidden than there is hidden from me as I sing that psalm what and how much proceeded from its beginning and what and how much remains to the end. (11.31.41)

Augustine makes an indirect reference to this creature in his meditation on transience and transformation in Book IV. In a crucial passage of that meditation, he says,

> . . . If fleshly sense had been capable of comprehending the whole, and had not, for your punishment, been restricted to but part of the universe, you would wish that whatever exists at present would pass away, so that all things might bring you the greater pleasure. (4.11.17)

This passage suggests that the creature in question exhibits a created consciousness from which we have fallen away and to which Augustine is pointing when he speaks about the contrast between our state and our original condition.[85]

In this original condition, created time manifests itself in the ability of a human being to comprehend the whole of time, just as Augustine comprehends the Psalm he recites. It is a created consciousness of this kind, and not the consciousness of an angel that Augustine is presupposing when he extends his account of the nature of time to include not only the life of an individual, the life of the entire human race, and the life of the superhuman creature that is able to know the entire past and the the entire future. Though angels are mutable, they are not in time because they never mutate. As a consequence, they cannot be the superhuman creatures that Augustine has in mind in this passage. The unfallen Adam, who is the superhuman creature to which Augustine is referring here, can hold the past, the present, and the future together in a present that leaves nothing out of account by analogy with the way in which we hold memory, attention, and expectation together in a present that abides.

Created time is cosmological time that has been unified in the past, the present, and the future of an undistorted consciousness. Fallen time is the distortion of this unity that expresses itself in bondage to temporal paradoxes that lead us to ask foolish questions about the relation between time and eternity. Converted time is the unity of the past, the present, and the future in delimited domains, the structure of which is analogous to the global unity to which created time gives us access. And fulfilled time is the unity of the past, the present, and the future in relation to God as the ground and the goal of human existence.

In suggesting that the unfallen consciousness can comprehend the whole of time, Augustine is not claiming that in its original innocence, it is able to adopt a divine perspective in which it knows the past, the present, and the future from the standpoint of eternity. God is eternal because he knows the past, the present, and the future all at once without making transitions from one temporal modality to another. By contrast, even though the unfallen consciousness participates in the vertical axis of experience and holds the past, the present and the future together in the guise of memory, intuition, and expectation, it is also temporal because it transfers expectation into memory through attention that abides through traces in the present (11.31.41). In addition, there is a crucial difference between the unfallen consciousness and the kind of consciousness that we exhibit. This difference expresses itself in the fact that the range of its knowledge is the world as a whole rather than a fragment of the world to which we are restricted because of our fallen condition (4.11.17).

In his analysis of the nature of time, Augustine is attempting to express a created concept of time and to reclaim the temporal unity that he has lost through the fall; and he does this by seeking a concept of time that brings stability to the soul. When he says that he will stand firm in his original form and in God's truth, he is remembering the act of creation and calling our attention to the fact that the conversion of time is a new creation (11.31.41). Augustine is committed to the view that he is created in the image of God, where one of his most important tasks is to bring the cosmological flux to a standstill; and he believes that the conversion of time is a way of embracing this image at the distinctively reflective level.[86]

The final question to be considered is the relation between the converted concept of time that Augustine has developed and the cosmological conception of time with which he begins his analysis. According to the cosmological conception, the past, the present, and the future do not exist; and the now moves so quickly from the future to the past that it cannot be measured. Yet moving beyond this concept of time to the view that time is a distention of the soul seems to make the human being prior to nature and to subsume the cosmological dimension of temporality under a psychological conception. When we remember that even the Genesis account of creation suggests that the creation of the world is prior to the creation of the human being, we might be tempted to insist that the cosmological conception of time is more fundamental than the concept of time that Augustine has been elaborating. This temptation is accentuated when we notice that if the present abides, it must abide in relation to something, leading us to wonder whether the reality to which it is related is time in the cosmological sense of the term.

At least one commentator has been puzzled by this question into claiming that Augustine has two theories of time, one cosmological and the other psychological, where the psychological concept is to be subordinated to the cosmological conception, or where there is no obvious relation between them.[87] However, in moving from time as a domain in which things come to be and pass away to time as a distention of the soul, Augustine does not deny that cosmological time is and is not (*esse et non esse*), but only that it is (*esse*) in the canonical sense of the term. Once this is understood, we can acknowledge the fact that cosmology is prior to psychology in the order of nature. Among other things, this means that human beings are parts of the cosmological flux in which they change and develop. However, this does not imply that these same beings do not rise above nature by stabilizing (stability$_1$) the flux of which they are proper parts. It is important to notice that time in the cosmological sense of the term would have existed, even if the soul had not existed. However, it would have have been stabalized if this had been the case.

In appraising the results of Augustine's analysis, it is important to emphasize once more that he has not reduced an objective to a subjective account of the nature of time. What he has done instead is to claim that time exists (*esse*) in the canonical sense only if it is construed as a modification of the soul in the present, where the present abides when it is brought into relation with intentional contents, acts of awareness, and actions, on the one hand, and with eternity on the other. The reason that the soul is a crucial element in this analysis is not that it is a subject in contrast with an object, but because it is higher than the cosmological flux and is able to stabilize the flux in relation to the temporal and the eternal presents.

The relative "length" of the present in which memory, attention, and expectation are bound together is not a metrical concept, but presupposes existential stability, expressing the intensity with which the soul longs for God and stretches beyond itself to make the transition from conversion (finite-infinite) to fulfillment (finite-infinite).[88] In this case, length is transformed into longing, and time and eternity are bound together in a present that transcends the temporal flow. Augustine also extends the domain of this intensity to nature, and by implication, to cosmological time insofar as it is intertwined with us. As he says in addressing God, the creator,

> Your whole creation does not cease or keep silent from your praise, nor does every spirit through a mouth turned to you, nor do animals and corporeal things through the mouths of those who meditate upon them, so that our soul may arouse itself to you out of its weariness, resting first on the things that you have made, and passing on to you who made those things in so wonderful a way. (5.1.1)

In this sentence, Augustine moves from creation, to the fall, through conversion, to fulfillment, where the essence of his life is expressed in remembering the conversion of Adam and in anticipating the fulfillment of the resurrection. In doing so, he not only suggests that nature and the human realm can be unified by a converted concept of time, but also points beyond time and the soul to the ground of existence that creates and sustains them.

One of the most important tasks of philosophical reflection is to focus on the ontological conditions that make experience possible and to indicate how these conditions are related imagistically to the experience of which they are the ground. As a consequence, thinking is not cut off from experience, but is a way of grounding and reflecting the structure of experience within a medium appropriate to philosophical reflection. It is because of Augustine's capacity to move so richly in both regions that he is able to solve the problem of experience and reflection. The *Confessions* is his solution to the problem of how to think concretely, where he does this, not only by answering the question, "Who am I?" (9.1.1), but also by answering the seemingly unrelated question, "What is time?" (11.14.17). In answering them both, he unifies experience and reflection by understanding philosophy as a domain that grounds and reflects the stages of the process of development that he has undergone.

3

The Hermeneutics of Creation
(Books XII–XIII)

This chapter focuses on Augustine's exegesis of Genesis 1:1–2:3, beginning with the creation of form and matter and ending with the telos of the new creation. In between these sections, it concentrates on diverse interpretations of the text that Augustine says are equally valid and develops an allegorical interpretation of verses 1:3–2:3 that allows him to move from a cosmological to a soteriological way of understanding the drama of creation. This shift from cosmology to soteriology permits Augustine to develop a creative interpretation of Genesis in response to his creator and makes it possible for him to bring the last two Books of the text into relation with the first nine. As in the experiential parts of the text, the problem that continues to preoccupy him is the relation between God and the soul and the language appropriate to it. The hermeneutical principles that he develops allow him to address both issues, mobilizing the richness of language that an adequate account of the relation between God and the soul presupposes.

Augustine's interpretation of the first chapter of Genesis correlates it with the metanarrative that makes his journey toward God possible and reflects the structure of his experience at the distinctively reflective level. This metanarrative begins with creation, moves toward the fall, points to salvation, and culminates in fulfillment. Augustine's allegorical interpretation of the text also comes to focus on symbolic personages, some of whom experience the transformation of every aspect of their being when the new creation comes to completion. Though it is tempting to believe that Books XII and XIII confirm the view that Augustine is a Neoplatonist, who repudiates embodied existence and embraces the separation of the soul from the body (7.10.16), these Books provide the strongest confirmation of the belief that Augustine develops a distinctively Christian conception of God and the soul and of the relation between them (12.7.7).

One of the most important implications of this belief is that when Augustine pictures his ultimate relation to God, he claims that both his soul and his body will stand before God as a transformed unity. As a consequence, he suggests that the relation between God and the soul will not collapse into an overarching unity, but that each of its terms will preserve its integrity as participants in a divine celebration. As he tells us on more than one occasion, when we see God, we will be like him, where our knowing will become loving, and where our loving will express itself in praise that never ends.

The hermeneutical method that Augustine develops not only allows him to speak about the relation between God and the soul, but also permits him to repudiate philosophical and theological dogmatism, to embrace the possibility of several interpretations of creation *ex nihilo*, and to point to the infinite richness of Truth that makes these interpretations possible (12.6.6–12.13.16). As a consequence, Augustine's hermeneutics is a way of moving toward fulfillment by understanding the Bible as a place where God continues to speak to the one who interprets it. However, the hermeneutics that Augustine develops comes to its richest expression only when it focuses on the relation between the act of creation and the trinitarian conception of God it presupposes. In discussing the Trinity, Augustine formulates the conditions that make the original and the new creation possible and introduces the kind of language that we must learn to speak about the intersection of time, space, and eternity (12.12.15). From the side of God, the Godhead is the place where the persons of the Trinity presuppose one another; from the side of man, creation and redemption are the places where these persons make God accessible to the experiential and reflective consciousness; and in between, figurative, performative, and intelligible discourse merge in a language appropriate to the dynamic interaction between God and the soul.

One of the most important structural features of the transitions between Books XI, XII, and XIII is the way in which they overlap as stages of Augustine's interpretive enterprise. He deals with Genesis 1.1 in Book XI, Genesis 1.1–2 in Book XII, and Genesis 1.2–2.3 in Book XIII. This connects the last three Books of the text as links in a chain, where they might otherwise appear to involve a sequence of reflections that are separated from one another. The hermeneutical principles that Augustine embraces also allow him to accomplish three purposes in the last two Books of the text: first, he discusses creation *ex nihilo* as the ground of the temporal unity that he develops in Book XI (11.26.23–11.27.36); then he indicates how creation is the larger context within which memory and time can be understood (12.1.1–12.15.21); finally, he embraces the hermeneutics of creation without needing extended prayers for enlightenment of the kind he prays at earlier stages of the *Confessions* (12.18.27–12.32.43*)*.

Book XIII completes the *Confessions* by generating an allegorical community of images of Augustine's journey toward God in Books I–VI and of his encounters with God in Books VII–IX. This is the final community to be found in the *Confessions*, and it points to the Place of places where the temporal, the spatial, and the eternal dimensions of the relation between God and the soul intersect.[1] In Book XIII, the paradise that Augustine experiences as an infant in the arms of his nurses (2.6.7), the negative communities that his education and the pear-stealing episode lead him to embrace (4.4.9), the positive community to which his conversion (8.12.29) and the mystical experience with his mother (9.10.24) lead, and the community of temporal modes that condition and image his journey toward God (11.11.13) become a community of "days," where the fragmented soul seeks rest and where it can continue to uncover the inexhaustible richness of God even after it has already found it.

FORM AND THE ABYSS (12.1.1–12.13.16)

Augustine begins Book XII by calling our attention to the fact that the Bible is the context that permits him to move from conversion to fulfillment. Though he knows that he is preoccupied with many things and that his intellectual distraction often prevents him from finding the fulfillment he seeks, he is confident that he can achieve it because God is for him rather than against him (12.1.1).[2] He is also sustained by the promise that if he asks, he will receive, if he seeks, he will find, and if he knocks it will be opened unto him (12.1.1).[3] In this case, faith moves toward understanding, where the door of Scripture swings open to give Augustine access to the infinite richness of God (12.1.1).

At the outset, Augustine returns to the first verse of Genesis that he has discussed already in Book XI. However, in the present context, he focuses his attention upon heaven and earth rather than upon the act of creation and upon the resulting contrast between time and eternity. His first reference to heaven and earth is familiar and conventional, where heaven (heaven$_1$) is identified with the heavenly bodies that we see, and earth (earth$_1$) is equated with the ground upon which we walk and with the source from which our bodies are made (12.2.2). In this context, Augustine is apparently distinguishing the creation of the soul from the creation of the body; but it is also important to notice that in speaking about our bodies, he is implying that the human being is a composite. Augustine's complex semantics and the rhetoric that depends upon it presuppose that the soul and the body are both united and separated, where metaphors bind them together and analogies hold them apart.[4]

Having distinguished the heaven (heaven$_1$) from the earth (earth$_1$) in the familiar sense of the terms, Augustine asks where the heaven of heaven (heaven$_2$), which is identical with what he will later call "the spiritual creature" or "the intellectual creature" is to be found. The psalmist answers the question when he says, "The heaven of heaven is the Lord's, but the earth he has give to the children of men" (12.2.2). Compared with the heaven of heaven (heaven$_2$) that we do not see, the visible heaven (heaven$_1$) and the visible earth (earth$_1$) are only earth (earth$_2$). Taken together, the visible heaven and the visible earth are a corporeal whole that can be divided into parts, where the lowest part has received form and beauty, and where the part in question is earth (earth$_1$) in the familiar sense of the term. Yet since the heaven (heaven$_1$) of our earth (earth$_1$) is only earth (earth$_2$) in comparison with the heaven of heaven (heaven$_2$), it is not unreasonable to claim that both "these great bodies [are] but earth before that indescribable heaven which is the Lord's and not the sons' of men." (12.2.2).

It is easy to conclude that Augustine finds a distinction here for which the Hebrew text does not provide a warrant. In that text, we find a typical nominal sentence that can be rendered, "The heavens are the heavens of Yahweh." The Latin translation available to Augustine seems to derive from a variant Hebrew text that is translated too literally as "the heaven of heaven." Perhaps it should be translated simply as the "highest heaven," which is a way of emphasizing its superlative status. Translated in this way, it would be analogous to the King of kings or the Song of songs, where a singular thing can be described superlatively only in terms of itself.[5]

To proceed in this way might bring us closer to the literal meaning of the text, but this is not the most important consideration from Augustine's point of view. Though he wants his interpretation of this and every other verse of Scripture to be true, he is not concerned primarily about whether his interpretations reflect the intentions of the author (12.2.2). Indeed, Augustine agrees with many postmodern philosophers in claiming that we can never know what an author intends to communicate by examining what he says.[6] We should also notice that even if Augustine had focused his attention on the Hebrew idiom that expresses the superlative status of the heaven of heaven (heaven$_2$), he would still have drawn a distinction between the visible heaven (heaven$_1$), on the one hand, and the highest heaven (heaven$_2$) that is closer to God on the other. This is an ontological contrast to which Augustine is deeply committed, and he will soon give his reasons for believing that it marks an important distinction among the things that God brings into existence.

Having drawn a distinction between the heaven of heaven (heaven$_2$) and the earth (earth$_2$) that stands in contrast with it, Augustine calls our attention to the fact that earth in this sense of the term (earth$_2$) is originally invisible and without order and that it is a "profound abyss" upon which there is no light because there is no form in it (earth$_3$). He also claims that this is the reason why the Bible says that darkness is upon the face of the deep (12.3.3). Darkness is the absence of light, just as silence is the absence of sound, where the absence of light is what we mean by the presence of darkness (12.3.3). Augustine equates the abyss that is deprived of light with unformed matter (earth$_3$); and he tells us that before it is fashioned into kinds, "there [is] no separate being, no color, no shape, no body, no spirit" (12.3.3). However, he is careful to call our attention to the fact that this does not imply that formless matter (earth$_3$) is absolutely nothing (*nihil*), but only that it is "a certain formlessness devoid of specific character" (12.3.3).

Yet what should unformed matter (earth$_3$) be called so that we can have at least a minimal understanding of it? Augustine replies that it is appropriate for formless matter (earth$_3$) to be designated by a familiar word, where nothing is "closer to utter formlessness than earth and the deep" (earth$_1$) (12.4.4). These two products of God's creative act are lower than any other formed creatures on the chain of being, and they are less beautiful than the higher parts of creation that God has brought into existence. However, this suggests that the formlessness of matter, which lacks beauty in itself, but from which this beautiful world has been made, can be indicated effectively by the phrase, "earth invisible and without form" (12.4.4).

A crucial point must not be overlooked in trying to understand Augustine's initial attempt to make formless matter (earth$_3$) accessible to us. When he says that invisible and formless matter (earth₃) is appropriately called earth (earth₁), he is extending a familiar term from one context to another, where the ground for this extension is the analogy between the relative lack of beauty on the part of earth and the deep (earth₁), and the absolute lack of beauty on the part of formless matter (earth₃). Yet even here there is a sense in which formless matter (earth₃) is "beautiful"; for as Augustine suggests, it is the material out of which beautiful things are made (12.4.4).

As a way of developing his account of the formless material (earth₃) from which things are made, Augustine says that he formerly conceives of it as having countless and varied forms, and that as a consequence, he does not conceive of it at all. Indeed, at an earlier stage of his development, Augustine believes that matter contains foul and horrid forms in a confused array, and that it is called "formless," not because it lacks all form, but because it has the kind of form from which the mind turns away (12.5.5). Right reason, which may well be the result of reading Aristotle and Plotinus, persuades him that he ought to remove altogether all vestiges of form if he wishes to conceive matter as completely formless.[7] However, when he first encounters this suggestion, he is no more able to do this than to conceive of a spiritual substance at an earlier stage of his development. As a consequence, it is easier for him to conclude that matter lacks all form because it does not exist than to conceive of anything between form and nothing—something that is neither formed nor nothing, but unformed and nearly nothing (12.6.6).

Augustine is able to move beyond this inadequate conception of matter by turning away from his imagination, by fixing his attention on bodies themselves, and by attempting to understand the mutability by virtue of which they cease to be what they are and begin to be what they are not. By proceeding in this way, he begins to suspect that the transition from one form to another is made through something formless (earth₃) rather than through absolute nonbeing (*nihil*). However, Augustine wants to know that this is so rather than to suspect it; and he tells us that if he were to recount all the stages of his reflections about this issue, none of us would be patient enough to listen to what he dictates (12.6.6).[8] Yet at least this much is clear without having to follow a lengthy process of inquiry: the "mutability of mutable things is . . . a capacity for all the forms into which mutable things are changed" (12.6.6). This capacity cannot be identified with either a mind or a body; and if we could say that it is a "nothing-something" or an "is-is-not" (earth₃), this would perhaps be appropriate. However, it is clear that formless matter (earth₃) exists somehow so that it might receive forms that are visible (*visibiles*) and ordered in an intelligible fashion (*compositas*) (12.6.6).

In calling our attention to the existence of unformed matter (earth$_3$) and in pointing to the mutability of mutable things, Augustine is suggesting that unformed matter (earth$_3$) carries with it the possibility of all the forms into which they can be changed. Though he may not have known the Platonic doctrine of relative nonbeing,[9] he is probably influenced here by the writings of Plotinus, where matter is analyzed as a substratum without quantity or quality,[10] and where it is described as absolutely indeterminate.[11] However this may be, Augustine agrees with Plotinus in maintaining that unformed matter is sheer possibility, from which it follows that the material out of which the world is made is neither something nor nothing (12.3.3). Yet contrary to Plotinus, Augustine claims that formless matter (earth$_3$) is good because it is the product of God's creative act (12.7.7). In committing himself to the Christian doctrine of creation *ex nihilo*, he avoids the embarrassment that the existence of matter as the source of evil causes Plotinus in some of his writings.[12]

Augustine claims that unformed matter (earth$_3$) comes from God, from whom all things come in so far as they are. He also says that the more "distant" something is from God, the more unlike God it is (12.7.7). The distance in question is not a matter of place, but of ontological richness within the continuum of things that God has brought into existence. The act of creation also presupposes the Trinity, where the beginning of the act is equated with the second person of the Trinity "in" whom God creates something out of nothing (*nihil*) (12.7.7). In bringing the world into existence, God does not make heaven and earth out of himself; for if this were the case, what he makes would be equal with his Son, and as a consequence, equal with the Father 12.7.7).

Having reiterated the point that there is nothing (*nihil*) beyond God from which he could make heaven and earth, Augustine claims that God creates heaven (heaven$_2$) and earth (earth$_2$) out of nothing (*nihil*), where heaven (heaven$_2$) is a great thing and earth (earth$_2$) is a little thing (12.7.7). Of these two beings, the first is as close to God and as far from nothing (*nihil*) as any created thing can be; and the second is as far from God and as near to nothing (*nihil*) as any created thing can be. As a consequence, only God is superior to the first; and nothing is inferior to the second (12.7.7). On the other hand, since the extreme poles of creation are created together (12.7.7) and not as the result of a cascade of descending emanations from the One, even the undifferentiated potentiality (earth$_3$) that lies beneath formed matter (earth$_2$) is as good as (heaven$_2$), understood from a

distributive point of view, which Augustine equates with the angels. Formless matter (earth$_3$) is created in exactly the same way as the heaven of
heaven (heaven$_2$).[13]

The earth (earth$_3$) that God creates in the beginning is not in the
same state as it is when we now see and touch it (earth$_2$). Instead, it is
invisible and unformed (earth$_3$); and it is "an abyss above which there [is]
no light" (12.8.8). Alternatively, Augustine says that the words, "darkness
was upon the face of the deep," could mean that there is more darkness
over the deep than in it (12.8.8). This qualification is important because
the deep that is now visible to us (earth$_2$) has light even in its lowest parts
that is "proper to its character and can in some way be sensed by the fishes
and the animals creeping on its bottom" (12.8.8).

However this may be, the abyss that is almost nothing (earth$_3$) is
something that has the possibility of being formed; and it comes into
existence as a determinate region (earth$_2$) when God makes the world out
of formless matter (earth$_3$). In order to clarify the relations among absolute nonbeing (*nihil*), unformed matter (earth$_3$), and the material things
that God brings into existence (earth$_2$), Augustine uses an analogy based
on the relation between a letter and the words that can be generated from
it. In terms of this comparison, he says that God creates a "letter" from
absolute nonbeing (*nihil*). He equates this letter, in turn, with formless
matter (earth$_3$), where words correspond to the things (earth$_2$) that God
creates from the formless material (earth$_3$) that he makes (12.8.8).

The corporeal heaven (heaven$_1$) is a firmament that is established
between the water$_2$ and the water$_1$, where the first reference to water
points to the *fluidity* of the heaven of heaven (heaven$_2$) before it is given
form, and where the second reference calls our attention to the formless
material out of which the earth and the sea are made (earth$_3$). God gives
form to the heaven of heaven (heaven$_2$) by creating light before any reference to days, and he separates the light from the darkness on the first day
of creation. Then he makes the firmament on the second day; and he calls
it "heaven" (heaven$_1$) because it is the visible region that stands in contrast
with the earth and sea. Finally, God makes the earth and the sea (earth$_1$)
"on the third day by giving visible form to formless matter (earth$_3$), which
[he makes] before the beginning of . . . days" (12.8.8).

Augustine emphasizes the peculiar status of the heaven of heaven
(heaven$_2$) and of formless matter (earth$_3$) by claiming that they are
nontemporal creatures in the ordinary sense of the term (12.8.8). Yet
before he develops this theme, he returns to the claim that the earth
(earth$_3$) that is mentioned in the first verse of Genesis is formless because

it is "invisible, and not set in order, and darkness [is] above the deep." As a consequence, it will also prove to be prior to time, understood as the cosmological flux in which things come to be and pass away (12.8.8). With respect to formless material (earth$_3$), Augustine says,

> Out of this unordered and invisible earth, out of this formlessness, out of this almost-nothing, you made all things, out of which this mutable world stands firm, and yet does not stand firm, in which mutability itself is apparent, in which tracts of time can be perceived and numbered off. For tracts of time result from the changes of things, according as the forms, for which the aforesaid invisible earth is the matter, are varied and turned about. (12.8.8)

In this quotation Augustine commits himself to the view that God makes visible things (earth$_2$) out of unordered and invisible material (earth$_3$). In addition, he says that unlike the heaven of heaven (heaven$_2$) and formless matter (earth$_3$), visible things (earth$_2$) are subject to time and that they stand firm (*constat*), on the one hand, and do not stand firm (*non constat*) on the other (12.8.8). In this case, mutability is apparent; and tracts of time can be perceived and measured when we turn our attention to them (12.8.8). Finally, Augustine says that cosmological time results from the changes of things as they vary from one form to another (12.8.8). This means that time in the cosmological sense is a function of things rather than the other way about.

When Augustine claims that things in time stand firm (*constat*) and do not stand firm (*non constat*), and when he says that time is a function of things as they change from one form to another, he is implying that changing things are higher on the chain of being than the temporal matrix that depends upon them. Things that vary from one form to another both are (*esse*) and are not (*non esse*), while the past, the present, and the future in the cosmological sense of the terms do not exist (*non esse*). This implies that changing things stand in between time and eternity and that they participate in being (*esse*) and nonbeing (*non esse*) simultaneously. The sense in which changing things stand in between time and eternity rests on two considerations: first, time is a function of changing things (11.24.31), which implies that things are higher on the chain of being than temporality; second, the fact that time does not exist (*non esse*), that things are (*esse*) and are not (*non esse*), and that eternity (*esse*) is in an unqualified sense of the term places things in between time and eternity in a hierarchy of being. It is from this middle ground that

Augustine prays in Book XI, asking that his fluttering heart will be brought to rest (stability$_2$) so that he might stabilize (stability$_1$) the temporal framework that unfolds "below" him.

Creation is the ground of cosmological time; and conversion is the ground of the stabilized (stability$_2$) concept of time that permits Augustine to transcend his experiential and reflective predicament. One of the most important expressions of this moment of transcendence is that it gives Augustine the stability he needs to stabilize (stability$_1$) time by developing the account of it that he formulates in Book XI (11.26.33). It is also important to remember that both time and the changing things upon which it depends are created good and that they are a (finite-infinite)[14] reflection of the creative ground from which they emerge. As Augustine suggests, already, we need to stabilize (stability$_1$) the cosmological flux in order to convert it to form; and we need to recover (stability$_2$) this stabilized (stability$_1$) conception of time in order to overcome the discord of the fluttering heart and the disorientation of the flighty mind.

Having referred to changing things and to the temporal matrix that depends upon them, Augustine emphasizes the fact that when God's Spirit says that God creates heaven and earth in the beginning, it says nothing about times and is silent about days. He also claims that the heaven of heaven (heaven$_2$), which God makes in the beginning, is an intellectual creature. Finally, he says that even though this creature is not coeternal with God, it is a partaker of eternity (*sempiternitas*). Apparently, the intellectual creature is *in* eternity by standing in unwavering relation *to* eternity, where it contemplates God and "firmly checks its own mutability" (12.9.9).

This reference to the mutability of the heaven of heaven (heaven$_2$) brings it into relation with time, even though it would be inappropriate to say that the creature in question is temporal in the customary sense of the term. Perhaps it would be better to say that it is on the cusp between time and eternity, where this way of speaking would distinguish it from God, on the one hand, and from the souls and bodies that God creates on the other.[15] Augustine might have something like this in mind when he claims that without "any lapse from its first creation, it has clung fast to [God] and is thus set beyond all the turns and changes of time" (12.9.9). The light God gives to the intellectual creature (heaven$_2$) before the first day of creation informs its formlessness[16] and enables this creature to transcend time by clinging to eternity. As a consequence, even though the heaven of heaven (heaven$_2$) is temporal insofar as it is mutable, it is not temporal insofar as it mutates. Augustine also tells us that the formless material (earth$_3$) from which the earth (earth$_2$) is made is "invisible and without form" and is "not numbered among the days." He says this because where there is no shape or order, there is nothing that either comes to be or passes away; and where this does not occur, there are no days or any change of time (12.9.9). On the other hand, to claim that formless material (earth$_3$) is not in time in the strict sense of the term does not imply that it is not temporal in some sense. In this case, the "temporality" of prime matter (earth$_3$) consists in the fact that it serves as the material cause of temporal things. As a consequence, temporality can be predicated of it transcategorially.[17]

At this juncture, Augustine subordinates his interpretation of the first two verses of Genesis to God by praying that his source of inspiration will be the light of his heart rather than the darkness that covers it over. Augustine has good reason to do this, for he is keenly aware of the fact that he has fallen away from God toward material things and that he has become "darkened over" as a consequence of his sin (12.10.10). At this stage of his analysis, Augustine is pointing to the kind of allegorical interpretation that he will develop in Book XIII, where light and darkness refer to stages in the drama of salvation rather than to cosmological moments in the creation of the world (13.3.4). As a way of expressing this account of his development in a preliminary way, he claims that even in his fallen condition, he does not forget the one in whose image he is has been created. This image has not been effaced, and this fact makes it possible for him to hear God's voice calling him to return to the condition from which he has fallen (12.10.10).

When Augustine says that he falls away from God toward material things, he does not mean that the soul falls into the body, but that the entire human being turns away from God toward the world that God creates. This is a typical example of loving the creature rather than the creator, where in extreme cases, we attempt to return to the *nihil* from which God brings the organized universe into existence (12.10.10). When Augustine claims that he remembers God in spite of the fact that he has turned away from him (10.24.35), this need not point to the existence of the soul in a previous state from which it falls into the body, but to the fact that the image of God is to be found in every individual, existing alongside the negative condition into which we have fallen.[18] There may be a good reason for claiming that the soul is created prior to the body in a nontemporal sense of the term, for the soul is higher than the body and is the dimension of a man or woman that rules and judges both the body and the senses.[19] However, such a view does not imply that the soul is embodied by *falling* into time[20] rather than by being *conjoined with* the body as a stage in the process of creation.[21] It is only when both stages of this process have been completed that Augustine becomes preoccupied with the journey that leads from creation to the fall, from fall to conversion, and from conversion to fulfillment.

When Augustine hears God's voice in the garden in Milan, he turns toward God in a conversion experience that implicates both his soul and his body (8.12.29); and on this basis, be begins to move toward fulfillment in both practical and theoretical terms. The confession of his sins in Book X points to the practical dimension of his quest for fulfillment (10.5.7), while the interpretation of the nature of memory in the first half of the Book (10.6.8–10.27.38), and of the first chapter of Genesis in Books XI–XIII calls our attention to the theoretical dimension of his journey toward completion. In characterizing his existential journey, Augustine moves from creation to the fall, from the fall to conversion, and from conversion to fulfillment, where one of the most important ways in which fulfillment can be achieved is for God to speak *to* Augustine through the Bible and to speak *with* him as he attempts to unravel its mystery.

Augustine begins to summarize what he has learned by claiming that since God never changes from one temporal state to another, God is immortal. He also says that God has made every substance that is not identical with him but that still exists. The only "thing" that does not "come from [God] is what does not exist, together with any movement of the will" away from God toward what exists "in a lesser way" (12.11.11). In addition, Augustine reminds us that even the intellectual creature is not coeternal with God, even though it has "never asserted its own mutability" (12.11.12). As a way of elaborating some of our earlier suggestions, we should notice that this creature can be characterized in three ways: first, it is oriented toward eternity by clinging to God with all its power; second, it does not have a future from which to transfer what it expects into what it remembers; and finally, even though it is temporal because it is mutable, it is nontemporal because it never changes (12.12.15). The intellectual creature is happy in God, and Augustine says that he knows no better way to describe the heaven of heaven (heaven$_2$) than to identify it with such a creature. Indeed, he claims that the heaven of heaven (heaven$_2$) is "the house of the Lord" that contemplates God without turning away from him, where the unity it displays is expressed in the harmony of the citizens of the City of God that exist "in heavenly places above these present heavens" (12.11.12).

One of the most important notice about the heaven of heaven (heaven$_2$) is that Augustine identifies it not only with an intellectual creature (heaven$_2$)

in the singular, but also with intellectual creatures in the plural. However, we can bind these ways of speaking together by using the same kind of analysis that we adopted in discussing the meaning of "Adam,"[22] where the intellectual creature (heaven$_2$) is first a single being, then what it means to be a being of this kind, and finally a distributive collection of creatures, all of whom are oriented toward God. To the extent that we embrace the third prong of this analysis, it becomes possible to identify the intellectual creature (heaven$_2$) with the angels that Augustine mentions in Book XIII, where unfallen angels can be characterized in terms of their unwavering commitment to God.

The second point to notice is that once this identification has been made, it becomes possible to specify the distinction between the intellectual creature and the unfallen souls and bodies that God brings into existence. Though the intellectual creature is mutable (12.11.14), it is made of spiritual material (heaven$_3$), transcends time by clinging to God; and "suffers no change in time" (12.11.13). By contrast, souls and bodies change and develop in time (12.11.14), though they need not fall unless they turn their attention away from God and plunge toward the created things that God has made (12.11.11). The intellectual creature, together with the spiritual material (heaven$_3$) of which it is made, does not fall if it directs its attention toward God unwaveringly. By contrast, and somewhat paradoxically, the soul has the more difficult task of stabilizing (stability$_1$) time and bringing what it stabilizes into relation with God. This is one example of what Augustine means when he tells us that we must learn to love all things in God (12.11.12), where loving things in God is a way of not falling away from God toward other creatures that God has brought into existence.

The final point to notice about the relation between the intellectual creature (heaven$_2$) and unfallen souls and bodies is that they have different places on the ontological continuum. First, God creates everything *ex nihilo*, where God and the *nihil* are beyond the continuum altogether. In between, we find the heaven of heaven (heaven$_2$) that cleaves to God without wavering (12.11.12), the unformed material (earth$_3$) from which things are made (12.11.14), souls and bodies that are (*esse*) and are not (*non esse*), and cosmological time that is a function of changing things and that does not exist (*non esse*). When this spatialized hierarchy is ordered in terms of value, it begins with God and ends with absolute nonbeing (*nihil*), where the spiritual creature (heaven$_2$), souls and bodies, unformed material (earth$_3$), and cosmological time are placed in between. The reason that unformed matter (earth$_3$) is higher than cosmological time is that it is the material (earth$_3$) out of which bodies are made rather than a temporal matrix that results from changing things and requires conversion to form. At a later stage of our discussion, we will find that Augustine introduces a concept of spiritual material (heaven$_3$) and places the material (heaven$_3$) from which spiritual beings (heaven$_2$) are made on a higher level than bodies, issuing in a final revision of the order that the continuum before us exhibits (12.29.40).[23] However, the most important point to notice at this stage of our reflections is that the intellectual creature (heaven$_2$) and the soul have different places on the ontological continuum, where both of them are unfallen in their original condition.

By calling our attention to the intellectual creature (heaven$_2$) that is not coeternal with God, but that manifests both intellectual and volitional properties as it clings to God without suffering changes in time (12.12.15), Augustine not only enables us to distinguish this creature from the created Adam, but also encourages his readers to move beyond their fallen condition. He tells us that even though our pilgrimage has become long, we will be able to become citizens of the same city that the intellectual creature (heaven$_2$) inhabits by turning away from the world and by seeking God with the whole of our being. In this way, we will be able to dwell in God's house all the days of our lives, where doing this means to live without wavering in relation to eternity (12.11.13). By contrast with this unwavering relation, the fluttering heart focuses its attention upon the "mutations of the latest and [the] lowest things." A man of this kind "wanders about and tosses up and down amid his own fantasies (*phantasma*)" (12.11.14). Just as the flighty mind fails to understand the nature of time that needs to be stabilized (stability$_1$ and stability$_2$), it also says that even unformed matter (earth$_3$) can exhibit temporal change. However, Augustine says once more that "in no way could it be so, because without variety of motions there are no times, and there is no variety where there is no form" (12.11.14).

The time to which Augustine is referring here is cosmological, and it displays relative nonbeing (*non esse*) in all of its modes. By contrast, having indicated that God has begun to open the Scriptures to his knocking, he reiterates the claim that two things are immune to time, although neither of them is coeternal with God. As Augustine formulates the point,

One of them has been so formed that, without any interruption of its contemplation, without any interval of change, subject to change yet never changing, it enjoys eternity and immutability. The other was so formless that it could not be changed from one form into another whether of motion or of rest, and thus be made subject to time. (12.12.15)

However, Augustine also claims that God does not "abandon this second being to remain formless"; for before all days and in the beginning, he makes the heaven and the earth (earth$_2$) about which he has been speaking (12.12.15).

The previous sentence implies that the earth (earth$_3$) mentioned in verse one is the formless material out of which God makes the heaven and the earth (earth$_2$). Otherwise, it would be inappropriate to say that in creating them, he is not abandoning the earth (earth$_2$) to remain formless. Yet as I have suggested already, it is also important to notice that the creation of the intellectual creature (heaven$_2$) is a way of giving form to what is formless (heaven$_3$); and Augustine implies that the creative act in which God does this occurs in the beginning and before any reference to days. At a later stage of our inquiry, Augustine makes his account of this issue more perspicuous by saying that the formless earth (earth$_3$) to which he is referring here supplies the spiritual material (heaven$_3$) from which the heaven of heaven (heaven$_2$) is made, and that the formlessness of matter (earth$_3$) takes two forms, one of which is spiritual (heaven$_3$) and the other of which is material (earth$_3$) (13.2.2).

In that later context, Augustine tells us explicitly that the formation of the heaven of heaven (heaven$_2$) involves a process of bringing light to formless material (heaven$_3$). The formation of the heaven of heaven (heaven$_2$) does not occur until light is given to it, where what is formed is the formless material (heaven$_3$) that God makes before the creation of days (13.3.4). In so far as the creation of light is a way of bringing form to formless material (heaven$_3$), the creation of light is related to time only because the intellectual creature (heaven$_2$) that exhibits it is mutable. Since this creature has the capacity to change without ever changing, the created light that makes this possible is "temporal" without ever becoming subject to temporality (13.3.4).[24]

Having pointed to the fact that the intellectual creature (heaven$_2$) clings to God without wavering, either intellectually or volitionally, Augustine shifts his attention to the earth (earth$_3$) that is "invisible and without form" and in which "darkness [is] above the deep" (12.12.15). He says that these words are intended to instill the idea of formlessness into minds that "could not conceive complete privation of form without arriving at nothing" (12.12.15). He also suggests that God makes the visible heaven (heaven$_1$) and the visible earth (earth$_1$) from this formless material (earth$_3$) on the second and the third days of creation. Finally, he claims that in these things, "temporal changes . . . take place because of ordered alternations of movements and forms" (12.12.15).

This is Augustine's provisional interpretation of the first two verses of Genesis in which we find the words, "In the beginning God made heaven and earth, and the earth was invisible and without form, and darkness was upon the deep" (12.13.16). Since these verses do not mention a day upon which God does this, Augustine concludes that the heaven of heaven (heaven$_2$) is an intellectual creature,

> where it belongs to intellect to know all at once, not in part, not in a dark matter, not through a glass, but as a whole, in plain sight, face to face, not this thing now and that thing then, but, as has been said, it knows all at once, without any passage of time. (12.13.16)

Augustine also reminds us that he understands by the phrase, "the earth invisible and without form," an earth (earth$_3$) that never changes in time, "for where there is no form, there is [no] separation of this from that" (12.13.16).

Augustine brings this section of the *Confessions* to a conclusion by claiming that his interim judgment is that when the first two verses of Genesis mention the creation of the world without making any reference to days, they are referring to the heaven of heaven (heaven$_2$) that is formed from the beginning, and to the earth (earth$_3$) that is invisible and unorganized. The original status of the earth is made evident by the fact that the second verse of Genesis says that it is created without form, is void, and darkness is upon the face of the deep. It is equally clear to Augustine that the heaven that is mentioned in verse one is the heaven of heaven (heaven$_2$), for heaven in the usual sense (heaven$_1$) is created on the second day and stands in contrast with the heaven that is mentioned at the outset (12.13.16). In both cases, heaven (heaven$_2$) and earth (earth$_3$) have an ontological status that makes it possible for them to exist before time is created, even though they are products of creation *ex nihilo*.

AUGUSTINE AND HIS CRITICS (12.14.17–12.16.23)

As he reflects on the words of the first few verses of Genesis, Augustine is struck with wonder at the depth of Scripture that stands in contrast with the surface of the text that can even give delight to little children. In drawing this distinction, he returns to the contrast that he has mentioned earlier between the surface and the center of the Bible, where the text grows in richness as we penetrate more deeply into its depths (12.14.17). Augustine also denounces the enemies of the Bible; and he tells us that he wants God to slay them "with a two-edged sword" (12.14.17). However, just as the metaphor he uses points in two directions, the wish he expresses has a twofold significance. On the one hand, he hates the enemies of the Bible; on the other hand, he also loves them so they might be "slain to themselves" and might live for God (12.14.17).

At the beginning of Book X, Augustine turns away from a universal audience to address the Christian community; and this is the community to which he has spoken in the third part of his inquiry (10.1.1). The only exception to this has been the remarks in Book XI to flighty minds and fluttering hearts, which are unable to grasp the relation between time and eternity (11.11.13). Even there, his primary intention is to indicate to Christians how critics who stand outside the Christian community are to be dealt with. In the passage before us, the enemies of the Bible whom Augustine hates are also a secondary audience for what he has said and wishes to say about the intricacies of biblical interpretation (12.14.17). The only thing that Augustine can hope for in this case is that God slays them to themselves so they might enter the Christian community to which he has been speaking.

By contrast with those who stand outside the Christian community, there are others within it who praise the first chapter of Genesis, but do not agree with Augustine's interpretation of it. These interpreters say that the Spirit of God does not want all the things that Augustine has said to be understood from it, but something different that they themselves say. To these fellow Christians, who have been slain to themselves and are attempting to live for God, Augustine intends to reply within the circle of faith, asking God to judge between what he says and his critics' contradictions (12.14.17).

In order to prepare the foundation for his response, Augustine attempts to establish common ground upon which he and other interpreters of Genesis stand. Augustine has a specific audience of Christian philosophers and theologians in mind when he begins his response, and he wants to establish from the outset the assumptions that bind them together.

The philosopher tells us that the first thing that Truth speaks "with a strong voice into [his] inner ear" is that God the creator never changes and that "his will is not outside his substance." For this reason, God does bring things into existence in time, but "wills all that he wills" all at once. If this were not the case, God would be mutable rather than eternal (12.15.18). In addition, Augustine reminds his critics "that expectation of things to come becomes complete intuition when those things come to pass, and this same intuition becomes memory after they pass away." He also says that everything that varies in this way is mutable, and that "no mutable thing is eternal" (12.15.18). That is to say, both the acts and the contents of expectation and memory come to be and pass away through actions in which they are distended all at once, and which transfer the one into the other (12.15.18). Finally, Augustine claims that when he gathers up and fits together all these claims about time and eternity, just as he has been gathered up in time and oriented toward eternity in Milan (9.10.24–26), he finds that God does not establish "his creation by any new act of will, nor [does] his knowledge suffer any transmutation" (12.15.18).

In response to these presuppositions, Augustine's critics claim that they do not deny any of them. Yet then Augustine asks whether they deny "that every formed nature, or matter capable of formation, exists only from [God] because he is supremely good and because he supremely is" (12.15.19). And when they say that they do not, he asks whether they believe that a sublime creature exists that cleaves to God and that without being coeternal with him, does not detach itself from him, and "does not dissolve away into any variation and change of times." As Augustine has claimed already, this being does not fall away from God toward itself; and it is "the house of God," neither earthly nor celestial. As a consequence, he says once more that a spiritual creature (heaven$_2$) partakes of eternity, even though it is not coeternal with God (12.15.19).

Although the intellectual creature (heaven$_2$) is created before time, and even though it is to be identified with the "wisdom [that] has been created before all things," Augustine is careful to indicate that it is not the wisdom through whom heaven (heaven$_1$) and earth (earth$_1$) are created in the beginning (12.15.20). Instead, it is to be understood as created wisdom, which is to be identified with the intellectual creature that becomes light through the contemplation of Light. This transformation from darkness into light occurs in the beginning and without any reference to the days of creation. On the other hand, since the creature in question stands in an unwavering relation to the Wisdom that brings the world into existence, it is called "wisdom," even though it is to be understood only as "created wisdom" (12.15.20).

Augustine compares the difference between the Light that brings light and the light that is brought with the difference between the Wisdom that creates and the wisdom that is created. In this way, he points once more to the fact that the heaven of heaven (heaven$_2$) is informed by the light that transforms the darkness in which it would otherwise languish. The soteriological dimension of Augustine's intention is underscored by the fact that he also compares the difference between the Light that creates and the light that is created with the difference between the "justice that justifies and the justice that is brought about by justification" (12.15.20). This comparison prepares the way for understanding creation as conversion to form and for understanding conversion as a new creation.[25] Just as Augustine moves toward justification in the garden when he encounters the Justice of God that justifies him, so the wisdom that God creates in the beginning and without any reference to days "moves" toward the Light when its darkness is enlightened (12.15.20). This comparison is another indication that Augustine's theoretical conversion is a condition for and an image of his experiential conversion.

Augustine continues his reflections about the wisdom that God creates by claiming that it "was created before all things" and that it is "the rational and intellectual soul" (heaven$_2$) of the City of God that is "free and eternal in the heavens" (12.15.20). Then he tells us that created wisdom is in the heaven of heaven (heaven$_2$) that praises God without ceasing. Finally, he summarizes the relation between the one who brings light and the light that is brought by saying,

> Although we find no time in it, for that which was created before all things precedes the creation of time, yet the eternity of the creator himself is before it. For being made by him, it took its beginning from him, not indeed in time, for time itself was not, but in its very creation. (12.15.20)

Among other things, this means that the intellectual creature (heaven$_2$) is completely different from the one who brings it into existence.

Augustine claims that there is not only no time before the creation of the intellectual creature (heaven$_2$), but also no time *in* it because it beholds God's face forever and is never turned aside from it. As a consequence, it never changes from one state to another (12.15.20). As we have noticed already, there is "a certain mutability" in it in virtue of which it would become "dark and cold" if it ceases to cleave to God with a steadfast love (12.15.21). Yet the intellectual creature (heaven$_2$) never does this, while the soul has fallen away from God and has wandered in a region of destitution (end of 2). This leads Augustine to exclaim

O lightsome and beautiful house! I have loved your beauty and
the dwelling place of my Lord, your builder and possessor! May
my pilgrimage sigh after you! I speak to him who made you, so
he may also possess me in you, because he has likewise made me.
"I have gone astray like a sheep that is lost." Yet upon the shoulders of my shepherd, your builder, I hope to be borne back to
you. (12.15.21)

In this passage, Augustine need not be claiming that his soul once
exists in the City of God (heaven₂), that he wanders away from it, and
that he longs to recover the state from which he has fallen. Indeed, this
is only one of four theories about the origin of the soul that Augustine
considers; and he never decides which one to embrace, even at the end of
his life.[26] As I have argued already in Book X, and as I have indicated at
a previous stage of this chapter, Augustine is committed to the view that
the image of God has not been effaced by the fall and that original
innocence is the first word about the human situation. The reason for this
is that the world that God creates is good, however much it may be
marred by original sin. Against this background, and by remembering the
one who has created both his soul and his body, Augustine longs to
recover his original relation to the one who creates and sustains him; and
he wants to do this by returning to God on the shoulders of the shepherd
who has brought the heaven of heaven (heaven₂) into existence.[27]

At this stage of his argument, Augustine extracts agreement from
his critics about three other issues that have surfaced in his interpretation of the first two verses of the Bible. First, they agree that even
though the house of God (heaven₂) is not coeternal with God, it participates in eternity and exhibits no temporal variations. Instead, this
house (heaven₂), which clings unwaveringly to God, "surpasses all distention and all turning tracts of time" (12.15.22). This means that even
though a temporal creature can be stabilized in time by being distended
toward the past, the present, and the future simultaneously (11.11.13),
such a creature has a lower place on the chain of being than the house
of God (heaven₂) that never changes. Second, Augustine's critics agree
that the material from which the world is made is unformed (earth₃). It
follows from this that no order and no time are to be found in it. This
is true because where there is no form, there is no order; and where
there is no order, there is no time (12.15.22). Finally, the audience to
which Augustine is addressing himself agrees that the material (earth₃)
from which things are made is not completely nothing (*nihil*). They also

agree that God creates this material (earth$_3$), for everything that exists in any way comes from God (12.15.22).

Having established this broad base of agreement with his critics, Augustine says that he wants to converse with them for a little while in the presence of God (12.16.23). In this way, he reaffirms his commitment to the Christian community and to the hermeneutics of loves that it presupposes (12.16.23). Augustine begins to embrace this community at the end of Book VIII, where he, Alypius, and Monica first stand alongside one another as fellow Christians. The community in question is what Josiah Royce calls the "beloved community,"[28] and it develops in a series of stages through Augustine's later experience. First, the community expands when Augustine is baptized and becomes a member of the Church (9.6.14); and it expands still further when he prays, not only for his mother and father, but also for all the citizens of the City of God at the end of Book IX (9.13.37). Finally, it expands in practical and theoretical terms in Books X–XIII. In Book X, he confesses his present sins to "the believing sons" of men (10.1.1); and in Books XI–XIII, he speaks with charity to those within the Christian community who disagree with him. As their conversation continues, it finally leads to the threshold of the City of God, where the community of "days" to which the first chapter of Genesis calls our attention points to a day without an evening in which Augustine comes to rest.

Yet having embraced the Christian community and the Christian scholars to whom he addresses himself in the last four Books of the text, Augustine also makes reference to those who stand outside the circle of faith, barking at those who stand within it and succeeding only in making noise for their own ears. Augustine says that he will attempt to persuade those who stand outside the Christian community that what he has said is true. However, his primary purpose in doing so is not to have a theoretical discussion with them, but to make it possible for them to make a positive response to the Word of God (12.16.23). In this way, the author makes it clear once more that inquiry into philosophical and theological issues presupposes a transformed spirit and that unless those who stand outside the circle of faith are prepared to accept a transformation of this kind, they can never hope to understand what he is attempting to teach.

Even if these people refuse to be persuaded, Augustine asks God to speak within his own heart, permitting him to turn away from them to the place where God can address him. In making this request, Augustine seeks a place for meditation of the kind that emerges from his analysis of the nature of time (11.2.3); and he does so by saying,

I will enter into my chamber and there I will sing songs of love
to you, groaning with unspeakable groanings on my pilgrimage,
and remembering Jerusalem, with heart lifted up towards it, Jerusalem my country, Jerusalem my mother, and you who over her are
ruler, enlightener, father, guardian, spouse, pure and strong delight, solid joy, all good things ineffable, all possessed at once,
because you are the one and the true good. (12.16.23)

Finally, Augustine says that he will not be turned away from the City of
God until God gathers him up from his "scattered and disordered state"
into the peace of God where the "first fruits of [his] spirit" are to be found
(12.16.23). In speaking about everything that he is, Augustine is referring
to his soul and his body; and in mentioning the first fruits of his spirit,
he is calling our attention to his conversion in the garden in Milan[29]
(8.12.29). Against the background of this conversion, he wants to move
from conversion to fulfillment by understanding the words of Scripture.
Thus, he asks God to judge between him and his critics, all of whom
share the presupposition that the Bible is the Word of God.

ALTERNATIVE INTERPRETATIONS (12.17.24–12.22.31)

In turning to alternative interpretations of the first two verses of
Genesis, Augustine structures his initial remarks as if he were participating in a debate. Perhaps this debate has occurred or is still in progress,
pointing beyond a cluster of mere possibilities to positions that his critics
actually hold.[30] However this may be, the opponents whom Augustine
depicts believe that they know what Moses means when he says, "In the
beginning God created the heaven and the earth"; and though they believe that what Augustine has said about the first two verses of Genesis
is true, they maintain that it is not what Moses means when he utters the
words in question (12.17.24).

The first group of critics claims that when he speaks about heaven
and earth, Moses is not referring to the intellectual creature (heaven$_2$)
who contemplates God without wavering or to formless matter (earth$_3$)
from which things are made. Instead, they claim that when he speaks
about heaven (heaven$_1$) and earth (earth$_1$), he indicates universally and
briefly "the whole visible world (earth$_2$), so that afterwards by [an] enu-
meration of days he could point out," one by one, all the things that the
Holy Spirit has revealed in this way (12.17.24). They make this claim

because they believe that the people to whom Moses speaks are rude and carnal, making it plausible that he should mention only the visible works of God to them. However, this same group of critics agrees that it is not inappropriate to interpret "the invisible and unformed earth" and "the darkened abyss" as the unformed matter (earth$_3$) out of which "visible things were made and set in order" (12.17.24).

A second group of critics claims that the terms "heaven" and "earth" are first used to refer to formless material (earth$_3$); and they believe that this is so because the visible world (earth$_2$), which is called "heaven" (heaven$_1$) and "earth" (earth$_1$) in the usual sense, is "established and perfected" from it (12.17.25). By contrast, a third group of critics says that the phrase, "heaven and earth," refers to the invisible (heaven$_2$) and the visible (earth$_2$) parts of creation, where the whole created order that God makes in the beginning is comprehended in this way. This group also maintains that the world has been created, not out of God, but out of nothing (*nihil*). They say this because "there is a certain mutability in all things, whether they stand fast, as does God's eternal house, or are subject to change, as are man's soul and body" (12.17.25). Finally, this third group says that the material from which everything is made, both visible and invisible, is mentioned in the phrases, "the earth invisible and without form" and "darkness over the deep." Yet they also emphasize a crucial difference between the phrases in question. They say that "the earth invisible and without order," refers to *corporeal* matter (earth$_3$) before it is formed and that "darkness above the deep" refers to *spiritual* matter (heaven$_3$) "before any restraint was put upon its almost unbounded fluidity (*fluens*) and any enlightenment from wisdom" (12.17.25).[31]

Three important points emerge from Augustine's account of the opinions of this third group of interpreters. First, in claiming that God's eternal house (heaven$_2$) stands fast in contrast with the soul and the body that are subject to change, they imply that the heaven of heaven (heaven$_2$), on the one hand, and the soul and the body on the other have a different ontological status. The intellectual creature (heaven$_2$) is created before the creation of time, and it is "temporal" only in the sense that it is changeable without ever changing. By contrast, souls and bodies are created in time; and as a consequence, they change and develop. This implies that even though they have fallen away from God, they exist in time from the outset. Since the view that we are considering is a way of understanding creation rather than the fall, it also implies that the soul *does not fall into time and the body,* but is *created in time,* in contrast with the intellectual creature (heaven$_2$).[32]

The second point to notice about the position before us is that in distinguishing spiritual (heaven$_3$) from corporeal (earth$_3$) material, and in equating spiritual matter (heaven$_3$) with the darkness on the face of the deep, Augustine's opponents make explicit what is implicit in his earlier distinction between the Light that creates and the light that is created. These critics are committed to the view than in creating the world, God brings light to the darkness of the spiritual material (earth$_3$) that he creates in the beginning, where the creation of light occurs without any reference to the passage of time. Since the critics in question are speaking about creation rather than the fall, they are also committed to the view that even though spiritual matter (heaven$_3$) floats about and is unenlightened until it is converted to form, this does not imply that it is fallen, but simply that it is capable of being formed.

The final point to notice is that the distinction between the two kinds of matter that surfaces here, and that will become a crucial part of Augustine's understanding of the process of creation, points to a double hylomorphism in his thinking that will need to be explored. In fact, Augustine's complex semantics about the soul and the body rests on the view that the soul is a substance, that the body is a substance, and that the composite of the soul and the body is a substance as well. This implies that spiritual material (heaven$_3$) is required to create a soul, that corporeal material (earth$_3$) is required to create a body, and that a soul and a body are required to create a human being. Though this might seem odd from a systematic point of view,[33] Augustine's rhetoric moves back and forth between the union and the separation of the soul from the body. When he unifies them, they are bound together as a composite to which metaphorical discourse gives us access; and when he separates them, they stand over against one another as substances that analogical discourse holds apart.

The final interpretation of "heaven" and "earth" that Augustine mentions is a hypothesis that he might have conceived of himself rather than a theory that is defended by someone in the audience he is addressing.[34] According to this hypothesis, "heaven and earth" does not refer to the heaven of heaven (heaven$_2$) and to the visible heaven and the visible earth (earth$_2$), that have been "already perfected and formed" (12.17.26). Instead, it refers to "the still formless commencement of things" in which matter (heaven$_3$, earth$_3$) is created as capable of conversion to form. According to this view, the heaven (heaven$_3$) and the earth (earth$_3$) that are mentioned in the first two verses of the Bible contain "in a confused manner, and not yet distinguished by qualities and forms," the things that are "now arranged in order and called heaven and earth, the one being a spiritual and the other a corporeal creature" (12.17.26). As one of Augustine's translators says, this position involves a "striking anticipation of some modern evolutionary doctrines [about] the origin and development of the universe."[35] It is also consistent with Augustine's claim in Book XI that though God creates the world all at once, all the things that he makes are not created "simultaneously and eternally" (11.7.9).

Augustine's first response to these theories is to say that he does not wish to contend about words. Rather, he wants to respond to them with charity in accord with the "two commandments" upon which "the . . . law and the prophets depend" (12.18.27). The first of these commandments requires that we love God completely, and the second says that we must love our neighbors as ourselves.[36] Against this background, Augustine suggests that we should be free to embrace alternative interpretations of the biblical text, the richness of which outstrips authorial intention. Thus, in attempting to understand the Word of God and to respond to his critics in the spirit of charity, he asks what harm would come to him if various interpretations of the words of Moses could be given, all of which are true (12.18.27).

Augustine also asks what harm would result if he disagrees with others about what the author of the text means. He believes that everyone who attempts to interpret a text tries "to trace out and understand" what the author wishes to convey; and since he and all of those who share his presuppositions believe that Moses speaks truly, they dare not suppose that he has said anything that they either know or suppose to be false (12.18.27). Finally, even though Augustine believes that everyone who interprets the Bible attempts to understand what the author means by what he writes, he asks,

> What [harm] is there if anyone understands what you, O light of all truthful minds, reveal to him as true, even if the authors he reads did not understand this, since he also understood a truth, but not this truth? (12.18.27)

In making these remarks, Augustine does not intend to say that there is a plurality of truths in a single verse of Scripture, but a multiplicity of perspectives on Truth that involve different levels and interpretations of Truth[37] (12.18.27). What distinguishes these perspectives is their greater or lesser adequacy for us, which is not the same as a greater or lesser adequacy for God. This insight overcomes the fundamental sense of every Platonist hierarchy according to which each step down is a diminution of

the preceding principle,[38] and its corollary that each step up in understanding is better from the standpoint of God. As a consequence, Augustine sees the diversity of truth—as nearer and farther from God and a
greater and lesser understanding of him—as good in itself.[39] This means
that the philosophers' assumption that their knowledge is better, from the
divine perspective, than the knowledge of others not capable of it have
failed altogether.[40] The hierarchical foundations of antiquity, its sense of
the return as a flight from the lower to the higher, and the consequent
preference for the latter over the former are replaced at this juncture with
a different view in which Monica stands as firmly in the Truth as Victorinus,
Ambrose, or her brilliant son in which the incarnate Christ is no less the
absolute Truth than is the eternal Word. The consequences of this gentler,
more charitable view that is sanctioned by God are incalculable. They
start from the five true explanations of the same passage from Genesis
(12.10.10–12.32.43), which he has just explained in a sixth way—and
evident parallel to the diversity of good things in the six days of creation.[41]
These diverse interpretations will call Christians eventually to the widest
possible inclusion of every possible difference that can be shown to stand
in the Truth.[42]

Augustine expresses his willingness to embrace the possibility of
alternative interpretations by conceding the truth of the following claims
that have been made by those who contradict him:

1. God creates heaven (heaven$_1$) and earth (earth$_1$).
2. The beginning of creation is to be equated with Wisdom, in
   which God makes all things.
3. The greater parts of the visible world are heaven and earth (earth$_2$)
   by way of a brief description of everything that God has made.
4. Mutable beings suggest "a certain formlessness" (earth$_3$) to our
   minds that makes it possible for them to receive forms, or to be
   transmuted and changed.
5. The intellectual creature (heaven$_2$) that clings to God never
   changes even though it is mutable.
6. Unformed matter (earth$_3$) that is "almost nothing" cannot change
   in time.
7. The material out of which something is made (heaven$_3$, earth$_3$)
   bears, according to a figure of speech, the name of what is made
   from it.
8. Of everything that has been formed, nothing is closer to being
   unformed than earth and the deep (earth$_3$, heaven$_3$).

9. God has not only made created and formed beings (heaven$_2$, earth$_2$), but has also made whatever is capable of being created and formed (heaven$_3$, earth$_3$). As a consequence, creation from nothing must be distinguished from conversion to form.[43]

10. Finally, every being that is formed out of what is "without form (heaven$_3$, earth$_3$) is itself first unformed (heaven$_3$, earth$_3$) and then formed (heaven$_2$, earth$_2$)" (12.19.28).

Of all these truths, about which there is no doubt among those who believe that the words of Moses are true, some interpreters of the first verse of Genesis give one account and some give another. For example, Augustine has claimed that "In the beginning, God made heaven and earth" means that in his Word that is coeternal with himself, God makes both "intelligible and sensible, or spiritual (heaven$_2$) and corporeal (earth$_2$) creation" (12.20.29). By contrast, the positions expressed by the other four interpreters, with the exception of the third, correspond at least in outline to the theories of the critics whom he has discussed in the previous paragraphs.

In summarizing the views of his critics, Augustine says that the second interpreter claims that the first verse of Genesis means that in his Word that is coeternal with himself, "God made [the] universal mass of [the] corporeal world," with all the observable and known entities that it contains (12.20.29). A third interpreter says that the verse in question means that "in his Word, coeternal with himself, God made the formless matter of spiritual (heaven$_3$) and corporeal (earth$_3$) creation" (12.20.29). A fourth interpreter claims that the verse in question means that God makes the unformed matter (earth$_3$) of the physical creation, in which heaven and earth are first confused, but which we now perceive as separated and formed (12.20.29). Finally, a fifth interpreter claims that the first verse of Genesis means that in the beginning of creating and working, God makes unformed matter (earth$_3$) that contains heaven and earth (earth$_2$) undifferentiated within itself, from which both of them are formed and from which they now stand out as fully formed and observable, together with all the things that are in them (12.20.29).

On the basis of this recapitulation, Augustine begins to integrate various interpretations of creation by turning to the second verse of Genesis and by developing a list of options comparable to the one that he has just given, beginning with his own. According to Augustine's earlier account, the claim that the "earth was invisible and without form, and darkness was upon the deep" means that corporeal things are first to be equated with the formless material (earth$_3$) from which they are made, and in which there is no order and no light (12.21.30). By contrast, the second interpreter says that the second verse of Genesis means that heaven and earth (earth$_2$) is first formless and dark (earth$_3$) and that out of it the corporeal heaven (heaven$_1$) and the corporeal earth (earth$_2$) are made, together with everything in them (12.21.30). This second account differs from Augustine's by mentioning the heaven and the earth (earth$_2$) explicitly, and by referring to the things in them as well as themselves.

The third interpreter claims that heaven and earth (heaven$_3$, earth$_3$) are first "formless and darksome matter" (heaven$_3$, earth$_3$) from which the heaven of heaven (heaven$_2$) and the visible heaven and the visible earth (earth$_2$) are made (12.21.30). As we have noticed already, this interpretation differs from Augustine's by drawing a distinction between spiritual (heaven$_3$) and corporeal (earth$_3$) material from which two levels of the cosmos come into existence. The fourth interpreter says that though "heaven" and "earth" do not refer to formless material (heaven$_3$, earth$_3$), the formlessness to which the phrases "the earth (earth$_3$) invisible and without form" and "the darksome deep (heaven$_3$)" refer already exists as the material out of which God makes spiritual (heaven$_2$) and corporeal (earth$_2$) creation (12.21.30). The final interpreter claims that formless matter (earth$_3$) exists, out of which God makes heaven and earth (earth$_2$) and between which the world is divided into higher and lower parts, together with all the creatures in them (12.21.30).

In bringing his interpretation of alternative interpretations to a conclusion, Augustine says that someone might object to the last two opinions by claiming that if the phrase, "heaven and earth" does not refer to formless material (earth$_3$), there is something that God does not make out of which he makes heaven and earth (earth$_2$) (12.22.31). Yet Scripture has not told us that God has made matter (earth$_3$) unless we agree that it is signified by the phrase, "heaven and earth," or by "earth" alone when the first verse of Genesis says that God creates heaven and earth in the beginning. This objector also maintains that when the second verse of Genesis refers to formless matter (earth$_3$) by claiming that "the earth was invisible and without form," this material should be understood as what God makes when the first verse says that he creates heaven and earth (12.22.31).

Augustine continues to display the hermeneutics of charity by permitting those who hold these two opinions to respond to their opponents by claiming that they do not deny that God creates unformed matter (earth$_3$) (12.22.31). They make this claim because they believe that God makes everything very good, and that just as what is created and formed is a greater good, so what is created and formable is a lesser good. However, the proponents of these opinions have several reservations about the view that unformed matter (earth$_3$) is intended when the first verse of Genesis mentions heaven and earth (earth$_2$). First, they claim that Scripture has not said that God has made formless material (earth$_3$), just as it has not said that he has made many other things like the Cherubim and the Seraphim, even though these things clearly exist as products of God's creative act. Second, they say that if the first verse of Genesis includes everything that God has made, including the waters above which the Spirit of God moves, how can "earth" refer to formless material (earth$_3$), when the waters are so beautiful. Third, if the earth to which verse one refers is unformed matter (earth$_3$), they wonder why the firmament is made out of it, but why the water is made from it as well (12.22.31).

In elaborating this third reservation, those who defend the two opinions before us point to the fact that the beautiful waters that we see are not still formless and invisible (earth$_3$). Yet if they receive their beauty when God gathers the waters together in giving them form, what should be said about the waters that are above the firmament? If these waters are also formless (heaven$_3$), and since it has not been written that they have been given form, they do not deserve to have so high a place on the ontological continuum (heaven$_2$). Thus, if Genesis is silent about anything that God has made, no one will conclude that something mentioned in Genesis without a corresponding reference to when it is made is coeternal with God. This suggests that formless matter (earth$_3$), which the second verse of Genesis tells us is invisible, is without form, and is a darksome deep, is "made by God out of nothing, and . . . is not coeternal with him," even though the text may fail "to state when those things are made" (12.22.31).

In dwelling at such length on these responses, Augustine is preparing us for claims that he intends to make at a later stage of his argument. First, he wants us to see that the unformed matter (earth$_3$) with which he first identifies the earth will become the visible heaven and the visible earth (earth$_2$), including the waters that we often see arrayed before us. However, he also wants to claim that the reference to the earth in the first verse of Genesis mentions the matter (earth$_3$) from which all of these things are made rather than the things themselves. Second, Augustine is preparing us to notice that the waters that are above the firmament are to be equated with spiritual material (heaven$_3$) and that they are given form when they are enlightened by Wisdom. Augustine is committed to the view that the waters that are first unformed (heaven$_3$) have such a high rank on the ontological continuum, not because of what they are, but because of what they become in the process that converts them to form.

MEANING, TRUTH, AND INFINITE RICHNESS
(12.23.32–12.32.43)

Having examined various theories about the meaning of the first verse of Genesis, Augustine claims that two kinds of disagreement can arise about the meaning of an utterance, even when a trustworthy reporter makes it. On the one hand, we may disagree about the truth of what a man says; on the other hand, we may disagree about what he intends to communicate (12.23.32). For example, it is one thing to ask whether what Moses tells us about the process of creation is true; and it is quite another to ask what he intends for his readers to understand by his words.

With respect to the first kind of disagreement, Augustine has made it clear already that he wants to separate himself from those who make foolish objections about the creation of the world. In his interpretation of the rest of chapters 1.1–2.3, he wants to continue to do this, asking those who believe that what Moses says is false to depart from him (12.23.32). At this critical juncture, Augustine indicates once more that he has committed himself to the Christian community of charity, where the hermeneutics of love overcomes the hermeneutics of suspicion.[44]

This commitment to the Christian community of interpretation has two important consequences: first, it enables Augustine to feed upon the Truth of God within the context of charity. In the Neoplatonic visions of Book VII (7.10.16; 7.17.23) and in the account of his relation to the God beyond the mind in Book X (10.17.26), Augustine catches a glimpse of what he is able to "see" but is not yet able to "eat." Now he suggests that the interpretation of Scripture within the framework of the Christian community makes it possible for him to do this (12.23.32). This implies that the hermeneutics of creation is a way of bringing his journey toward God to fulfillment, where interpretation makes fulfillment possible and is a reflective image of the journey toward fulfillment that he begins in Book IX and describes in detail in the second half of Book X.

The second consequence of Augustine's commitment to the community of charity is that it makes it possible for him to bring his interpretation of the Bible into relation with the interpretations of other people who have embraced the same text. At the end of Book VIII, he begins to describe the Christian community that he enters after his conversion in the garden (8.12.30). Then this community expands to include all the people with whom he interacts during his retirement at Cassiciacum;[45] and as we have noticed already, it begins to achieve universal proportions when he places himself, his father, and his mother alongside one another within the larger context of the City of God at the end of Book IX (9.13.37). Finally, Augustine suggests that the Christian community to which he commits himself at the beginning of Book X has a reflective dimension (10.1.1), one of the most important aspects of which is the interpretation of Scripture. Thus, he addresses other members of the community of interpretation by saying,

> Let us together approach the words of your book, and let us seek in them for your will by means of the will of your servant, by whose pen you have dispensed those words. (12.23.32)

If we follow Augustine in approaching the Bible, we find that amidst the variety of true interpretations, we are unable to find any interpretation about which we can say with confidence that this is what Moses intends. For example, Augustine has claimed that the first verse of Genesis means that God creates all things in his immutable Word, both "visible and invisible" (earth$_2$, heaven$_2$) (12.24.33). However, even though he knows that this is true, he is not prepared to say that this is what Moses means when he says that in the beginning God makes heaven and earth. The disparity between truth and authorial intention results from the fact that Augustine is not able to see what Moses intends in the same way that he can see that his interpretation of what Moses says is true (12.24.33). In the first case, Augustine is unable to penetrate the content of another human being's mind; in the second case, he is able to apprehend the truth through divine illumination.[46]

Augustine considers the possibility that when Moses says, "In the beginning," he might be referring to the beginning of God's creative action. In addition, he could have intended for the words, "heaven and earth," to be understood, not as referring to what has been formed already, "whether spiritual (heaven$_2$) or corporeal (earth$_2$), but as meaning both as just started and as still unformed." Augustine claims that each of these interpretations is true, whichever might have been intended (12.24.33). Thus, he emphasizes the fact that truth is prior to meaning and that a text is prior to its interpretation, claiming that however the words of Moses are to be understood, Moses himself "saw it truly and expressed it aptly" (12.24.33).

Having drawn a radical distinction between truth and interpretation, Augustine admits that he cannot be certain about his own interpretation of Moses' intentions (12.25.34). However, he is equally insistent that other interpreters of the text should not claim that Moses means what they say rather than what he has suggested, even though they admit that what all of them have said is true. Claims of this kind anger Augustine, suggesting that even within the community of charity, conflict can arise between one interpreter and another. When this occurs, pride displaces love, causing members of the Christian community to love their own interpretations more than they love the Truth (12.25.34). Yet since Truth is public rather than private, we should love other true interpretations just as much as we love our own, not because these interpretations are theirs, but because they are true. Every true interpretation is "the common property of all lovers of truth"; and when we turn toward them, we are able to act in the spirit of charity (12.25.34).

Augustine emphasizes the seriousness of the issue before us by condemning the rash judgment of those who prefer their own opinions to the Truth, and he suggests that God himself joins him in this condemnation. Truth is not intended to be private,[47] but belongs to everyone whom God calls into the community of faith. Indeed, Augustine even claims that if we try to keep the truth to ourselves, we will be deprived of it (12.25.34). This points, in turn, to the proper relation between use (*uti*) and enjoyment (*frui*), where interpretations are to be used to give us access to the truth that we can then enjoy. As Augustine formulates the point,

> Whoever arrogates completely to himself that which [God proposes] for the enjoyment of all men, and desires that to be his own which belongs to all men, is driven from what is common to all men to what is really his own, that is, from truth to a lie. For he who "speaks a lie speaks of his own." (12.25.34)

According to this formulation, Truth is our common possession, while telling a lie is an attempt to stand outside the Truth in a realm of our own.

Augustine addresses those who contradict him by standing before God and his brethren and by speaking in the spirit of charity. In doing so, he emphasizes the fact that if several interpretations of an utterance are true, we do not see their truth in those who formulate them, but in Truth itself that is above our minds (12.25.35).[48] Yet since we do not contend with one another about the Truth, Augustine wonders why we contradict one another about what Moses means, which we cannot see in the same fashion. Even if Moses had appeared before us and had told us what he believes about the process of creation, we would not see that what Moses says is true, but would simply have to believe him (12.25.35). When we embrace the commandments to love God and to love our neighbors as ourselves, and when we embrace the Scriptures as the Word of God, we are committed to the truth of what Moses says, whatever it means. In the face of such a great variety of true interpretations, we are also committed to refrain from quarreling with one another about what Moses means by his utterances.

In claiming that the Truth exists above our minds (12.25.35), Augustine is returning to some of his earlier claims about the relation between God and the soul. In Book VII, he sees the one who transcends him with a trembling glance (7.10.16); and in Book X, he tells us that the structure of memory makes God accessible and reflects the structure of his encounter with God at the theoretical level (10.17.26). Now he says that it is possible to interpret Scripture because we can see its truth in the light of the standard of Truth that illuminates it. At this juncture, Augustine also returns to his earlier suggestion that if we are to make access to the truth of his confessions, we can do so only by believing him (10.3.3). By contrast with self-evident truths that we can see by coming to the Truth (10.25.35), what another human being intends to say is not available to public inspection (10.25.35). As a consequence, the same principle that governs our approach to Augustine within the community of love defines our approach to what the author of a biblical text intends to communicate by what he says (12.25.35).

At this stage of his argument, Augustine attempts to act on the basis of charity by suggesting that God would have scarcely given a lesser gift to Moses than he himself would have desired if he had written the first chapter of Genesis (12.26.36). The text in which this chapter is found has been the vehicle of salvation to the world, and it has been the authority by which proud and false teachings of other philosophies have been vanquished. Thus, it stands to reason that the author of Genesis is possessed of a divine gift that makes his words both powerful and effective (12.26.36). Since Augustine is made from the same clay as Moses, it might even have been possible that he could have been chosen to write Genesis, provided that he had lived at the same time and place. Indeed, had this possibility been actualized, Augustine knows what gift he would have wished for. On the hand, he would have wished to speak in such a way that even the simplest readers would understand what he says. On the other hand, he would have wanted every sophisticated reader to find his true interpretation of Genesis in what he says. In fact, he would have wanted this to be so, however many true interpretations of the book exist (12.26.36). In this way, Augustine begins to move beyond meaning and truth toward the affirmation of infinite richness.

Augustine appeals to an analogy to illustrate his way of understanding the relation between the original utterance of Moses and the many interpretations that can be given of it. Just as a single stream can be the origin of many rivers, so the words of Moses "pour forth floods of . . . truth" (12.27.37). The words of the text are more fruitful than any of the interpretations that can be derived from it, however profound they may be. In addition, these original words are the source from which an indefinite number of truths can be derived and expressed in longer and more detailed discussions.

As a way of elaborating what he has in mind, Augustine mentions an important class of readers of Genesis who have a temporal understanding of the process of creation. The readers in question are simple people who believe that when God creates the world, he acts like a man or like a power infused in a mass of material, "operating outside himself" and creating the heaven above and the earth below by making a "new and sudden decision" (12.27.37). People of this kind also believe that when God speaks, his words begin and end, sounding for a time and then passing away, at the end of which what God commands comes into existence. These readers interpret the Bible in the light of sensory experience; but even as they continue to do so, their faith can be strengthened as they develop from stage to stage (12.27.37). Readers of this kind also know with certainty that God has created the world that manifests itself around them in such a wondrous way. Nevertheless, Augustine warns them not to stretch too far beyond the nest of the Bible, suggesting that if they do so, they will fall away from God through prideful weakness. He also prays that more sophisticated members of his audience who pass along the pathway of biblical interpretation will not trample them and that God will send an angel to put them back into the nest where they may live until they can fly (12.27.37).

It is interesting to notice that Augustine employs the image of the fallen soul at this juncture, not to point to a fall from eternity into time, but to call the attention of immature readers to the dangers of turning away from the Bible.[49] In pointing to the distinction between living and flying, and despite the crucial role of the metaphor of the flight of the soul in Plato's *Phaedrus*,[50] he is also not concerned with the separation of the soul from the body as it attempts to return to its origins, but with the contrast between two ways of interpreting the Scriptures, one of which is simple and the other of which is mature. When we conjoin these two points with Augustine's earlier remark that he and Moses are made of the same clay (12.26.36), it is reasonable to believe that he is committing himself once more to the unity of the soul and the body.[51] In all three cases, the human being is confronted with two ways of living, one of which is oriented toward God, and the other of which turns away from God toward a world of its own. In posing these alternatives, Augustine indicates once more that he is more concerned with the problem of spiritual orientation than with the problem of ontological location (12.27.37).

Augustine elaborates the metaphor of flight by calling our attention to the way in which a mature reader of Genesis can "see the fruits that lie therein and joyously fly about, and pipe songs, and look carefully at them and pluck them" (12.28.38). An individual of this kind, for whom the words of the Bible are no longer a "nest," but a "shady thicket," and whose wings enable it to move from verse to verse, sees that all times past and future are transcended by God's stable permanence, even though there is no temporal creature that he has not made (12.28.38). In addition, he sees that God creates the world, not out of himself, but out of nothing—a "formless unlikeness" (earth$_3$) that can be formed to the likeness of God and that can return to God according to its "appointed capacity" (12.28.38). In this case, returning to God means conversion to form rather than the return of the fallen soul to the one from which it has fallen away, where conversion to form in this case is the condition for and the image of Augustine's conversion in the Garden in Milan (8.12.29). Finally, the interpreter in question sees that God has made all things very good, whether they abide around him, as does the intellectual creature (heaven$_2$), or whether they are arranged in an ontological continuum throughout space and time, producing beautiful gradations (12.28.38). This ontological continuum is presupposed and reflected by Augustine's journey toward God and by the structure of memory in which he encounters the God beyond the mind (10.17.26), and it is presupposed and reflected again by the various interpretations of the first verse of Genesis that he has considered. As a consequence, the journey toward God in the first six Books, the three pivotal experiences in which Augustine encounters him (7.17.23; 8.12.29; 9.10.24), and the conditions that make his transformation possible are bound together within the context of concrete reflection.[52]

Some of the ontological gradations to which Augustine refers at this stage of his argument are reflected in the interpretations of the first verse of Genesis that he has mentioned already. As a way of summarizing these interpretations for the last time, he says that one interpreter claims that the first verse of Genesis refers to Wisdom, the Beginning of things that also speaks to us in the incarnation (12.28.39). Another concentrates his attention on the same verse, claiming that it points to the commencement of created things, where "In the beginning he made" means "At first he made" (12.28.39). Still others claim that "heaven and earth" has a variety of meanings, calling our attention to the matter (earth$_3$) from which they are made, to natures that are formed and distinct (earth$_2$), or to the spiritual creature (heaven$_2$) and to the formless material (earth$_3$) from which corporeal things (earth$_2$) are brought into existence (12.28.39). Augustine also claims that those who understand "heaven and earth" as a way of referring to the formless matter (earth$_3$) of which things are made understand the phrase in question in two ways. On the one hand, it means that out of which both spiritual (heaven$_2$) and corporeal (earth$_2$) creation are formed; on the other hand, it means that out of which the corporeal mass (earth$_3$) is formed from which visible things (earth$_2$) will emerge eventually (12.28.39). Finally, Augustine tells us that those who believe that the first verse of Genesis refers to creatures that are arranged and organized already mean this in two senses. On the one hand, "heaven and earth" refers to both visible (earth$_2$) and invisible (heaven$_2$) creation; on the other hand, it refers only to visible creation (earth$_2$) in which we see "the luminous heavens and the darksome earth and the things that are in them" (12.28.39).

If we take these interpretations together, we are able to move once more beyond the contrast between truth and interpretation toward infinite richness. In fact, "Truth" as Augustine understands the term can be identified with infinite richness, where Truth itself is the highest truth, the meaning of Truth, and the distributive collection of all true propositions. Just as is the case with Adam and with the City of God, the concept of truth points in all three directions, calling our attention first to a clusters of truths, then to the standard by which they are measured, and finally to the arche to which they can be referred.

On the other hand, Augustine is not willing to accept every interpretation of the meaning of a statement, since at the very least, interpretations are always constrained by the demands of consistency. For example, if someone claims that "In the beginning he made heaven and earth" means "At first he made," the interpreter in question can only mean by "heaven and earth" the material (heaven$_3$, earth$_3$) from which intelligible (heaven$_2$) and corporeal (earth$_2$) creation are made (12.29.40). This becomes clear when we notice that if we intend to refer to the universe as formed already, we can be asked, "If God makes this first, what does he make later on?" Since nothing is made after the universe, it can scarcely be made before anything else. As a consequence, the interpretation in question must be rejected (12.29.40).

Augustine elaborates the acceptable interpretation of what it means to create one thing prior to another by claiming,

> If [someone] says that God first made formless and later formed matter, he does not contradict himself if he is able to discern what precedes by eternity, what in time, what by choice, and what in origin: by eternity, as God precedes all creatures; in time, as the flower precedes the fruit; by choice, as the fruit precedes the flower; in origin, as the sound precedes the melody. (12.29.40)

The second and the third ways of understanding the concept of priority are easy, while the first and the fourth are difficult. Though it is easy to understand how one thing proceeds another in time or in value, it is hard to understand how eternity is prior to time, and how sound can be prior to a melody (12.29.40).

With respect to the second of these difficulties, Augustine says that "a melody is formed sound," where "an unformed thing can exist," and where "what does not exist cannot be formed" (12.29.40). In this way, matter (earth$_3$) is prior to what is made from it: it is not prior because it makes its product, since it itself is made; and its priority does not pertain to an interval of time. For example, we do not first utter formless sounds without singing and then adapt or fashion them into the form of a song. Instead, when we sing a song, we hear its sound at the same time as the song itself; for there is not first a formless sound (earth$_3$) that afterwards is formed into a song (earth$_1$). Therefore, the song depends for its existence upon its sound; and the sound of the song is its matter (earth$_3$).[53] However, the sound is formed so that it may be a melody, and this is why the matter (earth$_3$) of the sound is prior to the form of the song (earth$_1$). The sound is not "prior" because it has the power to make a song; it is not prior in time, for it is uttered simultaneously with the song; and it is not prior by choice, since the song is better than the sound from which it is formed. However, it is equally clear that it is first in origin, because the song is not formed in order that it may become a sound, but the sound is formed in order that it may become a song (12.29.40).

Augustine applies these distinctions to the process of creation by claiming that the matter (earth$_3$) from which things are made is not made first in time, since the forms of things give rise to time. Instead, matter (earth$_3$) is first formless; and then it is perceived together with its forms in time. On the other hand, nothing can be said about unformed matter (earth$_3$) unless it is regarded as if it were first in time (12.29.40). It is also important to notice that the material (earth$_3$) from which things (earth$_2$) are made is "the lowest thing in value," for things that have been formed (earth$_2$) are obviously superior to things that remain unformed (earth$_3$). Things of this kind are "preceded by the eternity of the creator," so that the material (earth$_3$) from which things are made "would itself be made from nothing" (12.29.40).

In this final remark, Augustine is not only pointing to what is prior in origin, but also calling our attention to the two conceptions of nonbeing that have been important aspects of our earlier discussion. On the one hand, absolute nonbeing (*nihil*) is the "source" from which unformed material (earth$_3$) is brought into existence; on the other hand, relative nonbeing (*non esse*) that has been created from nothing (*nihil*) is the material (earth$_3$) from which things are made. When these points are taken together, we are able to understand the process of creation as unfolding in two stages. In the first stage, relative nonbeing (*non esse*) comes into existence through an act of *creation*. In the second stage, determinate things come into existence through an act of *forming*. The only thing that remains unclear is whether the intellectual creature (heaven$_2$) is created *ex nihilo* or is formed from spiritual material (heaven$_3$) that exists antecedently. It remains to be seen whether Augustine adopts the views of some of his critics about this issue.

Before he turns to this problem, Augustine moves away from the many interpretations that he has been considering to the Truth to which they point, asking that Truth itself might produce harmony between himself and his critics (12.30.41). The principle of charity continues to undergird Augustine's hermeneutics, and he is prepared to act on this principle by admitting that he does not know which of the interpretations that have been given of the first verse of Genesis reflects the author's intention. On the other hand, he insists once more that all the interpretations that he has mentioned except the ones that he has excluded explicitly are true. Augustine also expresses the hope that the words of the Bible, "lofty but humble and few but abundant" will not terrify the immature readers who approach it; and he reenvokes the two great commandments that enable us to stand along other interpreters of the biblical text in the spirit of charity. Finally, he gives pride of place to Moses as the author of Genesis, suggesting that when he writes under the impact of inspiration, what he says excels all other senses of the words of Scripture, both in truth and in profit to the reader (12.30.41).

The claim that the words of Moses excel all others meaning of his own words gives us a middle term between Truth, on the one hand, and interpretation on the other. Augustine has told us that even though he knows that the words of Moses are true, he is much less confident about how to interpret them. Now he suggests that Moses' own understanding of what he intends to say is the standard toward which all other interpretations converge.[54] However, it is also important to notice that the words of Moses are the instruments through which God speaks rather than the Word of God itself. There is an interpretive distance between Moses and God that is analogous to the space between our interpretations of what Moses says and what he intends to communicate. This suggests that no interpretation of the Word of God is perfect, even though the interpretation that Moses gives excels all others.[55] If this should prove to be the case, the interpretation of the one through whom God speaks would converge toward the Truth, just as our interpretations converge toward his.

Having pointed to the privileged place of Moses as the author of Genesis, Augustine returns to the concept of infinite richness by suggesting that many interpretations of what Moses says may be true and that Moses sees all of them simultaneously. He claims that this is so because he believes that God has "adapted the sacred writings to many men's interpretations. . . ." (12.31.42). As this stage of his argument, Augustine attempts to place himself once more in the position of Moses, suggesting that if he had been the author of Genesis, he would have preferred

> to write in such manner that [his] words would sound forth the portion of truth each . . . could take from these writings, rather than to put down one true opinion so obviously that it would exclude all others, wherein there was no falsity to offend me. (12.31.42)

Augustine suggests that this condition might also be true of Moses, permitting him to conceive all the truths that we have found in his words, together with "whatever we have been unable to find . . ." (12.31.42). In this way, Augustine suggests that Moses has access, not only to the highest interpretation of what he intends to convey, but also to the distributive collection of all the true interpretations of what he says.

Augustine also considers the possibility that the Spirit of God might reveal to later readers something that we have not yet found in the text, and that Moses might have had in mind only one of the many meanings that can be understood from his words (12.32.43). In this case, Augustine hopes that what Moses intends to communicate might be the highest interpretation, and that whether we understand his meaning or not, our own interpretation of his words might be true (12.32.43). Just as Adam might be understood as the primordial man or as the distributive collection of all individuals, so the interpretation of Moses might be regarded as the best and our own construal might be part of the distributive collection of all true interpretations. Finally, having recognized the fact that it will not be possible for him to interpret all of God's word in the way in which he has interpreted the first verse of Genesis,[56] Augustine prays,

> Permit me then, in these words more briefly to confess to you, and to choose some single true, certain, and good meaning which you shall inspire, . . . [recognizing] that if I should say what your minister intended, I will say what is right and best. For this I should strive, [but] if I do not attain it, I would still say that which your Truth willed to say by his words to say to me, which also spoke to him what it willed. (12.32.43)

In this way, Augustine makes the transition from what he has said already, and from what Moses intends to communicate, to what he will say about the remainder of the first chapter of Genesis.

CREATION AND THE TRINITY (13.1.1–13.11.12)

Augustine begins this part of his inquiry by calling upon the One who creates him, and who does not forget him, even when he forgets God (13.1.1). In doing so, he reminds us that the intellectual part of what it means to turn away from God involves forgetfulness, where the structure of memory makes forgetfulness possible (13.1.1). The author also returns to one of the central themes of the first page of the book, claiming that God has prepared his soul to receive its creator by the longing that he has breathed into it (13.1.1). The longing to which he refers points to the fact that he is a (finite-infinite)[57] being who stretches out toward God, where this fact about himself is part of what it means to claim the he has been created in the image of God.

The longing to which Augustine calls our attention reflects his belief that the image of God has not been effaced; and it suggests that a positive relation obtains between God and the soul, even when it falls away from the One who has brought it into existence. Augustine also reminds us that before he calls upon God, God calls out to him from afar, making it possible for him to be converted and to return to the

One from whom he has fallen away (13.1.1). As a consequence, the grace of God becomes Augustine's central theme; speaking and hearing come to the center of our attention once more; and creation, fall, conversion, and fulfillment reemerge as the conditions that make Augustine's journey toward God possible.

Augustine emphasizes the importance of the grace of God by claiming that he owes his being to the goodness of God, which precedes not only his existence, but also the material out of which he is made. He also tells us that God's motive in creating him is not to make a creature that will prevent him from tiring out or that he can use to accomplish a purpose that he is unable to achieve otherwise. Finally, he says that the purpose of creation is not to produce creatures that will cultivate God, as if the creator were a land that would not be cultivated otherwise. Rather, God's purpose in creation is to make it possible for the soul to be fulfilled; for he not only creates us, but also brings us back to himself as we participate in the journey toward fulfillment (13.1.1).

The claim that the created order depends upon the goodness of God reflects the conviction of the Platonic tradition that God is not jealous and that finite beings are expressions of his overflowing abundance. However, the claim in question also reflects the Christian view that God does not create the world out of himself, but out of nothingness (*nihil*), from which finite beings would not come into existence otherwise. This claim suggests that heaven and earth (earth$_2$) have no claim upon God to be brought into existence (13.2.2). However, it also leads to a more profound level of interpretation when Augustine reads the second verse of Genesis, not only as referring to the material (earth$_3$) from which corporeal things (earth$_2$) are made, but also as pointing to formless spiritual material (heaven$_3$) from which the intellectual creature (heaven$_2$) comes into existence. This reiterates the suggestion of some of his critics that heaven can be understood as formless spiritual material (heaven$_3$) alongside the formless corporeal material (earth$_3$) from which visible things (earth$_2$) are formed (13.2.2).

The suggestion that Augustine makes at this juncture is important for several reasons. First, it permits him to double back upon his earlier discussion, qualifying and deepening our understanding of the earlier stages of his argument. This way of proceeding is characteristic of Augustine,[58] and it expresses itself in the way in which the verses of Genesis overlap as he moves from step to step of his inquiry. The chain that emerges results from the fact that Augustine discusses verse one in Book XI, verses one and two in Book XII, and verses two through thirty-one in Book

XIII. The second reason that Augustine's introduction of the concept of spiritual material (heaven$_3$) is important is that it allows him to exhibit charity to other interpreters of the text whose views he has discussed already. In that earlier discussion, he claims that heaven refers to the intellectual creature (heaven$_2$) that clings to God without wavering, either intellectually or volitionally, and that earth refers to the formless material from which corporeal things are made. Yet now he expresses his willingness to adopt the suggestion of other interpreters by construing darkness on the face of the deep as a way of referring to formless spiritual material (heaven$_3$). The final reason that the concept of spiritual material (heaven$_3$) is significant is that it allows Augustine to develop a hint about the concept of darkness that he has given us already. At an earlier stage of his argument, he suggests that the darkness of the deep requires illumination and that this occurs before the beginning of days. Now he implies that formless spiritual material (heaven$_3$) is the unformed matter (heaven$_3$) upon which God works within this context.

We must be careful at this stage to draw all the relevant distinctions that will enable us to follow the course of Augustine's argument. First, he says that both spiritual (heaven$_3$) and corporeal (earth$_3$) material depend upon God's creative act and that each in its own genus is "inchoate and formless" (13.2.2). Second, he claims that both kinds of material "run off into immoderation and unlikeness far distant from [God]" (13.2.2). Third, he tells us that formless spiritual material (heaven$_3$) is more excellent than a formed body (earth$_2$) and that formless corporeal material (earth$_3$) is more excellent than if it were nothing at all. Fourth, he claims that both kinds of formless material (heaven$_3$, earth$_3$) depend upon God's creative act and that they have no claim upon God to exist. Finally, he says that these formless things (heaven$_3$, earth$_3$) depend upon God for their form and that in forming them, God calls them back to unity with himself (13.2.2).

In suggesting that both spiritual (heaven$_3$) and corporeal (earth$_3$) matter are formless, each in accord with its own genus, Augustine is extending the concept of a genus from distinguishable kinds of substances to distinguishable kinds of material. In this way, he employs what the Aristotelian tradition calls "transcategorial predication," moving from a literal context of predication to a context in which concepts are applied in a nonliteral way.[59] As a consequence, figurative discourse emerges once more as a crucial element of Augustine's philosophical project. It is also important to notice that in claiming that corporeal (earth$_3$) and spiritual (heaven$_3$) matter "run off into immoderation," Augustine is continuing to speak in a nonliteral fashion. As we shall see at a later stage of our argument, this figurative use of language will require us to distinguish between the "created down flow" of spiritual material (heaven$_3$) and the act of dissolution in which a spiritual creature (heaven$_2$) "falls away" from God.

Having committed himself to the distinction between spiritual (heaven$_3$) and corporeal (earth$_3$) material, Augustine calls our attention to the radical contrast between unformed matter (heaven$_3$, earth$_3$) and the nothingness (*nihil*) from which the world is created (13.2.2). In this way, he expands the chain of being to include the material (heaven$_3$, earth$_3$) from which determinate things (heaven$_2$, earth$_2$) on the chain in question are formed. In claiming that both formless matter (heaven$_3$, earth$_3$) and the things (heaven$_2$, earth$_2$) that are made from it have no claim to exist, Augustine also reiterates his distinction between two stages in the act of creation. On the one hand, God creates the material (heaven$_3$, earth$_3$) upon which determinate things (heaven$_2$, earth$_2$) depend; on other hand, he makes the things (heaven$_2$, earth$_2$) that are formed from antecedently existing material (heaven$_3$, earth$_3$) (13.2.2).

Augustine says once more that corporeal (earth$_3$) and spiritual (heaven$_3$) material have no claim upon God to exist, even in their formless condition, since they would not exist at all unless God had brought them into existence from nothing (*nihil*) (13.2.3). However, he expands his earlier discussion of the status of spiritual matter (heaven$_3$) by pointing to the concept of conversion, on the one hand, and the concept of enlightenment on the other. In this connection, he asks,

> What claim did inchoate spiritual creation have on you, even to float and flow about, darksome like the deep, but all unlike you, unless it were converted by that same Word to the Word by whom it was made, and were enlightened by him and made into light, although not equal to the form equal to you, yet conformed to it? (13.2.3)

As our discussion unfolds, two things will become increasingly clear: first, the down flow of the spiritual creature (heaven$_2$) points to a counterfactual situation rather than to an existing state of affairs; second, the "conversion" of this creature calls our attention to its enlightenment and to its conversion to form. Just as Augustine's concept of time is a way of bringing stability (stability$_1$) to the cosmological flux, so conversion to form is a way of stabilizing (stability$_1$) spiritual material (heaven$_3$). Conversion to form is also a reflective image of Augustine's intellectual conversion in Book VII (7.10.16; 7.17.23), and of his volitional conversion in Book VIII (8.12.29), and it is a cosmological reflection of his memory of the One who overcomes his blindness and shatters his deafness in Book X (10.27.38). This suggests that "conversion" is the inner structure of creation understood in cosmological terms, just as "creation" is the inner structure of conversion from a soteriological point of view. As I have suggested already, the analogy between these two contexts is important because it makes it possible for Augustine to speak about creation as conversion to form, just as the Apostle Paul speaks about conversion as a new creation.[60]

In the case of the intellectual creature (heaven$_2$) that has been converted to form and that has been enlightened by being brought to the Light, Augustine says that it is good for it always to adhere to God, "lest by aversion from [God] it lose the light gained by conversion, and fall back into a life similar to the darksome deep" (13.2.3). The possibility that Augustine envisages here is contrary to fact; for once it has been formed, the intellectual creature (heaven$_2$) will never turn away from God to embrace a world of its own. On the other hand, Augustine's point about the need to cleave to God is relevant to Augustine's existential situation. Unlike the intellectual creature (heaven$_2$), he turns away from the light toward the darkness when he orients himself away from God. As a consequence, he will continue to labor until he is given rest in the justice of God. As things now stand, and as a way of beginning to offer us an allegorical picture of our own situation, Augustine says that we have become God's "judgments, which are like a great deep" (13.2.3).

At this stage of his argument, Augustine finally moves beyond the first two verses of Genesis to verse three, claiming that at the foundation of the world, God says, "Let there be light, and light was made" (13.3.4). In making this claim, he confirms his earlier suggestion that light is created before the first day, where what is brought to the light is the intellectual creature. As Augustine formulates the point,

> I not improperly understand [the creation of light] as applying to spiritual creation, since there was already some sort of life which [God] could illuminate. But just as it had no claim upon [God] to be a life as could be illuminated, so also, now that it existed, it had no claim on [him] to be given light. Nor would its formlessness be pleasing to [God] unless it were made light, not by merely existing, but by beholding the light-giving light and adhering to it. (13.3.4)

Finally, Augustine claims that the intellectual creature (heaven$_2$) owes both its life and its happiness to the grace of God, where happiness in this case results from the fact that this creature has been converted to form (13.3.4). Conversion of this kind makes it possible for the spiritual creature (heaven$_2$) to be oriented toward God without wavering, where God himself is the only being who enjoys happiness without qualification (13.3.4).[61]

Several important points emerge from this stage of Augustine's argument. First, the fact that the creation of light pertains to the intellectual creature (heaven$_2$) implies that this "stage" of creation is nontemporal, not only from the side of God, but also from the side of the created product. Even though the intellectual creature (heaven$_2$) is "temporal" in the sense that it is mutable, it never wavers in clinging to God. Second, the act of creation in this case has two "stages." God creates spiritual material (heaven$_3$) "first," and he makes the spiritual creature (heaven$_2$) from it by a process of forming. Third, the forming process as it pertains to the intellectual creature (heaven$_2$) involves divine illumination.[62] Illumination of this kind is a way of bringing light to the spiritual creature (heaven$_2$) by permitting it to gaze upon the Light through which the world is brought into existence. Finally, Augustine claims that God would not have been pleased with spiritual material (heaven$_3$) if he had not brought it to finished form (heaven$_2$) by bringing it to the light (13.3.4). However, when spiritual material (heaven$_3$) has been converted to form, the intellectual creature (heaven$_2$) is able to find happiness by being oriented toward God.

Augustine continues to consider the issues raised by the creation and the formation of the spiritual creature (heaven$_2$) by reiterating his claim that God would not have been impoverished if these things had not existed or had not been formed. As he has told us already (13.2.2), God makes the world, not because he lacks something, but out of his infinite goodness. Augustine also says that God restrains and converts spiritual material (heaven$_3$) to form, not so he may enjoy the creatures that emerge from it, but so they may enjoy him. Finally, he tells us that the imperfection of spiritual material (heaven$_3$) is displeasing to God and that spiritual creatures (heaven$_2$) are perfected by God and are now pleasing to him (13.4.5).

This is not to say that God is imperfect and is made perfect by his creatures. When Genesis says that the Spirit is borne over the waters, it is not borne up by finite creatures, as if it rests on them. Rather, the Spirit causes the creatures in question to rest on God. When something depends upon God, to live is not identical with living happily, since the creature lives even as it floats about in darkness. The one thing that remains is for this creature to be converted to God and to live more and more by the fountain of life, and "in his light to see his light and to be perfected, enlightened, and made happy" (13.4.5).

At this stage of his reflections, Augustine turns his attention to the Trinity, which he claims that he is able to understand only in a fashion that is dark and shrouded in mystery (13.5.6). At the outset, he refers to the first and the second persons of the Trinity, claiming that God the Father makes heaven (heaven$_1$) and earth (earth$_1$) in the Beginning through his Son. Then he mentions the heaven of heaven (heaven$_2$) that he has considered already, where the earth (earth$_3$) is "invisible and without form," where the deep is dark "according to the constant down flow of its spiritual formlessness" (heaven$_3$), and where formlessness has been converted to form by illumination, permitting the heaven of heaven (heaven$_2$) to be placed between "the water and the water." Finally, he expresses his desire to find a reference to the Trinity within the first few verses of Genesis:

> By the name of God, who made these things, I now understood the Father, and by the name of Beginning the Son, in whom he made them. And believing my God to be the Trinity..., I searched into his holy words, and behold, your "Spirit was borne above the waters." Behold the Trinity, Father, and Son, and Holy Spirit, creator of all creation! (13.5.6)

Yet even after he has found a reference to the Trinity in the first chapter of Genesis, Augustine is puzzled about why the Bible refers to God's Spirit only after it has mentioned heaven (heaven$_1$, heaven$_2$), earth that is invisible and without form (earth$_3$), and darkness that is upon the face of the deep (heaven$_3$). His preliminary explanation for this omission is that it might be fitting to introduce the Spirit in this way so that it would be possible to describe it as being "borne over." This could not be said unless what God's Spirit is borne over were mentioned first. The Spirit is not borne above the Father and the Son, and it could not be said to be "borne above" if it were borne above nothing. Thus, what the Spirit is borne over had to be mentioned at the outset so that what is properly said to be borne over could be mentioned afterwards. However, this raises another puzzling question about why it is unfitting to mention the Spirit in some other way than to say that it is "borne over" (13.6.7).

Augustine answers this question by moving away from cosmological speculation and by turning toward soteriological and figurative ways of speaking about the relation between God and the soul. In doing so, he moves from the spiritual creature (heaven$_2$) to embodied beings (earth$_2$) by suggesting that the Holy Spirit is borne above the "waters" because its role in the economy of salvation is to bring us to God (13.7.8). The Apostle Paul captures the point when he claims that charity has been poured out on us by the Holy Spirit and "when he teaches us about spiritual things," bending his knee before God so we may come to know the love of Christ[63] (13.7.8). Since Paul is able to do this only because the Holy Spirit has been given to us, it is appropriate to say that the Spirit that is supereminent from the first is borne above the "waters" so they may be converted to form.

Augustine continues to speak figuratively when he suggests that the cosmological material (earth$_3$) from which the world is made can be reconstrued as the abyss (*nihil*) from which the soul needs to be redeemed. In speaking about it in this way, and in pointing to God's Spirit that can lead us beyond it, Augustine asks,

> How shall I speak of the weight of lust, dragging downward into the steep abyss, and of charity lifting up through your Spirit, who was borne above the waters? To whom shall I say this? How shall I say it? These are places into which we are plunged and from which we emerge. What is more like them, and yet what is more unlike them? They are affections; they are loves: the filthiness of our spirit, flowing away downwards with a love that brings but care. But here too is the holiness of your Spirit, raising us aloft with a love that is free from care, so we may lift up our hearts to you, where your Spirit was "borne above the waters," and come to super eminent rest, when our souls should have passed through the waters that are without substance. (13.7.8)

Several important points emerge from Augustine's depiction of the abyss (*nihil*) toward which we have fallen and of the Spirit of God that liberates us from it. First, his account of our relation to God transforms the concept of spiritual material (heaven$_3$) and the form into which it is converted (heaven$_2$) into a "place" toward which we plunge (*nihil*) and into a process of redemption that leads us back to God. Second, a more fine-grained analysis of our fall toward the abyss (*nihil*) points to affections that lead us away from God, permitting us to see that Augustine is more concerned with the orientation of the soul than he is with its place on an ontological continuum. Finally, Augustine compares the Spirit that leads us toward fulfillment with the Spirit that is borne over the waters, suggesting that fulfillment is the telos of the Spirit from a soteriological perspective, and that the Spirit is the arche of fulfillment from a cosmological point of view (13.7.8).

Augustine begins to bring his reflections about the intellectual creature (heaven$_2$) and the souls that God has created together by claming that the angel falls away from God and that man's soul also falls away (13.8.9).[64] In doing so, both the angel and the soul call our attention to "the abyss of all spiritual creation," which would have remained dark unless God had said, "Let there be light." When God says this, every obedient creature in the heavenly city (heaven$_2$) cleaves to him and finds rest in his Spirit, "which is borne unchangeably over every changeable thing. Otherwise, even the heaven of heaven (heaven$_2$) would be a darksome deep (heaven$_3$) within itself. . . ." Indeed, Augustine suggests that the purpose of claiming that both the angel and the soul have fallen away from God is not to point to the preexistence of the soul, but to indicate that in the restless down-flow of our spirits, and in the darkness that results from it, we reveal the greatness of the intellectual creature (heaven$_2$) that God has made.[65] Yet even in the case of the spiritual creature (heaven$_2$), the being in question is unable to give rest and happiness to itself (13.8.9).

Augustine continues to merge his account of the "conversion" of the intellectual creature (heaven$_3$) with his account of the conversion of the soul by suggesting that God enlightens the darkness of all the spiritual creatures that he has made. In expressing the point he has in mind from a soteriological point of view, Augustine asks God to give himself to him. The basis for this request is that he loves God and that he wants to love him more strongly. Augustine does not know how to measure the extent to which his love is insufficient to permit God to embrace him. However, he knows that apart from God, all his abundance, both outside and within, is a wasteland (2.10.18; 13.8.9).

Before we bring our reflections on creation and the Trinity to a conclusion, we should notice once more how Augustine develops his interpretation of the first chapter of Genesis, not only in the first two verses, but also in the remainder of the chapter. His initial reading of verses one and two is cosmological, leading to a detailed discussion of what is meant by "heaven and earth" and by the phrases, "without form and void" and "darkness over the deep." Having intimated that the waters are illuminated by the light, he then turns to verse three to suggest that the creation of light is what makes it possible for spiritual material (heaven$_3$) to be converted to form (13.3.4). Having chosen to remain silent about verses four and five in which the light is separated from the darkness and the first day is made, he mentions verses six and seven in order to suggest that the formation of spiritual material (heaven$_3$) permits it to separate the waters from the waters, where the heaven of heaven (heaven$_2$) that is formed emerges on the second day (13.5.6).

When he suggests that the heaven of heaven (heaven$_2$) is the heaven to which verse one refers, it is important for us to understand that it is *created* before the creation of time. However, when he focuses on the *formation* of the heaven of heaven on the first and the second days, it becomes necessary for us to understand that the days in question point to a logical as opposed to a temporal distinction. In comparing our fallen situation with the formlessness of spiritual material (heaven$_3$) and in contrasting the transformation we need with the conversion to form that permits the intellectual creature (heaven$_2$) to cling to God, it is also important to notice that Augustine begins to speak figuratively, indicating how verses two through eight apply to us as well as to the intellectual creature (heaven$_2$) upon which he has focused so much attention.[66] Finally, he will soon begin to give a figurative interpretation of the entire first chapter of Genesis, doubling back to verses one through eight, and then moving forward to the end of the chapter. In this way, he will not only continue to follow his customary procedure, but will also be able to show the relevance of a figurative interpretation of the text to our existential journey from creation and the fall to conversion and fulfillment.

Before he moves in this direction, Augustine returns to his earlier problem about how the Spirit of God is borne upon the waters, asking whether the Father and the Son are not borne over the waters as well (13.9.10). He answers this question by claiming that if we think of the Spirit as above the waters in a literal sense, even the Spirit is not borne over them. In addition, if we are referring to the supremacy of God to mutable things, both the Father and the Son, as well as the Holy Spirit, are borne over the waters. However, this leads us back to the question about why only the Spirit is spoken of in this way, where he is in a "place" that is not a place in the literal sense, and where only the Spirit is said to be the gift of God to us.

Augustine responds to this question by claiming that the Spirit is borne over us because he is the one in whom we rest, making it possible for us to have joy in God (13.9.10) and lifting us up "from the gates of death" (13.9.10). Earlier Augustine distinguishes between use and enjoyment,[67] where only God should be enjoyed, and where everything else ought to be used. Now he suggests that the enjoyment that emerges from fulfillment in God (13.9.10) is made possible by the work of the Spirit, permitting us to find the peace that results from a transformed will.

In moving from the soul to the body, Augustine draws some significant distinctions in one of the most memorable passages of the *Confessions*. In this passage, he says,

> By reason of its weight, the body strives toward its own place. Yet a weight strives not so much to sink to the very lowest depths, but rather to its proper place. Fire tends upward; a stone down-wards. They are impelled by their own weights; they seek their own places. Oil poured out beneath water is raised up above the water. Water poured on top of oil sinks down beneath the oil. They are impelled by their own weights; they seek their own places. Not put in proper order, they are without rest; when they are set in due order, they are at rest. (13.9.10)

Then Augustine continues,

> My love is my weight! I am borne about by it, wheresoever I am borne. By your gift we are enkindled, and we are borne upwards. We glow with inward fire, and we go on. We ascend steps within the heart, and we sing a gradual psalm. By your fire . . . we glow with inward fire, and we go on, for we go upwards to "the peace of Jerusalem. . . ." There will good will find us a place, so that we may desire nothing further but to abide therein forever. (13.9.10)

The first thing to notice about this passage is that everything is good if it remains in its proper place on the ontological continuum. This implies that the body is good and that it becomes evil only when we permit it to have an inappropriate relation to the soul. According to Augustine, the soul is intended to regulate the body; and the body is good just to the extent that this is the case. The second point to notice is that when things are in their proper order, they are at rest. This suggests that both the body and the soul can be at rest if they have a proper relation, not only to one another, but also to the one who has brought them into existence. The implication of Augustine's remarks is that both the soul and the body are able to return to God, just to the extent that they recover their relation to one another in the proper ontological order. Finally, Augustine brings the soul and the body together metaphorically by claiming that his love is his weight.[68] When he has turned away from God, weight in this special sense of the term points to the separation between God and the soul. Yet when he turns in the opposite direction, the *weight of love* that sometimes separates him from God becomes the *weight of fire* that leads him upward, pointing to a distinction between a corrupted and an uncorrupted soul and body, and making is possible for him to dwell in the "house of God" forever.

By contrast with the soul and the body, the proper role of the spiritual creature (heaven$_2$) is to stand in relation to eternity, where it engages in unwavering contemplation of the one who has brought it into existence. However, Augustine is careful to indicate that the intellectual creature (heaven$_2$) ". . . would have been different . . . unless as soon as it was made, without any intervening time, it was raised up" by the Spirit of God and by the creation of light (13.10.11). In our case, there is distinction in *time* between our darkness and the moment in which we are made light. In the case of the spiritual creature, there is only a distinction in *origin* as Augustine characterizes the term at an earlier stage of his analysis. This confirms our suggestion that Augustine has been intending all along to distinguish between the temporal status of the human soul and the status of the intellectual creature (heaven$_2$), which is temporal because it is mutable, but is sempiternal because it never mutates.

Augustine's final remarks in this section are intended to turn our attention back toward the Trinity, where a chasm exists between what we understand and what we often say. As is so often the case when we know less than we say, it is easy for quarrels to arise that obscure our access to the Truth (13.11.12). However, Augustine proposes to deal with these disagreements by asking his readers to reflect upon three aspects of ourselves about which we can be certain, so that having considered and assessed them, we can perceive how different they are from the Trinity. In this way, he begins to explore some of the analogies and disanalogies between the soul and God that he will consider in more detail in *The Trinity*.[69]

First, Augustine distinguishes three primary functions within the soul: "to be, to know, and to will." Then he indicates how these functions overlap by claiming, "I am a knowing and a willing being, and I know that I am and that I will, and I will to be and to know." On this basis, he asks us to notice how inseparable these functions are from one another, even though there is a distinction between them. Finally, he suggests that when we have explored the unity and the differentiation of these functions, it is still important to notice that we have not yet grasped the immutable being that is above us, "which is immutably, knows immutably, and wills immutably" (13.11.12).

Augustine expresses his uncertainty about the nature of the Trinity by wondering whether there is a Trinity in God because of these three functions, or whether these functions are in all three persons, or even whether both are true (13.11.12). If this third option were to be embraced, we would be committing ourselves to the view that the Godhead "exists immutably by its great and plenteous unity, in some marvelous way both simple and multiple, . . . whereby it is, and is known to itself, and suffices to itself . . ." (13.11.12). This way of understanding the nature of the Trinity would also permit Augustine to introduce a dimension of difference and dynamism, not only into the Godhead, but also into each person, and into both the Godhead and the persons taken together. In this way, Augustine supplements his earlier claim that God is incorruptible, inviolable, and immutable, implying that God is never fully present to us as a static content of consciousness, and that he is never fully present to himself without transcending himself. However, Augustine also insists that we must never encroach upon the mystery of God, suggesting that in our quest for understanding, we can never "conceive such things with any ease," speak about them in any way, or make rash pronouncements about the nature of the Trinity.

FIGURATIVE INTERPRETATION (13.12.13–13.34.49)

At this stage of his argument, Augustine continues to make his confession, where his confession of praise and his confession of sin become his confession of faith. As a way of emphasizing the fact that he is moving within the context of faith, he reminds us that he has been baptized in the name of the Father, the Son, and the Holy Spirit; and in only his second reference to his official role within the Church, he points to the fact that he has committed himself to the task of baptizing others (13.12.13). Then he begins to retrace his journey toward God by drawing an analogy between the first two verses of Genesis and his place in the Church. He does this by suggesting that from a metaphorical point of view, heaven (heaven$_2$) and earth (earth$_2$) can be regarded as "the spiritual and the carnal parts of [the] Church" that Christ brings into existence. Before it receives "the form of doctrine, our earth [is] invisible and without order," and we are "covered over by the darkness of ignorance. . . ." However, because God's Spirit is "borne over the water," God does not abandon us, but says, "Let there be light." In this case, the creation of light presupposes our memory of God (13.12.13); and out of our darkness that is unpleasing to us, we are converted to God when light is made. As a consequence, we who are once "darkness" are now "light in the Lord" (13.12.13).

Three terms must be distinguished in the kind of interpretation in which Augustine is beginning to engage. First, he makes reference to his own experience by using words like darkness, light, and conversion to remind us of his existential situation. Second, he uses the language of the first chapter of Genesis to remind us of the literal interpretation of the creation of the world in which he engages in Book XII and in the first section of Book XIII. Finally, he extends his use of language from literal to figurative ways of speaking in the remainder of Book XIII, permitting cosmological discourse to have a soteriological significance when it refers to stages in the birth and development of the Church. By speaking in all three ways at once, Augustine indicates how his journey toward God, his cosmological account of creation *ex nihilo*, and his figurative description of the development of the Church are images of one another. As he moves toward the conclusion of the book, he also makes it clear that creation, fall, conversion, and fulfillment at the cosmological level and in these same stages in the emergence of the Church are the conditions for and images of his existential journey.[70]

Before I continue to indicate how Augustine brings these ways of speaking together, it is important to distinguish between literal and figurative discourse as Augustine understands these terms. In his book about the interpretation of Scripture, the first three Books of which are written at roughly the same time as the *Confessions*, Augustine says that signs are "literal when they are used to designate those things on account of which they are instituted. . . ." By contrast, he claims that "figurative signs occur when that thing which we designate by a literal sign is used to signify something else. . . ."[71] If we apply these definitions to what Augustine has done and to what he is about to do in the *Confessions*, we find that his cosmological interpretations of the first eight verses of Genesis are literal, where an indefinite number of literal interpretations can be given of what Genesis says about the creation of the world. However, when he uses the words of Genesis to describe stages in the emergence of the Church, he uses the referents of these words to characterize something other than themselves. As Augustine has told us already, "heaven and earth" (heaven$_2$, earth$_2$), understood figuratively, point to the spiritual and carnal parts of the Church, where the former emerges from the latter by acquiring the form of doctrine. Insofar as Augustine understands himself as part of the Church, these figurative ways of speaking also apply to his own experiential development, pointing once more to the unity of the personal, the cosmological, and the figurative ways of speaking in which he engages.

Augustine continues to move in all these directions by speaking about the "deep" to which he has referred already, by calling our attention to his existential situation, and by distinguishing once more between the spiritual and the carnal parts of the Church. As he expresses the point, the deep is not only the spiritual material (heaven$_3$) from which the intellectual creature (heaven$_2$) is made, but also the depths of the mystery of God that he is unable to comprehend in his journey toward fulfillment. Augustine also claims that he is saved by faith rather than by sight, and that even the Apostle Paul is unable to find absolute fulfillment by comprehending the richness of God (13.13.14). Finally, having claimed that Paul must often speak to carnal rather than to spiritual members of the Church, he says that the Apostle nevertheless wants to be "clothed . . . with his habitation . . . from heaven" and that he "calls to the lower deep, and says, 'Do not be conformed to this world, but be reformed in the newness of your mind' "[72] (13.13.14). In this way, he points beyond Christian immaturity to the possibility of Christian perfection.[73]

At this point, Paul begins to speak, not in his own voice, but in the Voice of the One who sends his Spirit from heaven so the citizens of the City of God may be made joyful (13.13.14). In this case, God not only creates the world, and the Spirit of God is not only borne above the waters at the moment of creation, but God also enriches the lives of members of the Church by pouring out the gifts of his Spirit upon them (13.13.14). When Augustine reflects upon these gifts, he notices that even though the Apostle Paul possesses "the first fruits of the Spirit" that he receives at his conversion, he still "groans within himself" and waits for "the redemption of the body"[74] (13.13.14). In this way, Augustine indicates once more that the Christian quest for fulfillment pertains to the entire human being as a whole rather than to the separation of the soul from the body.

Paul is a member of the Church, and he says that he sighs for the founder of the Church and is zealous for him rather than for himself (13.13.14). Thus, Paul speaks with the voice of God to that part of the "deep" about which he is fearful, lest the minds of those who live in it are lead away from chastity (13.13.14). Just as spiritual material (heaven$_3$) must be converted to form (heaven$_2$) in order to achieve perfection, so the inhabitants of the deep who might be tempted to turn away from God must be called back to the One who has made it possible for them to become God's children. If Paul succeeds in this, the quest for fulfillment of those whom he addresses will be brought to completion; and when they see Christ, all their tears will be wiped away.

Against the background of the vision of Christ to which Paul calls his attention, Augustine still struggles with the fact that his own quest for fulfillment has not yet been brought to completion. He expresses this point by combining a description of his existential situation with the language of the first chapter of Genesis and with the language of the Bible taken more generally. First, he tells us that he slips back from God again and again, claiming that he "becomes a deep," or that he perceives himself "to be a deep" (13.14.15). Second, he says that when the language of faith asks the question, "Why are you sad, O my soul, and why do you trouble me?" he responds in the language of hope by exclaiming "Hope in the Lord" (13.14.15). Finally, Augustine's hope points beyond itself toward fulfillment in the following injunction:

Hope and persevere, until the night . . . passes, . . . for we were heretofore darkness, the relics whereof we carry in our body, "dead because of sin"—"until the day breaks and the shadows retire." Hope in the Lord. "In the morning I will stand, and I will see." (13.14.15)

Augustine elaborates this expression of hope by suggesting that the purpose of salvation is to lead us to fulfillment, which will express itself in the resurrection of the body instead of the flight of the soul into heaven.[75] He then uses the language of Genesis to express his existential situation by claiming that the Spirit of God dwells in him because he is "borne above our dark and fluid inner being" (13.14.15). As he begins to turn back toward God by means of his conversion and his quest for fulfillment, he receives assurances from God that he is a child of light rather than a child of darkness (13.14.15). However, Augustine does not presume to decide which of us fall within one category and which in the other. Only God can do this; for we have nothing that we have not received from him, having been made "vessels of honor" from the same lump of clay from which others have been made "vessels of dishonor" (13.14.15).

Augustine continues to weave existential, cosmological, and figurative language together by speaking of a "firmament of authority" that is placed over us in the form of Scripture. Earlier he defends the authority of Scripture as a crucial vehicle for bringing us to God. Now he claims that the Scriptures can be compared to the heavens (heaven$_2$) that are "folded together like a book" and that are "stretched over us like skin" (13.15.16). The fact that the Scriptures may be understood as a firmament suggests that they have greater authority now than they do when the ones by whom they are written are still alive. In addition, the claim that they are stretched out like a skin reflects the fact that God places coverings of skin on Adam and Eve after they eat the forbidden fruit and become subject to death.[76] It also expresses Augustine's conviction that he is redeemed from death by putting on a new garment called "Jesus, the Christ" in the garden in Milan (8.12.29). In this way, the language of Genesis is brought into relation with the existential and the allegorical language that surfaces in this part of the text.

When Augustine asks us to contemplate "the heavens" (heaven$_2$) that are to be compared with Scripture, he claims that no books are more effective in giving wisdom to immature readers and in destroying the pride that they often bring to the text. These books are also useful in urging Augustine to make his confession and to serve God without complaint. As a consequence, he prays that he will be able to understand them, being placed under them as a man who needs to move from faith to understanding (13.15.17). Earlier Augustine compares the Bible with a mystery cave that he must bend down in order to enter, and with a book that is simple on the surface, but profound at the center (3.5.9). Now the Bible is stretched over him like a skin, inviting him to understand what his faith makes accessible initially.

Augustine returns to a cosmological way of speaking by comparing his own situation with the situation of the intellectual creature (heaven$_2$) who clings steadfastly to God. He does this by confirming his earlier suggestion that the waters above the firmament are the spiritual material (heaven$_3$) from which this creature is made and that they are "kept free from earthly corruption" (13.15.18). Augustine also identifies the creature in question with the angels (heaven$_2$), who differ from us by contemplating God directly, rather than by looking up at the firmament and reading the Word of God that is expressed there. Even though these creatures are "temporal" insofar as they are mutable, they transcend time because they never change; and they read upon God's face what his eternal will decrees. As Augustine formulates the point, they read (*legunt*), they choose (*eligunt*), and they love (*diligunt*), where "they read forever, and what they read never passes away." The book they read is "never closed, nor is their scroll folded up . . ." because God himself is the "Book" upon which they focus their attention (13.15.18).

Augustine contrasts our existential situation with the spiritual condition of angels (heaven$_2$) by suggesting that the mercy and the truth of God, which is accessible to angels (heaven$_2$) intuitively, is accessible to us through the authors of the Bible, whom he identifies with the "clouds" in the "heavens" (13.15.18). Just as the clouds in the sky pass away, but the heavens remain, so the writers of the biblical books cease to exist, while the Scriptures are "extended over [all] the nations . . . to the end of the world." Yet even when heaven and earth pass away, and when the "skin" of the Bible is folded up, the Word of God that it expresses endures forever (13.15.18). Now the Word of God appears to us in the figurative discourse of the authors of the Scripture and in the "mirror" of the "heavens" to which Paul refers in the thirteenth chapter of First Corinthians. Yet Augustine also claims that one day the eternal Word of God will appear, just as it is, and we will know him face to face (13.15.18). Finally, Augustine tells us that the body of Christ is to be compared with a "lattice" through which he looks at us, speaking tenderly and arousing our affections. However, he also claims that the quest for fulfillment will be brought to completion in the resurrection of the body; for he says that when Christ appears, "we shall be like him, because we shall see him as he is" (13.15.18).

Lest we believe that the transformation to which Augustine is pointing is a human achievement, it is important to remember that a radical contrast exists between God, on the one hand, and his creatures on the other. As Augustine has told us, God is, knows, and wills immutably, where his "essence knows and wills immutably," his "knowledge is and wills immutably," and his "will is and knows immutably" (13.16.19). It is also important to emphasize the fact that we do not know God in the same way in which God knows himself. In God's case, the immutable Light knows itself, while in our case, a mutable being knows God because it has been enlightened. Thus, Augustine is able to combine existential, cosmological, and figurative language once again by claiming that our souls are "like earth without water," where just as we cannot enlighten ourselves, so we are unable to be sufficient to ourselves. As a consequence, we find both light and life in God, where the first enables us to see, and the second enables us to be.

Augustine finally moves beyond the first eight verses of the opening chapter of Genesis, turning to an allegorical interpretation of verses nine through thirty-one. In doing so, he places these verses from the Old Testament side by side with relevant verses from the New Testament, pointing beyond the letter of the Law to the Spirit by which it is fulfilled.

The passages in the New Testament to which Augustine refers will come most often from the Apostle Paul, and he puts them to use as if they were self-explanatory. This is significant because it points to the fact that Paul is often the ultimate authority for Augustine, where his authoritative status is reflected in the fact that Augustine often paraphrases him.[77] Though it cannot be denied that Plotinus influences Augustine decisively, it is also important not to overlook the Pauline roots of his thinking.[78]

In turning to the figurative interpretation of the last twenty-three verses of the first chapter of Genesis, and before he begins to put the epistles of Paul to a constructive use, Augustine first distinguishes between those who are oriented away from God and those who are oriented toward him. As a way of anticipating the distinction between the City of God and the City of Men,[79] he says that God has gathered all the individuals who are oriented only toward "temporal and earthly happiness" into a single society, where they "waver back and forth" among "a countless variety of cares" (13.17.20). In a figurative reading of verse nine, Augustine then compares the City to which he is referring to the waters that are gathered together (earth$_3$), in the midst of which the dry land of embodied beings (earth$_3$) appears at the beginning of the third day of creation. However, he claims that the dry land thirsts after God, and he is careful to say that the sea to which the verse in question refers is not the water, but the gathering together of the waters that he equates with the lusts of those who turn away from God. In the "sea" that he creates, God restrains "the wicked lusts of souls" and places limits on them. As a consequence, God demonstrates his sovereignty even over those who reject him (13.17.20).

In speaking about verse eleven, Augustine also claims that the water that he has been describing figuratively has a positive role to play in relation to the souls that thirst after God, where the earth with which they are equated is kept apart from the sea so they can bring forth fruit (13.17.21). Augustine then completes his figurative interpretation of the third day of creation by claiming that the citizens of the City of God generate "works of mercy" according to their kind, where they act in accord with the second great commandment by relieving the bodily necessities of those in need. They do this because they recognize their own infirmities, helping the needy just as they would wish to be helped if we were ever in the same kind of situation (13.17.21). Augustine also claims that it is important to act in this way, not only in easy things, "like a herb yielding seed," but also by giving "the protection and assistance of a mighty oak, like the fruit bearing tree." Assistance of this second kind expresses itself in rescuing those who suffer injury and in giving "shelter and protection" under the "great oak tree" of the judgment of God (13.17.21). Augustine begins his figurative interpretation of the fourth day of creation by exclaiming, "Let there spring up truth from the earth, and let justice look down from heaven, and 'let there be lights made in the firmament' " (13.18.22). He then mobilizes other parts of the Bible, urging his readers to feed the hungry, to bring those who are homeless into their houses, and to clothe the naked, claiming that when works of this kind spring up from the "earth," they are always good. Works of this kind are possible only when the "light" breaks in on us; and in order for these works to be sustained, we must pass from the "fruit of action to the delights of contemplation," where we appear as lights to the world, "holding fast to the firmament of . . . Scripture" (13.18.22).

Just as he engages in conversation with other interpreters of Genesis to generate a hermeneutical community, Augustine says that God holds a discussion with us in the Bible as we move toward fulfillment, making it possible for us to distinguish between "souls dedicated to intelligible things and . . . souls given over to things of sense" (13.18.22). The purpose of this discussion is to enable the spiritual children of God, who have been given a place in the "firmament," to "shine upon the earth," to "divide night and day," and to "mark off the seasons" (13.18.22). Some of these spiritual children are given wisdom (*sapientia*), which is a greater light that is intended for those who are delighted by the light of truth. Others are given other fruits of the Spirit, including knowledge (*scientia*),[80] faith (*fides*), the gift of healing, the working of miracles, prophecy, the discerning of spirits, and divers kinds of tongues. Speaking figuratively, and in this case, comparing different kinds of souls with material objects, Augustine tells us that the souls in question may be compared with the stars that shine upon the earth (13.18.23).

With this framework in the background, Augustine claims that knowledge (*scientia*), in which all the mysteries of God are contained, is like the moon, which together with the other gifts that have been compared with the stars, rule the night. These gifts are necessary for immature Christians to whom Paul has been unable to speak words of wisdom (*sapientia*) (13.18.23). As Augustine formulates the point,

The natural man, like a babe in Christ, and a drinker of milk until he becomes strong enough for solid food, and can steady his eye so as to look at the sun, let him not hold his night to be bereft of all light, but let him be content with the light of the moon and the stars. (13.18.23)

It is these things that God discusses with us in the firmament of his book, making it possible for us to move from action to contemplation, even though we can do so now only "in signs and times, and in days and years." Formulated in a somewhat different way, "Now we see through a glass darkly, but then face to face. Now we know in part, but then we shall know, even as we also are known"[81] (10.5.7).

The first step in moving in this direction is to wash ourselves and to take away the evil from our souls so "the dry land may appear." When this occurs, and when we learn how to do well, to judge on behalf of the fatherless, and to plead for the widow, the "earth" will bring forth green herbs and fruit-bearing trees (13.19.24). In order to illustrate the point he has in mind, Augustine mentions the rich man who comes to Jesus to ask what he must do to find eternal life. The first thing Jesus says is that he must obey the Ten Commandments, where in the figurative language that Augustine has been using, doing so will make it possible for the dry land to appear. When the young man replies to the demand of Jesus that he has done all these things, Jesus says that he must

> root up the spreading thickets of covetousness, "sell what [he has]," and be filled with fruits by giving to the poor, [which will make it possible for him to] have treasure in heaven. (13.19.24)

Jesus speaks wisdom (*sapientia*) to the rich young man so that he may become perfect, making it possible for him to distinguish the day from the night so that light may be created in the "firmament." Yet Augustine knows that this will not occur unless the young man's action comes from the heart and unless it expresses an ultimate commitment to perfection itself. In the language of the Bible, where our treasure is, there will our hearts be also;[82] and in the language of Augustine, where the light may be found, it will become possible to turn away from the darkness (13.19.24). However, in the case of the rich young man, his "barren earth" becomes sorrowful because thorns choke the Word of God.

As this juncture, Augustine combines his use of figurative discourse with his earlier use of cosmological language by claming that those who have forsaken everything to follow God "shine in the firmament" so the heavens may declare the glory of God (13.19.25). This makes it possible for him to distinguish the light of those who are "perfect," even though they are not yet like the angels, from the darkness of immature Christians, who are not like those who are without hope. In this way, he not only gives a figurative picture of the fourth day of creation, but also points to a hierarchical arrangement among the things that are made on that day. In this context, the day, "brightened by the sun," utters "the speech of wisdom" (*sapientia*) and the night, "shining with the moon," declares "the word of knowledge" (*scientia*) (13.19.25).

At this juncture, Augustine gives an account of the lights of the firmament that pertain to the founding of the Church at Pentecost. He says that the moon and the stars shine in the night and that the night does not darken them. Yet having placed these lights in the firmament, he also tells us that a "sound" comes from heaven and that "tongues of fire appear," making it possible for the lights of the firmament to hold the word of life[83] (13.19.25). In the words of Jesus, these fires are the light of the world; and they are not to be placed under anything that makes it impossible to see them.[84] Indeed, Augustine claims that because Christ has been exalted, these "fires" have been exalted as well, where their most important task is to make Christ known in every nation.

Having moved through the first four days of creation, both sequentially and hierarchically, Augustine turns to the fifth day of creation by claiming that the sea brings forth God's works, where the works in question do not include the living soul, but are to be identified with the "creeping creatures" that have life and "fowls that fly over the earth" (13.20.26). From a figurative point of view, these creations represent the mysteries of God, which are made accessible through the work of the saints and are present "amidst the waves of the world's temptations," making it possible for citizens of the City of Men to turn away from them and to embrace baptism (13.20.26). Among the deeds of the saints, great wonders are wrought, "like great whales"; and the voices of the "winged creatures above the earth" sound fourth by proclaiming the "firmament" of God's Book, which is in authority over them and under which they fly. The voices of the messenger of God have spoken in every nation; for by his blessing, God has multiplied them (13.20.26).

In developing this aspect of his figurative interpretation of Genesis, Augustine is careful to distinguish between the knowledge of God that is available in the Bible, and which he has identified already with the firmament of heaven, from corporeal works within the "restless sea" that make God accessible initially (13.20.27). In the case of wisdom (*sapientia*) and knowledge (*scientia*), our knowledge is made complete without reference to any "increase in generations." By contrast, we can express this knowledge through many corporeal operations, where one grows out of the other and where they are multiplied by the blessing of God. Because of the weakness of the senses in our mortal condition, our knowledge "may be pictured and expressed in many ways" (13.20.27). The waters have been brought these things, not because the sea has produced them, but because it needs to hear the Word of God. As Augustine formulates the point

> The needs of people alienated from [God's] eternal truth have brought them forth, but in [the] gospel. For these waters have cast them forth, of which waters a bitter disease was the cause whereby these things came forth in [God's] Word. (13.20.27)

At this juncture, Augustine reiterates some crucial points that he has made on a number of occasions and points by implication to his creation, his fall, his conversion, and his quest for fulfillment as the pivotal stages through which he moves in his own experiential and reflective development. First, he says that everything that God creates is beautiful, suggesting that the first word about the created order is positive (13.20.28). Second, he points to the fall and to the freedom of the will that it presupposes by claming that if Adam had not fallen away from God, the salt water of the human race—"so deeply active, so swelling in storms, and so restlessly flowing"—would not have poured forth from his womb (13.20.28). In the third place, he says that if the fall had not occurred, it would have been unnecessary for the messengers of God, who are to be identified with creeping creatures and with flying animals, to work corporeally among the waters to make conversion possible (13.20.28). Finally, he points toward fulfillment by claiming that those who respond to corporeal rites, and who are "instructed and initiated" by signs of this kind, "would not make further progress unless the soul began to live spiritually on another plane, and after words of admission would look forward to their consummation" (13.20.28).

The points that Augustine is making here are important because they presuppose the goodness of creation, point to the contingency of the fall, and call our attention to the conditions that make it possible for us to move toward conversion and fulfillment. If we focus first upon the goodness of creation and upon the human being as a positive expression of it, the most important point to notice is that since "Adam" means "man," and since to be a man is to be a composite of a soul and a body, both the soul and the body stand in a positive relation to God from the outset. As a consequence, the unfallen soul about which we have spoken earlier is embodied and is given a place in space and time, from which it is able to orient itself toward God. The second thing to notice is that when this embodied being turns away from God, the fall becomes a contingent act with disastrous consequences for every human being who emerges from Adam's "womb." In our earlier discussions of what it means to live and die in Adam, we have emphasized the fact that "Adam" is the first man, is what it means to be a man, and is a distributive collection of all individual men. While some passages in the *Confessions* reflect the last two interpretations more readily than the first, this passage implies that sin originates in the act of the primordial man to whom all of us can be referred and in whose actions all of us are implicated (10.16.25). The final crucial point about the issues before us is that we must distinguish two levels of individuals as we attempt to move away from the consequences of Adam's sin. On the one hand, fallen individuals are transformed into immature Christians by the signs and wonders of the creeping creatures and the flying animals; on the other hand, it is the task of the Church to make it possible for Christians to move from the corporeal to the spiritual level, where the contrast in question is a way of distinguishing two kinds of embodied individuals rather than the soul from the body.

As Augustine begins to move from conversion to fulfillment and to focus his attention on the sixth day of creation, he suggests that it is not "the depths of the sea," but the earth (earth$_3$) that has been separated from it that brings forth "a living soul"[85] (13.21.29). This claim reflects the seventh verse of the second chapter of Genesis where the Bible says that man is created from the dust of the ground and that God breathes into his nostrils the breath of life and he becomes a living soul. From a cosmological point of view, the claim that the earth brings forth a living soul points to the fact that a human being is a both a soul and a body; and it suggests that Augustine has no intention of identifying himself with his soul. However, from a figurative point of view, the emergence of the living soul from the earth points to the spiritual maturity of one kind of soul in contrast with another. A soul of this kind is not in need of baptism as unbelievers are, and as is once the case in their own situation (13.21.29). In a masterstroke of rhetoric that inverts the original construal of water as unformed spiritual material, Augustine tells us that being covered by the waters of baptism is a necessary condition for entrance into God's kingdom. However, once it has been baptized, the soul no longer needs "signs and wonders" to establish its faith (13.21.29).

Augustine continues to elaborate the difference between the fifth and the sixth days of creation by claiming that the earth that has emerged from the waters does not need the "flying fowl" that has been brought forth to speak to unbelievers. Instead, the Word of God addresses the dry land through its messengers, working upon it to produce a living soul (13.21.29). In this figurative context, the soul emerges from the earth (earth$_3$) because it is the material cause that makes the spiritual work of God's messengers necessary, just as the sea calls the "creeping creatures" and the "fowls of the air" into existence. Once the earth has been established, it no longer needs these creatures to provide a pathway to God, but it still "feeds upon the Fish" that has been

> raised out of the deep and put upon the table which [God has] prepared in the sight of believers. [For] he was taken out of the deep to the end that he might nourish the dry land. (13.21.29)

The word for fish in Greek is "ichtus,"[86] where it serves as an anagram for "Jesus Christ, God, Son, Savior." Having put on Jesus, the Christ in the garden in Milan (8.12.29), Augustine is now suggesting that the sacraments of the Church point in the same direction and indicate the reasons why putting on this kind of garment can make salvation possible.

Having said on the first page of the *Confessions* that preaching and hearing make it possible for us to call upon God, Augustine tells us on this occasion that our infidelity calls forth the preaching of the first evangelists (13.21.29). However, he also claims that faithful Christians are exhorted and blessed by these evangelists in manifold ways. As a consequence, he challenges his fellow ministers to work upon "the earth" and not simply upon "the waters of infidelity," where one needs to preach and speak by miracles, and mysteries, and mystical expressions (13.21.30). Augustine continues to combine existential, cosmological, and figurative language by claiming that even though signs and wonders of the ministers of God make faith possible for the sons of Adam who are forgetful of God, who hide themselves from his face, and who have become a darkened abyss, it is equally important for these ministers to work on the "dry land" that has emerged from the whirlpools of the abyss. The principle way of doing this is to become an example to the faithful, living before them and stirring them up to imitation.

Augustine claims that we hear God speak, only when we do what he says (13.21.30). As a consequence, thought and action are connected intimately as they pertain to the emergence of a living soul from the earth. The words of the Apostle Paul are directed to a soul of this kind when he says, "Do not be conformed to this world"[87] (13.21.30). As Augustine indicates in Book X, pride, sensuality, and false knowledge are the kinds of sin to which he is subject even after his conversion (10.30.41), where he equates pride with "wild beasts" that must be tamed, where he claims that sensuality is identical with the "cattle" that must be mastered, and where he understands false knowledge as "serpents" that must be rendered harmless (10.30.41–10.39.64). In figurative terms, he describes the passions of the soul in these ways, where the "haughty pride, lustful delight, and poisonous curiosity" that he expresses in this way are motions of "a dead soul." Souls of this kind do not cease to exist altogether; but as Augustine has suggested again and again, they die in a spiritual sense by forsaking God and by being conformed to the world.

The Word of God that does not pass away restrains our departure from God, so that the earth brings forth a living soul that imitates "the imitators of Christ." This is one of the figurative meanings that Augustine gives to the phrase, "being born according to kind." In the living soul, there will be beasts that are "good in meekness of conduct," cattle that will "neither have too much if they eat, nor if they do not eat, will they be in need." Finally, serpents will be good rather than pernicious, "searching only so far into temporal nature as suffices for eternity to be 'clearly seen, being understood by the things that are made.'" Formulated in literal rather than in figurative terms, "these animals are obedient to reason," living wisely because they are restrained from a deadly course by the Word of God (13.21.31).

Augustine now begins to elaborate what it means to be obedient to reason when he claims that when we turn our affections from the love of the world, when we begin to be "a living soul" by living well, and when the word, "Be not conformed to this world," has been fulfilled in us, what follows immediately is the command, "But be transformed by the renewing of your mind"[88] (13.22.32). This transformation will not result from imitating our neighbor "after their kind," or by following the example of a better man. As a consequence, when God turns to the creation of man, he does not say, "Let man be made after his kind," but rather, "Let us make man in our image and likeness,"[89] so that we may be able to prove the will of God (13.22.32).

Following the Apostle Paul, Augustine suggests that we will be able to move toward fulfillment only by the renewing of our minds, where renewal of this kind will permit us to discover the good, the acceptable, and the perfect will of God.[90] As a consequence, God does not say, "Let man be made," but "Let us make man"; and he does not say, "according to his kind," but according "to [his] image and likeness" (13.22.32). Indeed, it is only when he has been renewed that he does not need another man as his director so that he may "imitate his own kind." It is also important to notice that since a renewed mind is capable of moving from faith to understanding by comprehending God, God teaches him to see the Trinity of Unity and the Unity of the Trinity. Augustine claims that this is why the statement in the plural, "Let us make man," is connected with the statement in the singular, "And God made man." This is also the reason why the plural, "after our likeness," is conjoined with the singular, "after the image of God" (13.22.32). Augustine concludes his remarks about the image of God by suggesting that in a figurative context, creation in God's image is the condition that makes it possible for us to be transformed in the knowledge of God.

In continuing to discuss the sixth day of creation, Augustine says that the capacity to judge all things gives the spiritual man dominion over the "fish of the sea," the "fowls of the air," the "herds" and the "wild beasts," and all the "creeping things that creep upon the earth." We have this capacity only if we have moved from faith to understanding, which makes it possible for us to perceive "the things that are of the Spirit of God." Otherwise, when we are placed in positions of honor, we do not have understanding, are like "senseless beasts," and "are made like them" (13.23.33).

Augustine now begins to apply this figurative interpretation to the structure of the Church by claiming that those who preside spiritually and those who are subject to them from a spiritual point of view judge spiritually. However, this does not mean that the individuals in question ought to judge the distinction between wisdom (*sapientia*) and knowledge (*scientia*), or the Bible itself, even though some things in it are not clear. In this special case, we must submit our understanding to the Word of God and believe that what is hidden from our sight is spoken rightly and truly. Thus, even though a man may be spiritual and may be renewed by the knowledge of God according to the image of the One who created him, he must be a doer of the Law rather than its judge. In addition, it is not appropriate for us to judge the distinction between "spiritual and carnal men," who are known to God, but have "not yet become apparent to us, so that we might know them by their fruits." It is also important for us not to judge unbelievers, not knowing which ones will remain outside the Church and which will come to God through grace and faith (13.23.33).

Augustine also claims that even though mature Christians are made after God's image in the spiritual sense of the term, they do not have power over the lights of heaven, the hidden heaven (heaven$_2$), the day and the night (earth$_2$, earth$_3$) that God brings forth before the creation of the heaven, and the gathering of the waters, which is called sea (13.23.34). Instead, he says that Christians have received dominion over the fish of the sea and the fowls of the air, over all the cattle and the earth, and over all creeping things that creep on the earth. From a figurative point of view, this means that the Christian can judge and approve what he finds right and disapprove what he finds wrong, either in the celebration of the mysteries (baptism) by which individuals who have been redeemed from the waters are initiated; or in the sacrament (the eucharist) in which the Fish (Christ), having been raised from the depths of the sea (the crucifixion), the earth (members of the Church) feeds upon; or, in the sign and the symbols that are subject to the authority of Scripture, bursting forth from the ministers of God under the firmament (the Bible), interpreting, expounding, discoursing, disputing, blessing, and invoking God, so the people may answer, "Amen," which means, "I believe it." Augustine claims that these words must be pronounced vocally and must strike upon our ears because of the abyss of the world and because of the blindness of the flesh in which thoughts cannot be seen directly. Although the flying fowl are multiplied upon the earth, they still take their origins from the waters, where men must be addressed in order to bring them to God. Finally, Augustine says that the spiritual man may approve what he finds right and disapprove what he finds wrong in "the deeds and habits of the faithful," passing judgment upon the things "over which he . . . has the power of correction" (13.23.34).

Having proceeded in a relatively self-confident way in giving a figurative account of verses nine through twenty-seven of the first chapter of Genesis, Augustine encounters a difficulty in verse twenty-eight where he finds that God blesses men so they may "increase and multiply and fill the earth" (13.24.35). The literal interpretation of this phrase is clear, but how is it to be construed from a figurative point of view? One might think that if a figurative interpretation were possible, God would have spoken in the same way to the light, the firmament, the lights and the stars, and the earth and the sea (13.24.35). If we reply that the Bible does not do so because this blessing is restricted to human beings, we should then be puzzled by the fact that God has already blessed the fishes, the whales, and the birds in the same way, telling the fishes and the whales to be fruitful and multiply in the sea and the birds to multiply on the land (13.24.35). As a way of intensifying our puzzlement, Augustine says that we might be tempted to believe that the blessing in question pertains to creatures that propagate through themselves, provided the blessing in question had also been given to trees, plants, and beasts of the earth. However, when we turn to the text, we find that "increase and multiply" is not said to plants, trees, beasts, or serpents—although all of these, along with fishes, birds, and men, increase by propagation to preserve their species (13.24.35).

Augustine points to one of the most important principles that undergirds his approach to biblical interpretation when he asks whether the phrase before us "means nothing" and whether it is included in the first chapter of Genesis "for no purpose." Yet having asked the question, Augustine replies immediately that a servant of the Word of God should never suggest such a thing (13.24.36). This implies that when a reader of the Bible does not understand a passage that he wishes to interpret, he should subordinate himself to the text rather than the text to himself. In this way, the reader can remain open to the infinite richness of the text rather than bring the process of interpretation to a standstill.

Augustine attempts to follow the principle that he has enunciated by claming that even if he might not understand what a passage means, other men who are more intelligent than he might provide the interpretation he needs, according to the powers of understanding that God has given to them (13.24.35). However, in the case before us, Augustine is confident that God has not spoken the words, "increase and multiply" in vain, even to him. As a consequence, he says that he will not keep silent about what God has said to him through the phrase in question; for since he believes that the text itself is both true and infinitely rich, he does not believe that anything should prevent him from understanding the figurative statements in the Bible (13.24.36). Formulated in a somewhat different way, Augustine is expressing his confidence that out of the many meanings that the text might embody, it is reasonable to expect that he will find at least one of them.

The interpretation that Augustine gives of the phrase before us is significant, not only because he believes that it is one of many true interpretations, but also because it points to another principle of the method that Augustine adopts in interpreting the Bible. He formulates this principle by claiming that when a thing is understood in only one way in the mind, it may be expressed in many different ways by the body; and that when a thing is expressed in only one way through the body, it may be understood in many different ways in the mind (13.24.36). For example, the two great commandments can be expressed corporeally in many rites, many languages, and many ways of speaking, permitting the earth that emerges from the waters to increase and multiply. Correspondingly, the single statement, "In the beginning God created the heaven and the earth" can be understood by various true interpretations, as Augustine's earlier discussion of the verse in question indicates (12.28.38–12.29.40).

Augustine tells us that if we approach the words, "increase and multiply," from a cosmological point of view, these words pertain to things that have been begotten from seed (13.24.37). Yet if we interpret these same words figuratively, they can be applied to the spiritual and corporeal creatures of "heaven" and "earth"; to just and unjust souls of "light" and "darkness"; to the authors of the "firmament" that separates the "water" from the "water"; among the society of embittered people in the "sea"; in the zeal of holy souls on "dry land"; in the works of mercy that belong to the "present life, as in herbs bearing seed and trees bearing fruit"; among spiritual gifts that profit us, as in the "lights of heaven"; and among affections that have been brought under rational control, as in the "living soul" (13.24.37). In all these ways, we meet with multiplicity, fertility, and increase from an allegorical point of view.

However, when we apply the phrase, "increase and multiply," to "a single thing [that] may be stated in many ways and a single statement [that] may be understood in many ways," this can be the case only with respect to signs expressed corporeally and things conceived intelligibly. Signs that are expressed corporeally are necessary to communicate with the "fleshly depth" of the "waters" on behalf of which they are generated, and things that are conceived mentally are necessary to satisfy the rational dimension of the human being. Thus, Augustine believes that the words, "increase and multiply," have been spoken to both corporeal and spiritual individuals (13.24.37). In the form of another principle that undergirds his hermeneutical approach to the Bible, Augustine concludes that we have been given the power to express in many ways what we understand in only one, and to understand in many ways what we read expressed obscurely only in a single way. Thus, the "waters of the sea" are replenished because they are moved "by various significations"; and the "human offspring" of the "earth" are replenished because its "dryness" appears in its longing for God (13.24.37).

At this stage of his argument, Augustine turns to verses twenty-nine and thirty to conclude his account of the sixth day of creation. Yet in doing so, he speaks to God directly, asking for inspiration to speak out of the ground of Truth itself, rather than out of himself. In the first case, speaking will be true because it reflects the Truth out of which it emerges; in the second case, it will be false because it reflects the attempt to speak out of the source of oneself. Augustine expresses the point when he says, "He who 'speaks a lie speaks of his own.' Therefore, that I may speak the truth, I will speak out of [God's] gift" (13.25.38).

Augustine attempts to speak in this way by claiming that herbs and trees have been given to us to eat, but not to us alone, but also to the birds, the beasts of the earth, and the serpents. On the other hand, this food has not been given to the fish and to the "great whales" (13.25.38). From a figurative point of view, Augustine has claimed that the fruits of the earth signify works of mercy that are provided for the needs of life. For example, Onesiphorus, whom Paul mentions in 2 Timothy, is "earth" of this kind, because he had often shown mercy to Paul without being ashamed of Paul's bonds.[91] Yet as he thinks about other individuals whom Paul mentions, but who fail to act in this way, Augustine claims that we owe "fruits" to those who minister spiritual doctrine to us through their understanding of the divine mysteries. He also says that we owe these fruits to them, not only as men, but also as "living souls," since thy offer themselves as examples for us in their continence. Finally, Augustine tells us that we owe fruits to "the flying creatures" because of the blessings that have emerged from the fact that "their sound has gone forth into all the earth" (13.25.38).

In elaborating what he means by the fruits that we own to mature Christians, Augustine draws a distinction between what the Spirit gives and the Spirit itself. In the first case, fruit is what nourishes the one to whom it is given; in the second case, it is the good works that fruit of the first kind expresses (13.26.39). For example, when the Apostle Paul says that fellow Christians have sent something for his needs, he rejoices about this fact, not because of the gift, but because of the fruit (13.26.41). As Augustine elaborates the point, it is important to distinguish between the gift and the fruit. A gift is what is given to take care of the recipient's necessities, while the fruit expresses itself in the good will of the giver. In further examples that can be found in the Bible, the "gift" involves receiving a prophet,[92] receiving a righteous man,[93] and handing a cup of cold water to a disciple[94]; but the "fruit" is to do these things in the name of a prophet, in the name of a righteous man, and in the name of a disciple. In the Old Testament, a widow feeds Elijah with "fruit," for she knows that she is feeding a man of God. As a consequence, the outer man is fed by a "gift" from a raven, while the inner man is fed with fruit[95] (13.26.41).

Augustine summarizes his reflections about the figurative interpretation of the first chapter of Genesis by claiming that it is necessary to begin with fish and whales to respond to those who stand outside the Christian community. The fish and the whales point to the sacraments and the miracles that make access to the mystery of the faith accessible. When this has been accomplished, and when those who have become part of the Church give something useful to the servants of Christ, they do not "feed" them in a spiritual sense of the term because they do not understand why this is to be done. Those who give the gifts do not do so out of a good will, and those who receive them do not rejoice at what they receive because they do not see any fruit. The spiritual individual is able to feed only on what brings joy, where a gift must always be understood as something to be used (*uti*) rather than to be enjoyed (*frui*) (13.27.42).

Having brought his figurative interpretation of verses nine through thirty of the first chapter of Genesis to a conclusion, Augustine returns to his cosmological reading of the text in verse thirty-one by claiming that God looks at the world that he creates and that he finds it "very good" (13.28.43). Then he tells us that with respect to each of the kinds of work that he produces, God says that the work in question is good. The text says this in seven places (13.28.43), where we might remember that in giving an account of the pear-stealing episode as a way of attempting to negate the goodness of creation, Augustine says seven times that he would have never stolen the pears alone (2.8.16). However, Augustine emphasizes the fact that if we move behind the negativity with which we often choose to deal with the created order, God says that the days of creation taken separately are good, but taken collectively, are very good. Returning to his earlier reflections about the beautiful and the fitting, Augustine tells us that beautiful bodies express this truth; for a body that consists of several parts, each of which is beautiful, is itself more beautiful than any of its individual parts taken separately, where the well-ordered whole is completed through the parts that are beautiful taken separately (13.28.43).

Augustine continues to deal with some of the cosmological implications of the first chapter of Genesis by asking how God can stand outside of time in creating the world and can nevertheless see on seven different days that the things that he has created are good (13.29.44). He responds to this problem by claiming that the voice of God speaks to him "in his interior ear," breaking through his deafness and crying out,

> O man, true it is that what my Scripture says, I myself say. Yet that Scripture speaks in time, but time does not affect my Word, because that Word exists along with me in equal eternity. [Thus] the things that you see through my Spirit I see, just as those things which you speak by my Spirit I say. [But while] you see those things in time, I do not see them in time, even as when you say those things in time, I do not say them in time. (13.29.44)

In this way, Augustine returns to the God of creation, to the one who shatters his deafness and make it possible for him to find God (10.27.38), and to the one who helps him understand the faith that has been unfolding in him, where on this occasion, he is able to grasp the distinction between Words that are spoken from eternity, and words that are apprehended in time.

Augustine says that when we see things through God's Spirit, God himself sees them in us (13.31.46). As a consequence, when we see that the things in question are good, it is God who sees that this is so, where God gives us pleasure in whatever is pleasing because of God. Augustine continues to bring God and the soul together by claiming that the things that please us through God's Spirit are pleasing to God in us; for no one knows the things of God but the Spirit of God in us. If we are mature members of the Christian community, Augustine claims that we have not received the spirit of the world, but the Spirit of God, so we may know the things that are freely given to us by God. Finally, Augustine says that when we see, know, and speak in God, it is not we ourselves, but God who sees, knows, and speaks in us.

In a final formulation of the difference between various kinds of soul in relation to God, Augustine says that some individuals believe that what is good is evil (the Manicheans); that some find the whole of creation to be good, but do not find God in it (certain philosophers); and that still others are able to find the goodness of God expressed in the goodness of creation (Christians and Christian philosophers) (13.31.46). Individuals of this third kind do not enjoy (*frui*) the finite order, but use (*uti*) what God has created to make access to the one who has brought them into existence. It is individuals of this kind about whom Augustine says that they are able to love God through the Spirit of God that has been given to them. In doing so, they see that whatever exists is good, since everything has been created by God who is good in himself.

Augustine brings the penultimate section of the *Confessions* to a conclusion by summarizing the results of his interpretation of the first chapter of Genesis, first cosmologically, then existentially, and finally figuratively. From a cosmological point of view, he begins with heaven and earth, whether the corporeal heaven (heaven$_1$) and the corporeal earth, (earth$_1$) or the spiritual (heaven$_2$) and the corporeal (earth$_2$) creation. Then we turn to the world's universal mass or to the whole of creation in which light is separated from the darkness. At this stage, we consider the firmament, whether we understand it as the intellectual creature (heaven$_2$) that is located between the higher spiritual waters and the lower corporeal waters, or as the space through which the fowls of the air fly from place to place between the waters above them and the heavier waters that flow upon the earth.

In cosmological terms that he has used before, Augustine claims that the waters are gathered together into the seas and that the dry land, "whether bare or formed so as to be visible and put in order," is the source of herbs and trees. In the same way, he tells us that of the light in the sky, the sun suffices for the day, the moon and stars for the night, and that time which comes into existence when everything other than the intellectual creature (heaven$_2$) is brought into being, is used to mark and signify the passage of time. In cosmological terms, the creation of the heavenly bodies (heaven$_1$) is the first occasion upon which the days corresponding to them can be regarded as twenty-four hours in length. Finally, Augustine says that fish, beasts, and birds emerge from the water, that the density of the air supports the flight of birds, that earthly creatures and man live on the earth where man subordinates the nonrational animals to himself through the power of reason, and that the human race is divided between male and female with respect to gender, even though there is equality of nature between them. As a way of binding these cosmological remarks together, he says that each of these things is good, and that all of them taken together are very good (13.32.47).

Turning now in an existential direction, Augustine tells us that the works of God praise their creator so that we may love him, and that we love him so his works can praise him. Despite the fact that every creature in the natural order other than man has "beginning and end, rising and setting, growth and decay, beauty and privation,"[96] and even though each of them participates in the transition from morning to evening, they also point beyond themselves to their creator. In doing so, they call our attention to the one we seek, the one we praise, and the one we love (13.33.48).

The beings that God creates are made from nothing (*nihil*)—not out of God, not out of anything that is not God's, and not out of anything that is created beforehand. Instead, they are created from *concreated* matter, that is to say, from matter that is created "at the same time" that God forms its formlessness, without any interval of time (13.33.48). Since the matter of heaven and earth (earth$_2$) is one thing and the form of heaven and earth (earth$_2$) is another, God creates matter out of absolutely nothing (*nihil*), but he makes the form of the world (earth$_2$) from formless matter (earth$_3$). Yet both are done "at the same time," so that form follows matter in origin without the delay of any temporal interval (13.33.48).

Finally, Augustine returns to a figurative way of understanding the first chapter of Genesis, according to which God makes the stages of creation, either in a certain order, or so we can describe them in that order. In fact, just as he has extended his cosmological account to that part of the text that he had interpreted figuratively, he now extends his figurative account to the part that he had first interpreted cosmologically. As we have discovered, things taken one by one are good, but things taken together are very good, where in the Word of God, the heaven and the earth that can be regarded as the head and the body of the Church exist without morning or evening.

Yet when God begins to accomplish things in time, to reveal hidden things to us, and to reorder our disorders, God justifies the ungodly and divides them from the wicked. Then he establishes the Scriptures as a firmament between the intellectual creature (heaven$_2$) that cleaves stead-fastly to him and those below who are subject to them. Finally, God gathers the society of unbelievers into a single conspiracy so that the zeal of the faithful might become manifest, and in order that they might bring forth works of mercy, giving their earthly riches to the poor to obtain heavenly riches.

Against this background, God creates lights the firmament, which are followers of God, have the Word of Life, and shine with the manifest authority of their spiritual gifts. Then as a way of instructing those who are outside the Church, God produces sacraments from corporeal matter (earth$_3$)—miracles, words, and voices that reflect the firmament of God's Book. On this basis, God forms the "living soul" of the faithful whose affections are kept in order by continence. Finally, God renews the minds of his creatures after his image and likeness, which is subject to God alone and does not need to imitate human authority. To those who are ministers of the Church and are necessary for perfecting the faithful, God has willed that the works of the faithful should be offered for their temporal use. Thus Augustine can say,

> We see all these things, and we see that they are very good, because you see them in us, who have given to us your Spirit, by whom we might see them and in them love you. (13.34.49)

THE TELOS OF THE NEW CREATION (13.35.50–13.38.53)

In bringing the *Confessions* to a conclusion, Augustine moves beyond the six days of creation to the Sabbath rest, where he asks God to grant him the peace of quietness and the peace without an evening (13.35.50). His life has been filled with turmoil, and though he finds peace in the garden in Milan (8.12.29), he is under no delusion that final peace will ever come as long as he is still engaged in the quest for fulfillment. Thus, in this cosmological summary of his situation from an eschatological point of view, Augustine calls our attention to the fact that the whole creation will pass away when its purposes have been fulfilled, making it possible for the world to move from creation to fulfillment (13.35.50).

The fulfillment that Augustine anticipates will occur on the seventh day, where the day in question is without an evening and where God has sanctified it with an everlasting duration that points beyond time to eternity. After all the works of creation that are very good, God rests on the seventh day, even though he creates them all in unbroken rest. He does this in order to assure us that after our works have been completed, which are very good because God has given them to us, we may find rest in God on the Sabbath of eternal life.[97] In this way, Augustine returns to the first page of the text, pointing to a resolution of the problem generated by the fact that our hearts are restless until we find our rest in God (1.1.1, 13.36.51).

Augustine tells us that when we come to rest in God, God comes to rest in us so that God's own rest is in us just as his works are through us (13.37.52). God, who is ever at work and ever at rest, does "not see for a time," is not "moved for a time," and does not "rest for a time." However, God is responsible for the fact that things are "seen in time," for "times themselves," and for "the rest that comes after time" (13.37.52). Augustine also says that we can see the things that God has made because they are, while things exist because God sees them (13.38.53). In addition, we see with our eyes that things exist and see with our minds that they are good, while God sees them all at once as what has been created. Finally, Augustine looks back on his life and looks forward toward the future by moving for a final time through the progression from creation, to the fall, to conversion, to fulfillment. He says,

At one time we have been moved to do good, after our heart conceived this after your Spirit, whereas at a former time, having forsaken you, we were moved to do evil. But you, O one good God, have never ceased to do good. There a certain works of ours, done indeed out of your gift, but they are not eternal. After such things, we hope to find rest in your great sanctification. But you, the Good, needful of no good, are forever at rest, for your rest is yourself. (13.38.53)

Augustine's final words in the *Confessions* point to the journey from creation to fulfillment, and they take us back once more to the first page of the text where he frames his introduction to the confessional enter-prise. Having suggested that it is impossible for one human being to teach another about the culmination of our quest for fulfillment, Augustine says that we must ask about it from God, seek it from God, and knock for it from God (13.38.53). Only in this way can we move from faith to under-standing, first by knocking, then by seeking, and then by having the door opened to us.

Notes

Notes to Preface

1. *Contemporary Themes in Augustine's Confessions: Parts I and II*, Carl G. Vaught, ed., *Contemporary Philosophy* 15 (1993).

2. Carl G. Vaught, "Theft and Conversion: Two Augustinian Confessions," in *The Recovery of Philosophy in America: Essays in Honor of John Edwin Smith*, ed. Thomas P. Karsulis and Robert Cummings Neville, 217–49. (Albany: State University of New York Press, 1997).

Notes to Introduction

1. F. J. Sheed, trans., *The Confessions of Saint Augustine* (Indianapolis, IN and Cambridge, MA: Hackett, 1993), xxvii.

2. Ibid., xxix.

3. Pierre Courcelle, *Recherches sur les Confessions de Saint Augustin*, 2nd ed. (Paris: E. de Boccard, 1968), 49, 248.

4. References to the *Confessions* and Augustine's other writings are given in parentheses in book, chapter, and paragraph form. The purpose of this convention is to permit readers to find the references in any Latin edition and in any translation.

5. Augustine makes all of these dimensions explicit without ever binding them together in an overarching framework. He does this with respect to time by distinguishing stages of the life cycle. He does it with respect to space by describing the communities of which he is a part in the course of his development. And he does it with respect to eternity by pointing to the ultimate significance of many of the experiences that he undergoes. By holding all of these dimensions together, I am pointing to ways in which they intersect at various stages of Augustine's development.

6. See Carl G. Vaught, *The Journey toward God in Augustine's Confessions* (Albany: State University of New York Press, 2003).

7. Peter Brown comments on the inner dimensions of his own approach in his extensive biography of Augustine. See Peter Brown, *Augustine of Hippo: A Biography*, new edition with an epilogue (Berkeley: University of California Press, 2000), ix.

8. Brown remarks that a reciprocal relationship exits between Augustine and his surroundings, so that new settings and routines affect his inner life as his developing preoccupations affect both the meanings inherent in these circumstances and the people who surround him. See Brown, ix.

9. I use the familiar phrase from Paul Tillich, not because it is to be found in the *Confessions*, but because it expresses Augustine's fundamental intentions. It is not by accident that Tillich locates himself within the Augustinian tradition. See Paul Tillich, "Two Types of Philosophy of Religion," in *Theology of Culture*, ed. Robert C. Kimball, 10–29 (New York: Oxford University Press, 1959).

10. This is the first reference to the (finite-infinite) structure of the soul that I make in this book to express the transitions from creation to the fall, from the fall to conversion, and from conversion to fulfillment. As I will attempt to indicate, these categories are not imposed on the text, but are ways of pointing to distinctions that emerge from it.

11. Augustine, *Retractations*, trans. Sister Mary Inez Bogan (Washington, D.C.: Catholic University of America Press, 1968), 32,1.

12. As quoted in Brown, 436.

13. Paul Ricoeur, *Time and Narrative*, vol. 1 (Chicago: University of Chicago Press, 1984), 4.

14. Despite what Gerard O'Daly states in *Augustine's Philosophy of Mind* (London: Gerald Duckworth, 1987), 152–61, there are two forms of distension in Augustine's discussion of the nature of time, where one is positive and the other is negative.

15. This separation is greater than the one that obtains between the One and what emanates from it, since creatures are created from nothing, while everything other than the One emanates from it.

16. See Frederic E. Van Fleteren, "Augustine's Ascent of the Soul in Book VII of the Confessions: A Reconsideration," *Augustinian Studies* 5 (1974): 29–72.

17. There are a number of indications in the text that Augustine believes that we must have a concept of God before we can come to know him. In Book VII, for example, he acquires a concept of God (7.1.1) before he recognizes him; in Book X, he suggests that a necessary condition for finding God is that we must be able to recollect what we know already (7.16.25). On the other hand, Augustine says on a number of occasions that he believes that God exists, but that he does not understand who God is (3.7.12; 4.15.26; 5.10.20; 6.1.1; 7.4.6). It is not easy to see how these strands in Augustine's thinking are to be reconciled; and one of our central tasks in this book will be to attempt to do so.

18. See Etienne Gilson, *The Christian Philosophy of Saint Augustine*, trans. L. E. M. Lynch (New York: Random House, 1960) and Ronald H. Nash, "Some

Philosophic Sources of Augustine's Illumination Theory," *Augustinian Studies* 2 (1971): 47–64.

19. Absolute nonbeing, which Augustine distinguishes from prime matter (12.3.3) is more elusive that the lower limit of the Neoplatonic continuum, since Plotinus equates this limit with matter, which has determinate properties. See Plotinus, *Enneads*, trans. A. H. Armstrong, 7 vols. in *The Loeb Classical Library* (Cambridge: Harvard University Press, 1966–1984), 2.4.8.

20. In Augustine's first version of evil as privation, evil does not exist and is simply a part abstracted from its place within a larger whole (7.5.7). When his analysis becomes more sophisticated, privation means deprivation, on the one hand, and distortion and absence on the other (7.12.18). Finally, in the developing the view of evil that is most typical of the existential dimension of his thought, he claims that evil is a willful orientation of the soul away from God (2.10.18; 7.16.22).

21. Augustine does not use these terms in formulating his account of the relation between God and the soul. However, his description of this complex relation presupposes the concepts to which these terms call our attention. Finitude points to the bounded dimension of the human situation, and infinitude points to the aspect of it that transcends itself in relation to God.

22. The (finite-infinite) structure of the soul that Augustine presupposes and that we will develop in this book unfolds on four levels. In the moment of creation, man is a (finite-infinite) reflection of God, where the finite dimension holds the creator and the creature apart, while the infinite dimension binds them together. In the Fall, the (finite-infinite) creature turns away from its finitude and attempts to embrace its infinite dimension without qualification, causing it to become a negative reflection of the creative source that brings it into existence. In the incarnation, the infinite God becomes finite, and having emptied himself, enables the (finite-infinite) creature to come back to itself by embracing its finitude. And in the resurrection, the (finite-infinite) being returns to its infinite source as a reflection of the original infinitude from which it has fallen away. Creation, fall, conversion, and fulfillment are the four pivotal moments in the cosmic drama Augustine reenacts; these moments are bounded by God, on the one hand, and by absolute nonbeing on the other; and each of these moments involves unity and separation between God and the soul that requires metaphorical and analogical discourse for their adequate articulation.

23. Martin Luther, *Bondage of the Will*, in *Luther and Erasmus: Free Will and Salvation*, trans. E. Gordon Rupp (Philadelphia: Westminster Press, 1969).

24. Augustine develops this theme in his analysis of memory in Book X of the *Confessions* (10.9.16).

25. See Leo Charles Ferrari, "The Theme of the Prodigal Son in Augustine's *Confessions*," *Recherches Augustiniennes* 12 (1977): 105–18; and James J. O'Donnell, *Augustine: Confessions*, vol. 2 (Oxford: Clarendon Press, 1992), 95–98.

26. This is the insight expressed in Augustine's claim that he becomes a Christian when he "puts on" Jesus, the Christ (8.12.29).

27. Alfred North Whitehead, *Religion in the Making* (Cleveland: The World Publishing Company, 1963), 50.

28. For authors that move in a Neoplatonic direction, see for example Prosper Alfaric, *L'évolution intellectuelle de saint Augustine. Vol. 1: Du Manichéennes au Néoplatonisme* (Paris: Nourry, 1918); A. Hilary Armstrong, *The Cambridge History of Later Greek and Early Medieval Philosophy* (Cambridge: Cambridge University Press, 1967); Robert J. O'Connell, *St. Augustine's Confessions: The Odyssey of Soul* (New York: Fordham University, 1989) and *St. Augustine's Platonism* (Villanova, PA: Villanova University Press, 1984); J. J. O'Meara, "Augustine and Neo-Platonism," *Recherches Augustiniennes* 1 (1958).

29. Augustine, *Retractations*, 130.

30. Max Zepf, "Augustine's *Confessions*," *Lutheran Church Quarterly* 21 (1948): 214.

31. O'Donnell, *Augustine: Confessions*, vol. 3, 154.

32. John J. O'Meara, *The Young Augustine: The Growth of St. Augustine's Mind up to his Conversion* (New York: Longmans, Green, 1954), 13–17.

33. I have dealt with the first two topics in previous books, and the present book brings my account of the Augustine's *Confessions* to a conclusion.

34. O'Donnell, *Augustine: Confessions*, vol. 3, 154.

35. See H. Kusch, "Studien über Augustinus," *Festschrift Franz Dornseiff* (Leipzig, 1953), 124–200; Colin Starnes, *Augustine's Conversion: A Guide to the Argument of Confessions I–IX* (Waterloo, ONT: Wilfrid Laurier University Press, 1990); L. Verheijen, *Eloquentia pedisequa* (Nijmengen: Dekker & van de Vegt, 1949).

36. See Starnes, *Augustine's Conversion*.

37. See O'Meara, *The Young Augustine*.

38. See O'Connell, *St. Augustine's Confessions*.

39. See O'Donnell for a discussion on *libido*, *superbia*, and *curisositas*.

40. See Frederic E. Van Fleteren, "Augustine's Ascent," 29–72.

41. A paradoxal problem is pointed out in *De Magistro*, the dialogue between Augustine and Adeodatus, relating to the problem of signs. Augustine explains that in order to teach, one must utilize signs. However, unless the human being already understands the reality of these signs, then the use of such signs would be meaningless. Augustine provides the solution to the enigma by the doctrine of the "inner teacher." The ability of humans to acquire knowledge is made possible by consultation of the inner teacher, God.

42. Again, the divine teacher about whom Augustine speaks in *The Teacher* has a crucial role to play in the *Confessions*.

NOTES TO CHAPTER ONE

1. Matthew 5.12. See Colin Starnes, "Prolegomena to the Last Three Books" (paper presented at Celebrating Augustine's *Confessions*: Reading the

Confessions for the New Millennium, Pruitt Memorial Symposium, Baylor University, Waco, TX, October 4, 2001, 1–3).

2. For a thorough discussion of the three encounters see my earlier work *Encounters with God in Augustine's Confessions* (Albany: State University of New York Press, 2004). This book is a detailed analysis of Books VII –IX in Augustine's *Confessions*, and it comes to focus on three pivotal encounters between God and the soul. The first is the culmination of Augustine's philosophical conversion (7.10.16; 7.17.23), the second is the crucial moment in his conversion to Christianity (8.12.29), and the third is the mystical experience he shares with his mother a few days before her death in Ostia (9.10.24).

3. Augustine illustrates the doctrine of the "inner teacher" in a dialogue that involves the ability of humans to acquire knowledge made possible by Christ, the divine teacher. See Peter King, trans., *On the Teacher*, in *Against the Academicians and The Teacher* (Indianapolis and Cambridge: Hackett, 1995).

4. Gilson, 75.

5. O'Donnell, *Augustine: Confessions*, vol. 3, 150.

6. Ibid., 153.

7. Augustine's sexual addiction is made clear in Book VI. The difference between addiction and curiosity is illustrated in a comparison between himself and Alypius. Alypius begins "to desire to marry, not because he was overcome by lust for such pleasure, but out of curiosity" (6.12.22). Here we find once more the fundamental difference between Augustine and Alypius. Augustine's erotic consciousness seeks sexual satisfaction because a sexual addiction drives him toward it, while Alypius contemplates marriage out of curiosity.

In addition, Augustine must face one of the most traumatic experiences of his life when his mother tears his mistress from him because she is an impediment to his marriage, and his heart that continues to cling to her is torn and wounded until it bleeds. In spite of his bleeding heart, Augustine cannot wait two years to obtain the bride he seeks; he informs us, "Since I was not so much a lover of wedlock as a slave of lust, I procured another woman, but not, of course, as a wife" (6.15.25). The emerging philosopher remains addicted to a lasting habit. As in so many similar cases, this habit points, not primarily to a determinate problem, but to the deeper predicament of the bondage of the will. As he formulates the crucial point himself, the wound caused by cutting away the one he loves has not healed, and "it festered, and still caused [him] pain, although in a more chilling and desperate way" (6.15.25).

8. See Starnes, "Prolegomena to the Last Three Books," 3.

9. My second book on the *Confessions* focuses on the three experiences that transform Augustine's life: the philosophical conversion in 7.17.23, the conversion to Christianity in 8.12.29, and the mystical experience with his mother a few days before her death in Ostia in 9.10.24. See Vaught, *Encounters with God in Augustine's* Confessions*: Books VII–IX*.

10. The form of the verbs makes it possible to translate them both as present subjunctives or as future indicatives. I am following O'Donnell's suggestion in

rendering the first as a present subjunctive and the second as a future indicative. See O'Donnell, *Augustine: Confessions*, vol. 3, 154.

11. Augustine is referring to the passage in Matthew when God demands perfection: "You therefore must be perfect just as your heavenly Father is perfect" (Mathew 5.48). See Starnes, "Prolegomena to the Last Three Books," 2–3.

12. In order to sustain the kind of inquiry in which we are engaged, there is a need for details rather than a thesis. The details provide a mode of thought that incorporates narrative, analysis, system, and concrete reflection. The narrative of Augustine gives us concrete richness, the analysis makes the meaning of pivotal concepts available, the systematic dimension of our undertaking holds these concepts together in a systematic unity, and the concrete reflection brings the first three elements together by allowing the first three to interplay with one another as we move through the text. The text itself and our account provide the crucial fourth term that expresses itself most clearly by allowing us to describe the conditions for Augustine's experiential journey and by permitting us to develop a mirror image of that journey at a reflective level.

13. O'Donnell first draws the distinction between making confessions and coming to the light or "doing the truth." See O'Donnell, *Augustine: Confessions*, vol. 1, Prolegomena.

14. See Starnes, "Prolegomena to the Last Three Books," 4–5.

15. Augustine identifies human beings as having two parts (the soul and the body) that make up a single composite. See *Tractates on the Gospel of John*, trans. John W. Rettig in *The Fathers of the Church*, vol. 92 (Washington, DC: Catholic University of America Press, 1988), 19.5.15; *On the Catholic and the Manichean Ways of Life*, trans. D. Gallagher and I. Gallagher in *The Fathers of the Church*, vol. 56 (Washington, DC: Catholic University of America Press, 1966), 1.4.6; and *The Happy Life*, trans. Ludwig Shop in *The Fathers of the Church*, vol. 1 (New York: CIMA Publishing, 1948), 2.7.

16. There are three types of curiosity for Augustine: epistemological, moral, and metaphysical. The epistemological aspect for Augustine is form of curiosity that is simply a misplaced desire for knowledge. The misguided pursuit involves a search merely for the sake of knowing (10.35.55). Augustine's attack on epistemological curiosity is most evident in his writings on the Manicheans and their "intense and eager curiosity" derived from sensory experience only. See *On the Catholic and the Manichean Ways of Life* (1.21.38); N. Joseph Torchia, "Curiositas in the Early Philosophical Writings of Augustine," *Augustinian Studies* 19, (1988): 111–19. The moral significance of curiosity can be found in the triad of sins including pride and sensuality. In this sense, curiosity is linked to the "concupiscence of the eyes" forbidden in 1 John 2.16 (10.35.54–55). Finally, the metaphysical element of curiosity is a diversion from eternal peace as a result of the soul's restless temporal existence due to our fallen nature. See *On True Religion*, trans. John H. Burleigh in *Augustine Earlier Writings, The Library of Christian Classics*, vol. 4 (Philadelphia, PA: Westminster Press, 1953), 38.69, 52.101.

17. The hermeneutics of trust is replaced with a hermeneutics of suspicion by some secondary scholars of Augustine, which in turn causes us to qualify, amend, or recant some positions on the *Confessions*. Paul Ricoeur coined the phrase "hermeneutics of suspicion" and named Marx, Freud, and Nietzsche the preeminent "masters" of that art. "Hermeneutics of suspicion" approaches the text not so much to clarify it as to unmask its myths and contradictions. As Ricoeur claims, "All three clear the horizon for a more authentic word, for a new reign of Truth, not only by means of a 'destructive' critique, but by the invention of an art of interpreting." See Paul Ricoeur, *Freud and Philosophy: An Essay on Interpretation* (New Haven, CT: Yale University Press, 1970), 33.

18. There is evidence from documents written soon after his conversion that seem to contradict Augustine's later recollections in the *Confessions* making it easy to conclude with Harnack, Alfaric, and others that Augustine is reconstructing his past or lying about it for prudential purposes. See Adolf Harnack, "Die hohepunkte in Augustins Konfessionen," reprinted in his *Redens und Aufsätze*, vol. 1 (Giessen: Ricker, 1904), 51–79 and Prosper Alfaric, *L'évolution intellectuelle de saint Augusti* (Paris: Nourry, 1918). See also Starnes, *Augustine's Conversion*, 5.

19. Vernon Bourke claims that Augustine is appealing to readers with an open mind. Bourke writes, "Augustine realizes that some open-mindedness is required of people who wish to understand his views. Either one has to start from some base of religious belief (as he did), or the benevolent reader must grant that if an ultimate answer to philosophy's problems is sought, then some ultimate supreme cause, and truth, and wisdom, must be considered." See Vernon Bourke, *Augustine's Love of Wisdom: An Introspective Philosophy* (West Lafayette, IN: Purdue University Press, 1992), 120.

Starnes argues contra Bourke and maintains that Augustine makes it clear that his audience is Christian. As Starnes suggests, "Whereas the first nine books were about the once-only move from error to truth (i.e., from birth to baptism), Augustine is now addressing himself to the continuing concerns of his fellow Christians, all of whom are engaged in a common struggle to conform their individual lives to the demands of Christ. What is true in this sense for Augustine is true for every Christian." See Starnes, "Prolegomena to the Last Three Books," 5.

20. See Starnes, "Prolegomena to the Last Three Books," 3–4.

21. See *Against the Skeptics* and *On Order*, trans. Denis J. Kavanagh in *The Fathers of the Church*, vol. 1 (New York: CIMA, 1948), (3.43; 2.16); *Soliloquies*. trans. with an intro. and notes Kim Paffenroth, in *The Works of Saint Augustine: Translations for the Twenty-first Century*, vol. 2, ed. John E. Rotelle (Brooklyn, NY: New City Press, 2000), 1.12–14.23. See also Robert E. Cushman, "Faith and Reason," in *A Companion to the Study of St. Augustine*, ed. by Roy W. Battenhouse (New York: Oxford University Press, 1955), 295–300 and Ragnar Holte, *Béatude et Sagesse: Saint Augustin et le problème de la fin de l'homme dans la philosophie ancienne* (Paris: Études Augustinienne, 1962), 321–27, 381–86.

22. See Vaught, *The Journey toward God in Augustine's Confessions*, 24–27.

23. Unlike Augustine, Thomas Aquinas emphasizes the discontinuity that divides God and the world. He crosses the divide with a cosmological argument for God's existence beginning with a posteriori assumptions that the universe exists and that something outside is required to explain its existence. Thomas gives a version of the cosmological argument based on the theory of causation. For example, Thomas writes:

> We find in our experience that there is a chain of causes: nor is it found possible for anything to be the efficient cause of itself, since it would have to exist before itself, which is impossible. Nor in the case of efficient causes can the chain go back indefinitely, because in all chains of efficient causes, the first is the cause of the middle, and these of the last, whether they be one or many. If the cause is removed, the effect is removed. Hence if there is not a first cause, there will not be a last, nor a middle. But if the chain were to go back infinitely, there would be no first cause, and thus no ultimate effect, nor middle causes, which is admittedly false. Hence we must presuppose some first efficient cause— which all call God.

See Thomas Aquinas, *Summa Theologiae*, trans. English Dominican Fathers (New York: Christian Classics, 1981), Ia.2.3.

24. Augustine's view regarding the immediate inference of God is similar to that of Charles Pierce. Pierce insists, "The variety of the universe which we see whenever and wherever we open our eyes, constitutes its liveliness, its vivacity. The perception of it is a direct, though darkling perception of God." See Charles Pierce, "The Neglected Argument," in *Collected Papers of Charles Sanders Pierce*, eds. Charles Hartshorne and Paul Weiss (Cambridge, MA: Harvard University Press, 1965), 372.

25. For further discussion see Ronald H. Nash, *The Light of the Mind: St. Augustine's Theory of Knowledge*, 48–51; and Margaret R. Miles, "Vision: The Eye of the Body and the Eye of the Mind in Saint Augustine's De Trinitate and Confessions," *Journal of Religion* 63 (1983): 125–42.

26. Compare this with the view of Gareth B. Matthews, *Thought's Ego in Augustine and Descartes* (Ithaca, NY: Cornell University Press, 1992), 49–51, who takes the alternative position.

27. Bourke, *Augustine's Love of Wisdom*, 7, 34–35.

28. Gilson, 44–45

29. Having called our attention to the fact that the soul, the body, and the composite are all substances on Augustine's view, Gilson suggests that such a confusion exists. See Gilson, 45–55.

30. Augustine acknowledges the persuasive nature of rhetoric in his writings. He writes that "one who tries to speak not only wisely but eloquently will

be more useful if he can do both." See *On Christian Doctrine* (4.5.8). Augustine used his rhetorical abilities to convince readers of his own scholastic interpretation of the Scriptures. He asks, "Why should not decent people use it in behalf of the truth when the wicked use it for corrupt and vain purposes, in the service of wickedness and error?" Ibid., (4.2.3).

31. This is also true of souls, where their finitude distinguishes them from God, and where souls differ from bodies because they are temporal rather than spatiotemporal. See Bourke, *Augustine's Love of Wisdom*, 32–33.

32. Augustine considers four theories as possible explanations for the origin of the human soul. The first theory, traducianism, presupposes that the souls of human beings evolve from the one soul that God created. Second, creationism claims that souls are created individually at birth. The third theory maintains that God sends the existing souls to the bodies when they are born. The soul then governs the individual. Finally, in the fourth theory, souls are not sent by God, but fall into bodies of their own accord. See *On Free Choice of the Will*, trans. Anna S. Benjamin and L. H. Hackstaff (Englewood Cliffs, NJ: Prentice Hall, 1964), 3.21.59; *Retractations*, 1.1.3; *Select Letters*, trans. James Houston Baxter in *The Loeb Classical Library*, vol. 239 (Cambridge: Harvard University Press, 1980), 1.66; and *The Literal Meaning of Genesis*, trans. John H. Taylor in *Ancient Christian Writers*, vols. 41–42 (New York: Newman Press, 1982), 10.1.

33. See Bourke, *Augustine's Love of Wisdom*, 39–40 and Nash, 40.

34. Nash, 48–51 and Miles, "Vision," *Journal of Religion* 63 (1983), 125–42.

35. For an alternate view see O'Daly, 199–203.

36. Jacques Derrida claims that a "metaphysics of presence" is central to all systems of Western philosophy. Derrida uses his deconstruction of speech and writing to develop a critique against the logocentrcism that percolates in Western philosophy. Derrida explains that the metaphysics of presence is a desire for a "transcendental signified" that transcends all signifiers, or a meaning that transcends all signs. Derrida deconstructs the metaphysics of presence in order to uncover the interplay between presence and absence in Western thought. For a discussion of the metaphysics of presence see Jacques Derrida, *Of Grammatology*, trans. Gayatri Chakravorty Spivak (Baltimore, MD: Johns Hopkins University Press, 1974), 49–50.

37. See Tillich, 10–29.

38. At this juncture, I am beginning to enrich my use of the distinction between the finite and the infinite. To say that man is a (finite-infinite) being is to say that limitations and self-transcendence intersect in our journey toward God. If we accept our limitations, we are (finite↑infinite) beings; and our souls stretch out toward God without denying our created limitations. On the other hand, if we attempt to encroach upon the mystery and the majesty of God, we turn away from our finitude to accentuate our infinite dimension. As a consequence, we become (finite↓infinite) beings who are separated from God. Søren Kierkegaard makes a similar characterization of the condition of the self when he

writes, "A human being is a synthesis of the infinite and the finite, of the temporal and the eternal, of freedom and necessity, in short, a synthesis" Cf. Søren Kierkegaard, *The Sickness unto Death*, trans. Howard Vincent Hong and Edna H. Hong (Princeton, NJ: Princeton University Press, 1980), 13.

39. Bourke, *Augustine's Love of Wisdom*, 151–54; Gilson, 74–75; and O'Donnell, *Augustine: Confessions*, vol. 3, 181–82.

40. Nash, 84.

41. See Plato, *Meno in Five Dialogues*, trans. G. M. A. Grube (Indianapolis, IN: Hackett, 1981), 84b–86c.

42. For an alternative view, see O'Daly, 199–203.

43. Bourke, *Augustine's Love of Wisdom*, 158–59.

44. See O'Donnell, *Augustine: Confessions*, vol. 3, 185.

45. Ibid., 186.

46. O'Daly, 207.

47. O'Connell regards these experiences as dramatic ways of summarizing doctrines that Augustine had come to hold after his encounter with the Platonists in Milan. See O'Connell, *St. Augustine's Confessions*, 75–89. There is no reason that they cannot be both, where the doctrines provide the discursive content for the experiences.

48. See O'Donnell, *Augustine: Confessions*, vol. 3, 186–87.

49. Genesis 3.23.

50. Genesis 3.17–23.

51. See Augustine, *The Teacher* in *Philosophy in the Middle Ages*, trans. J. H. S. Burleigh, ed. Arthur Hyman and James J. Walsh (Indianapolis, IN: Hackett, 1973).

52. Augustine is speaking about forgetfulness itself rather than an image of it. For example, his argument specifically addresses the loss of memory as forgetfulness (10.16.24).

53. See Plato, *Sophist in The Collected Dialogues of Plato*, ed. Edith Hamilton and Huntington Cairns (New York: Pantheon Books, 1961), 236c–237b.

54. The reason for this claim is the volitional nature of the fall within both contexts.

55. The reason that this is the case is that God has a transcendent side that is accessible only if God reveals himself to the soul that is oriented toward him (7.10.16).

56. For Plotinus, the *Nous* comprises the domain of intelligence and intelligible beings referred to as primary reality. The *Nous* emanates from the ineffable One. As he formulates the point,

The One, perfect because It seeks nothing, has nothing and needs nothing, overflows, as it were, and Its superabundance makes something other than Itself. Its halt and turning towards the One constitutes being, its gaze upon the One, Nous. Since it halts and turns towards the One that it may see, it becomes at once Nous and being. Resembling the One thus Nous produces in the same way, pouring forth a multiple power. Just as That, Which was before it, poured forth its likeness, so what Nous produces is a likeness of itself. This activity springing from being is Soul, which comes into being while Nous abides unchanged: for as a necessary consequence of its own existence: and the whole order of things is eternal: the lower world of becoming was not created at a particular moment but is eternally being generated: it is always there as a whole, and particular things in it only perish so that others may come into being. (5.2.1)

57. This is the other side of the point about the transcendence of God that makes it impossible for Augustine to reach God through recollection alone. Perhaps we should say that he has a concept of God that he has not forgotten completely (7.1.1), but that an encounter with God is necessary to find him (7.10.16; 7.17.23).

58. Plato, *Republic*, trans. G. M. A. Grube (Indianapolis: Hackett, 1992), 509a–511e.

59. Luke 15.8.

60. See Plato, *Meno in Five Dialogues*, 80d.

61. Augustine, *The Happy Life*.

62. O'Donnell, *Augustine: Confessions*, vol. 3, 190.

63. Augustine considers four theories about the origin of the soul. The first theory of the soul is known as traducianism and presupposes that "the souls of human beings who are born are drawn from the one soul God created." In this case, original sin originated with Adam and Eve and it was passed on to us through our parents, or more especially Adam. See *On Free Choice of the Will*, 3.20.56–3.20.57.

64. The second theory of the soul is creationism. It claims that "souls are created individually in those who are born." The original innocence being referred to in creationism pertains to the original innocence of Adam in which we still participate, in spite of original sin. Otherwise, God would be responsible for sin in the act of creation. Ibid., 3.20.56–3.20.57.

65. The third theory of the soul maintains that God sends existing souls to bodies when they are born and that the soul in question then governs the individual. Ibid., 3.20.56–3.20.5.

66. According to the fourth theory, souls are not sent by God, but fall into bodies of their own accord. Ibid., 3.20.56–3.20.57.

67. This is an important point to notice when one considers work of authors who seem to be confident about the position Augustine holds. For example see, O'Connell, *St. Augustine's Confessions; St. Augustine's Platonism*; and *The Origin of the Soul in St. Augustine's Later Works* (New York: Fordham Press, 1987). Courcelle, *Recherches sur les Confessions de Saint Augustin*. See also O'Daly, "Did Augustine Ever Believe in the Soul's Pre-existence?" *Augustinian Studies* 5 (1974): 227–35; Frederic E. Van Fleteren, "Augustine's Ascent of the Soul in Book VII of the *Confessions*: A Reconsideration," *Augustinian Studies* 5 (1974): 29–72.

68. If all Augustine means by "the image of God" is rationality, as he sometimes suggests, it is not possible to infer original innocence from the fact that the image is not obliterated by the fall (1.7.11; 2.10.18; 4.11.16). However if the concept of the image points to the unfallen state in which Adam was created, it suggests that the one participates in original innocence as well. Augustine himself points in this direction (1.6.7; 13.22.32), where he speaks about our participation in Adam before the fall. For a discussion of original sin and innocence, see Vaught, *The Journey toward God in Augustine's* Confessions, 28–37.

69. Gilson, 82.

70. In the *City of God*, Augustine develops the view that all human beings are identical with the soul of Adam prior to the fall, presumably as a way of getting around the difficulties of blaming God for sin and permitting original sin to be the first word about the human situation. See *City of God*, trans. W. Dyson in *Cambridge Texts in the History of Political Thought* (Cambridge: Cambridge University Press, 1998), (14.13); *The Literal Meaning of Genesis*, 11.30. However, these references fail to take into account the fact that Augustine mentions the "in Adam" doctrine in Book X of the *Confessions*. In addition, "in Adam" can mean "participate in" rather than "being identical with."

71. In terms of our earlier distinctions, they move though four stages: the (finite⌐infinite) that is oriented initially toward God, the (finite⌐infinite) that falls away from God, the (finite-infinite) that comes back to itself, and the (finite⌐infinite), that moves toward fulfillment.

72. Plato, *Republic*, 509a–511e.

73. Aristotle, *Nicomachean Ethics* in *A New Aristotle Reader*, trans. W. D. Ross and J. O. Urmson, 365 (Princeton, NJ: Princeton University Press, 1987).

74. It is important to notice that the truth that Augustine is seeking is not a principle that can be articulated discursively, but a standard according to which judgments of value can be made (7.17.23). A standard of this kind is a guide to inquiry, as both Plato and Pierce recognized; it has nothing to do with truth as a means by which one philosophical position attempts to exercise hegemony over another in this respect.

75. O'Daly, 207.

76. Genesis 3.7.

77. A paradoxal problem is pointed out in *On the Teacher*, trans. Peter King. In this dialogue between Augustine and his son, Adeodatus, Augustine explains that, in order to teach, one must use signs. However, unless the human being already understands the meaning of these signs, the use of them would be meaningless. Augustine provides the solution to the enigma with the doctrine of the "inner teacher." The ability of humans to acquire knowledge is made possible by consultation with the inner teacher, or illumination from Christ.

78. Augustine returned to North Africa after his mother's death in Ostia at the end of Book IX. He was ordained in 391 and became Bishop of Hippo in 395. In a sermon, Augustine explains how he became the Bishop of Hippo (Sermon 355.2):

I, whom you see, with God's grace as your bishop—I came as a young man to this city, as many of you know. I was looking for a place to set up a monastery, to live with my "brethren." I had given up all hope in this world. What I could have been, I wished not to be: nor did I seek to be what I am now. For I chose to be humble in the house of my God rather than to live in the tents of sinners. I kept apart from those who loved the world: but I did not think myself the equal of those who ruled over the congregations. At the Lord's Feast, I did not take up a higher position, but chose a lower and more retiring place: and it pleased the Lord to say "Rise up." I feared the office of a bishop to such an extent that, as soon as my reputation came to a matter of among "servants to God," I would not go to any place where I knew there was no bishop. I was on my guard against this: I did what I could to seek salvation in a humble position rather than be in danger in high office. But, as I said, a slave may not contradict his Lord. I came to this city to see a friend, whom I thought I might gain for God, that he might lie with us in the monastery. I felt secure, for the place already had a bishop. I was grabbed. I was made a priest . . . and from there, I became your bishop.

This passage is quoted in Brown, 131. Brown gives a detailed analysis of how Augustine became Bishop of Hippo and fills in the biographical chasm that is missing between Books IX and X. See Brown, 131–38.

79. In developing this distinctively Augustinian framework, it is not necessary to claim that Augustine is a Christian rather than a Neoplatonist at this point, as Boyer argued in his well-known controversy with Alfaric, who claimed that the Bishop of Hippo concealed the fact that his conversion in 386 was not to Christianity but to Neoplatonism. (C. Boyer, *Christianisme et néo-platonisme dans la formation de saint Augustin* [Paris: Beauchesne, 1920] and Alfaric, *L'évolution intellectuelle de Saint Augustin.* However, it *is* necessary to move beyond the mediating position of Courcelle according to which Augustine is more a Neoplatonist than a Christian. See Courcelle, *Recherches sur les Confessions de Saint Augustin,* 7–12, 138. See also A. Pincherle, "Sources platoniciennes di l'augustinisme," and the debate between them (*Augustine Magister,* vol. 3 [Paris: Etudes Augustiniennes, 1954], 71–93, 97, 100).

80. A more profound expression of the crucial points can be formulated by returning to our earlier distinction among the four modes of the (finite-infinite) dimensions of a human being. Since this hyphenated characterization of the individual remains constant from stage to stage in Augustine's development, he displays a continuity in which something is always preserved. However, since (finite-infinite) creation, (finite-infinite) fall, (finite-infinite) conversion, and (finite-infinite) fulfillment are so radically different, discontinuity is a crucial theme as well. Furthermore, even in these terms, Augustine is to be distinguished from Hegel; Augustine never suggests that what is essential in one of these stages is preserved in the next.

In this new formulation of what is at stake in the comparison between Hegel and Augustine, the (finite-infinite) matrix forms a common core in terms of which four *essential* modifiers can be expressed, no one of which can be taken into the next.

81. I John 2.16.

82. Notice how much more balanced Augustine is with respect to the problem of sexuality than many of his contemporaries, and many of ours. He does not make the sin that plagued him more than any other paramount in his discussion of his previous experience, or even in what he has to say about other sins that he regards as much more serious. One of the best ways of making the crucial point is that Augustine is prepared to move on from where he is, however much of the past presses in upon him, to the task of meditating on the Word of God that he will embrace at the end of Book X (10.43.70).

83. There are four modes of the (finite-infinite) dimension of the human being. Since this hyphenated characterization of a man or woman remains constant from stage to stage in Augustine's development, he displays a continuity in which something is always preserved. However, since a (finite-infinite) creation, a (finite-infinite) fall, a (finite-infinite) conversion, and a (finite-infinite) fulfillment are so radically different, discontinuity is a crucial theme as well. In this formulation of what is at stake in Augustine's position, the (finite-infinite) matrix forms a common core in terms to express the stages of his development. Yet even though this matrix is present in all four contexts to supply the moment of identity, the irreducible differences among them reveal to themselves the fact that none of them can be taken up into the others.

I have added arrows to all the modifications of Augustine's development to indicate the differences among the creation, the fall, the conversion, and the fulfillment in graphic terms. The arrow that goes up from the hyphen points to the relation of the self-transcendent creature to God. The arrow that points in the opposite direction expresses the fall. The arrow that curves from the infinite to the finite conveys the process of conversion; the arrow that begins with the hyphen and curves around the infinite strives for fulfillment. With reference to this schematic formulation, it is important to emphasize the fact that although original sin is conquered in conversion, the man or woman who has been converted continues to suffer from its stain in the fourth stage of development. In this connection, see Augustine's confession of his "present" sins in (10.28.39–10.40.65).

84. Ecclesiastes 18.30.

85. I Corinthians 8.8.

86. Philippians 4.11–13.

87. Philippians 4.13.

88. Tobit 4.2–4.

89. Genesis 27.1–40.

90. Genesis 48.11–22.

91. In this book, I develop the view that Augustine's thought tilts in the direction of Christianity, however Neoplatonic it may be. This tilt is expressed in

four ways: first, Augustine is committed to the doctrine of creation *ex nihilo* rather than to the Neoplatonic doctrine of emanation. Second, his doctrine of the fall is more radical than the fall of the soul in Neoplatonism because it involves the fall of the entire human being. Augustine, *On the Catholic and the Manichean Ways of Life*, 1.22.40; *The Literal Meaning of Genesis*, 6.25, 9.3; and *The City of God*, 13.3, 13.23. Third, Augustine believes that a Mediator is necessary if the infinite chasm between the divine and the human realms is to be bridged, and he differs from Plotinus by denying that the soul can be transformed by efforts of its own; see Plotinus, 4.3.17. Finally, Augustine is committed to the resurrection of the body, even in his early works; see *On the Greatness of the Soul* in *The Fathers of the Church*, vol. 2 (New York: CIMA, 1947), 33.76.

92. The relations among the creation, the fall, conversion, and fulfillment are not dialectical, but analogical, precisely because Augustine does not move from stage to stage through a series of positive negations that occur in time, philosophical or otherwise. Rather, he makes these transitions within the temporal, spatial, and eternal framework that we have presupposed and in which we can articulate the subsequent relations among the four stages of his development in analogical terms. The analogies in question presuppose that what we have called the (finite-infinite) structure of the human being provides the element of identity and that the four modifications of this structure provide the elements of difference. In addition, the proper understanding of these analogies does not presuppose that analogy is a function of identity and difference, but an expression of what might be called "irreducible similarity." For an analysis of this conception, see Carl G. Vaught, "Participation and Imitation in Plato's Metaphysics," in *Contemporary Essays on Greek Ideas: The Kilgore Festschrift*, ed. Robert M. Baird, William F. Cooper, Elmer H. Duncan, and Stuart E. Rosenbaum (Waco, Texas: Baylor University Press, 1987), 17–31; Vaught, "Hegel and the Problem of Difference: A Critique of Dialectical Reflection," in *Hegel and His Critics*, ed. William Desmond (Albany: State University of New York Press, 1989), 35–48; and Vaught, "Categories and the Real Order: Sellar's Interpretation of Aristotle's Metaphysics," *The Monist* 66 (1983): 438–49.

93. Genesis 2.8.

94. Genesis 3.6.

95. Genesis 3.6.

96. Genesis 3.5.

97. For a discussion of the "method of difference" see Francis Bacon, *The New Organon* (New York: Macmillan Publishing, 1960).

98. Augustine believes that a Mediator is necessary if the infinite chasm between the divine and the human realms is to be bridged. He confesses his present sins to the believing sons of men on this basis (10.4.5).

99. Matthew 19.19 says "Love thy neighbor as thyself." Christ is reformulating Leviticus 19.18 in this passage: "Thou shalt not avenge, nor bear any grudge . . . but thou shalt love thy neighbor as thyself: I am the Lord."

100. Here a self-referential dimension of Augustine's inquiry emerges once again, this time with reference to the problem of contempt.

101. Starnes compares the vision of Book X (10.40.65) with the vision described in book VII (7.17.24), where Augustine has not found the Mediator between man and God. I believe that Starnes' interpretation is correct, since the momentary visions of Augustine are now accessible to him because of the Mediator who is at work in the post-conversion vision with Monica described in Book IX. See Starnes, "Prolegomena to the Last Three Books," 8–10.

102. Ibid., 9.

103. Ibid., 6–9.

104. II Corinthians 11.14.

105. For authors who move in a Neoplatonic direction see, for example, Alfaric, *L'évolution intellectuelle de Saint Augustine*; A. Hilary Armstrong, *Cambridge History of Later Greek & Early Medieval Philosophy*; O'Connell, *St. Augustine's Confessions*; *St. Augustine's Platonism*; and O'Meara, "Augustine and Neo-Platonism," *Recherches Augustiniennes* 1 (1958): 91–111.

106. See Starnes, "Prolegomena to the Last Three Books," 8–9.

107. Augustine does not use these terms in formulating his account of the relation between God and the soul. However, his description of this complex relation presupposes the concepts to which these terms call our attention. Finitude points to the bounded dimension of the human situation, and infinitude points to the aspect of it that transcends itself in relation to God. I also use the (finite-infinite) distinction throughout this book in understanding the transitions from creation to the fall, from the fall to conversion, and from conversion to fulfillment. These categories are not imposed on the text, but are ways of pointing to crucial distinctions that emerge from it. For analogous uses of this distinction see the works of Søren Kierkegaard, *The Concept of Irony*, trans. and ed. by Edna H. Hong and Howard V. Hong (Princeton, NJ: Princeton University Press, 1992) and Reinhold Niebuhr, *The Nature and Destiny of Man*, vol. 1 (New York: Charles Scribner's Sons, 1953).

To say that a man or woman is a (finite-infinite) being is to say that limitations and self-transcendence intersect in our journey toward God. If we accept our limitations, we are (finite⟶infinite) beings; and our souls stretch out toward God without denying our created limitations. On the other hand, if we attempt to encroach upon the mystery and the majesty of God, we turn away from our finitude to accentuate our infinite dimension. As a consequence, we become (finite⟵infinite) beings who are separated from God. Søren Kierkegaard makes a similar characterization of the condition of the self when he writes, "A human being is a synthesis of the infinite and the finite, of the temporal and the eternal, of freedom and necessity, in short, a synthesis." Kierkegaard, *The Sickness unto Death*, 13. The image of God involves more than rationality and includes intentional activity in general, especially in self-transcendence. See John E. Smith, *The Analogy of Experience*, 10.

108. See Starnes, "Prolegomena to the Last Three Books," 8–9.

109. II Corinthians 5.15.

110. See Starnes, "Prolegomena to the Last Three Books," 9.

111. O'Donnell, *Augustine: Confessions,* vol. 3, 245–46.

NOTES TO CHAPTER TWO

1. For examples of texts that simply provide excerpts of Augustine's analysis of time see Kurt Flasch, *Was ist Zeit? Augustinus von Hippo, Das XI Buch der Confessiones* (Frankfurt am Main, 1993); Jean Guitton, *Le temps et l'éternité chez Plotin et Saint Augustin* (Paris: Boivin, 1933; 3rd ed. with new preface, 1959); Hugh M. Lacey, "Empiricism and Augustine's Problems about Time," *Review of Metaphysics* 22 (1968): 218–45; J. McEvoy, "St. Augustine's Account of Time and Wittgenstein's Criticisms," *Review of Metaphysics* 38 (1984): 547–77; C. W. K. Mundle, "Augustine's Pervasive Error concerning Time," *Philosophy* 41 (1966): 165–68; John M. Quinn, "Four Faces of Time in St. Augustine," *Recherches Augustiniennes* 26: 181–231; Roland J. Teske, "The World-Soul and Time in St. Augustine," *Augustinian Studies* 14 (1983): 75–92.

2. The kind of spatilization I have in mind does not involve space in the usual sense of the term, but "space" in an extended, analogical sense. In addition, the "space" in question remains temporal, just insofar as it involves the past, the present, and the future.

3. It is at this juncture that Augustine introduces the psychological dimension of time; but as we shall see, this does not imply that he characterizes time as merely subjective.

4. I am once more using the familiar phrase from Paul Tillich, not because it is to be found in the *Confessions,* but because Tillich stands within the Augustinian tradition. See "Two Types of Philosophy of Religion," 29.

5. In chapter 1, I have already characterized memory as a window to eternity. In this chapter, time will also be understood as such a window, where since memory is one of the modes of time, the window in the first is derivative upon the window in the second.

6. Once more I use the phrase from Paul Tillich because it points so well to the One from whom Augustine has been estranged and to whom he longs to return. See "Two Types of Philosophy of Religion," 10–29.

7. See a paper presented by Starnes, "Prolegomena to the Last Three Books," 11.

8. Matthew 5.3–10.

9. Augustine has expressed the experiential dimension of his quest for fulfillment by describing his journey toward God in Books I–VI and by depicting his encounters with God in Books VII–IX. Now he expresses both the experiential and the intellectual dimensions of his enterprise in Books X–XIII, and it is to the last stage of this enterprise that we now turn our attention.

10. Starnes, "Prolegomena to the Last Three Books," 11, 3–4; and O'Donnell, *Augustine: Confessions,* vol. 3, 250–52.

11. Starnes, "Prolegomena to the Last Three Books," 11.

12. I introduce the qualification to avoid the implication that what Augustine thinks is not a proper part of his autobiography. O'Donnell, *Augustine: Confessions,* vol. 1, Prolegomena.

13. Starnes, "Prolegomena to the Last Three Books," 4–6.

14. This matrix is finite because God creates it, and it is infinite because it has no limits at the horizontal level. Yet insofar as it is created and as the upward arrow indicates, time is also oriented toward God as the source from which it comes into being.

15. Once more, the temporal flux is both finite and infinite; but this time, the two orientations of the arrows point to an important distinction between created and fallen temporality.

16. There are a number of places in the text where Augustine attributes his ability to frame the theory he develops to the grace of God (1.1.1; 7.17.23; 10.23.33).

17. As we shall see, the flux is good, just insofar as it is created. However, we fall away from God when we turn toward the flux rather than God and to the respects in which the flux is grounded in God.

18. Courcelle, *Rechercehes sur les Confessions de Saint Augustin,* 23–25. O'Donnell, however, disagrees; see O'Donnell, *Augustine: Confessions,* vol. 3, 261.

19. O'Donnell, *Augustine: Confessions,* 193.

20. Starnes, "Prolegomena to the Last Three Books," 15.

21. One indication of the difficulty of Genesis 1–3 is that Augustine gives an exegesis of it on five separate occasions. See *On Genesis: Two Books on Genesis against the Manichees* and *On the Literal Interpretation of Genesis, an Unfinished Book,* trans. Roland J. Teske (Washington, DC: Catholic University of America, 1990), *Confessions,* 11–12; *City of God,* 11; *The Literal Meaning of Genesis.*

22. Starnes, "Prolegomena to the Last Three Books," 16.

23. Ibid., 11.

24. Genesis 1.1.

25. Hebrews 12.12.

26. Matthew 5–7.

27. Starnes, "Prolegomena to the Last Three Books," 14.

28. Plotinus, 5.1.6.

29. Ibid., 5.1.8.

30. Ibid.

31. O'Donnell explains that the Augustine credited the Platonists for having a tradiatic concept of God. See O'Donnell, *Augustine: Confessions,* vol. 2, 417.

32. It is important to notice that illumination differs from recollection because the first presupposes the active work of God in making the truth accessible rather than the human recovery of something that we know already, but that lies hidden from us. This distinction is expressed at a number of places in Book X where Augustine is discussing the memory of God (10.10.17; 10.11.18; 10.17.26; 10.25.36). Augustine's dialogue, *On the Teacher* also clarifies how illumination and

recollection differ due to the consultation of the inner teacher, Christ. See *On the Teacher*, trans. Peter King.

33. As I have said on a number of occasions, man is both finite and infinite, pointing up toward God, on the one hand, or down toward the world and toward the absolute nonbeing from which it is brought into existence on the other. The arrows in the two respective cases point to the directions in which the soul is oriented in these two respective cases.

34. Nash, *The Light of the Mind*, 90–93.

35. Matthew 3.17.

36. The second kind of nonbeing with which Augustine deals in Book XI is less radical that the first kind about which he speaks when he discusses the creation and the fall, and it is this second kind of nonbeing that is the integral element in his discussion of the nonexistence of time.

37. Once again, the expressions in parentheses point to the (finite-infinite) nature of the human being, where we are finite because we are delimitated, and where we are infinite because we are made in the image of God and are related to God along the vertical dimension of experience. I use the same formula in all four cases to point to the fact that our nature remains constant despite modifications, and I use the variations of the formula to point to the four conditions of the soul that the soul can exemplify.

38. Starnes, "Prolegomena to the Last Three Books," 14–15.

39. Genesis 1.

40. As I have noted in chapter one, there are two groups in the Christian community to which Augustine is speaking at the beginning of Book X. The first group is part of the community in a primarily ceremonial sense and remains external to the fundamental issues with which Augustine is struggling, while the second group shares his participation in the deeper issues about which he has and will be speaking in Books X–XIII. It is presumably the first group to whom he is speaking when he replies to the skeptical objection.

41. These passing movements constitute what McTaggart calls the "A series," where the members of this series are the past, the present, and the future. When he considers the members of this series, McTaggart believes that he can demonstrate that time does not exist. When the same event is past, present, and future, even at different times, he claims that this state of affairs is both self-contradictory and generates an infinite regress. It is interesting and important to compare Augustine's claims about the nonexistence of time and his reasons for them with the arguments of McTaggart. See John McTaggart Ellis McTaggart, *The Nature of Existence*, vol. 2, ed. C. D. Broad (Cambridge: Cambridge University Press, 1921), 10.

42. McTaggart claims that these passing movements cannot be present all at once because they are successive and because they cannot be held together in a specious present (McTaggart, 11). C. D. Broad replies to McTaggart, by trying to demonstrate that it is not self-contradictory to claim that a temporal moment

is past, present, and future, where the "is" is temporal, and where the past has been present, the present is present, and the future will be present. (C. D. Broad, *Examination of McTaggart's Philosophy*, Part I, vol. 3 (New York: Octagon Books, 1976), 271–72.) In addition, Broad argues that the specious present is long enough to contain the past, the present, and the future and that their copresence there permits these successive moments to be extended together. See Broad, 273, 281–98. Without resorting to the specious present, Wilfrid Sellars tries to deal with the problem of the nonexistence of the A series in a much less complicated way than either McTaggart or Broad, however complex the framework within which Sellars writes about the nature of time may be. Wilfred Sellars, "Time and the World Order," in *Minnesota Studies in the Philosophy of Science*, vol. 3, ed. Herbert Feigl and Grover Maxwell, 527–616 (Minneapolis: University of Minnesota Press, 1962). Again, it will be interesting to see how Augustine approaches the problems of successiveness and the problem of the specious present.

43. Though God speaks eternally, and only speaks once, it does not follow from this fact that from the standpoint of time, every temporal moment exists together.

44. In the language of McTaggart, there are two respects in which time is contained in eternity. On the one hand, the A series is contained there because time flows through it; on the other hand, what McTaggart calls the B series is contained there in the form of the sequence generated by the distinction between earlier than and later than. McTaggart, 10–13.

45. Once more, this means that the flux is a finite sequence of temporal moments that is infinite in extent, where the sequence in its original condition points toward God.

46. In the framework of our enterprise, God's relation to time is vertical rather than horizontal, eternal rather than temporal; and it is in these terms that we must learn to understand it.

47. G. E. Moore, *Some Main Problems of Philosophy* (New York: Collier Books, 1962), 222.

48. Plato, *Euthyphro*, in *Five Dialogues*, trans. G. M. A. Grube (Indianapolis, IN: Hackett, 1981).

49. Plato, *Lysis, Phaedrus, and Symposium*, trans. Benjamin Jowett, with selected retranslations by Eugene O'Connor (Amherst, MA: Prometheus Books, 1991).

50. Plato, *Laches*, in *Plato's Complete Works*, ed. John M. Cooper (Indianapolis, IN: Hackett, 1997).

51. Plato, *Republic*.

52. In the introduction to *Being and Time*, Heidegger makes a similar claim about the concept of being. In that case as well as this one, we have a prethematic awareness of what the fundamental issue under discussion means without being able to provide an adequate account of it. See Martin Heidegger, *Being and Time* (Albany: State University of New York Press, 1996), 2–35.

53. Though the paradoxes in question make distraction and disorientation possible, they do not make them necessary. As we shall see, these consequences result only when the (finite⌐infinite) being turns away from God to pursue a path of its own.

54. Wilfred Sellars rejects the claim that time is unreal by making the distinctions in question. (Sellars, 527–615). It is important to notice, by comparison, the reason that Augustine gives for his views about the unreality of time.

55. McTaggart, 272–76.

56. The thesis of McTaggart about the contradiction that a temporal episode exhibits, rests on the view that the "is" in which the past, the present, and the future are held together is timeless, while the efforts of Broad and Sellars to refute him presuppose that this same present is temporal. (McTaggart, 22–23, 27; Broad, 272–76, 352; Sellars, 583–91).

57. Insofar as the "is" is eternal, it points to the eternal present, and insofar as it is temporal, it points to temporal passage.

58. These dimensions correspond roughly to the A and the B series that McTaggart distinguishes. See McTaggart, 10–31. For an examination of the A and B series, see Broad, 289–92.

59. See Starnes, "Prolegomena to the Last Three Books," 15.

60. Note how this formulation is a way of combining what McTaggart calls the A and the B series respectively. See McTaggart, *The Nature of Existence*, 10–31; McTaggart, "The Unreality of Time," *Mind* (1908): 457–74.

61. McTaggart, *The Nature of Existence*, 19, 326; Broad, 315–16; Sellars, 583–91.

62. For a similar view see Sellars, 583–91.

63. For explanations of the specious present see McTaggart, *The Nature of Existence*, 27, 272–73; Broad, 281–88.

64. Ibid.

65. These three dimension of time correlate with the philosophical framework that we have used from the beginning to approach Augustine's experience and reflection. The static dimensions correlate with space, the dynamic dimensions correlate with time, and the psychological dimension brings us into a direct relation with the eternal present. Of course, this formulation is only an approximation, since all three dimensions pertain to time primarily and only point derivatively to the other dimensions that are involved in Augustine's relationship with God.

66. As Augustine makes clear (11.6.8) and as Ryan emphasizes in a footnote to his translation of the *Confessions*, to speak improperly is not to speak incorrectly, but to use whatever term is in question in an analogical sense of the term. See Ryan, *Confessions*, 409.

67. It is important to notice that what Augustine regards as the proper way to speak about time is what we would regard as an analogical extension of our usual way of speaking about it into what we would regard as an exclusively psychological context.

68. Once more these distinctions correspond the spatial, temporal, and eternal framework that our entire analysis of the *Confessions* presupposes.

69. In this case, time and space as elements of the philosophical framework that governs our analysis switch places.

70. It is important to compare the light to which Augustine refers at this juncture to the light that makes his intellectual conversion possible (7.10.46; 7.17.23), and to the light to which he refers at the conclusion of his analysis of the nature of memory (10.40.65). In the last two cases, the light serves an experiential purpose. In the first case, it serves an intellectual purpose where the divine light is the ground for and the image of the light in the first two cases.

71. This remark is simply a way of saying that the movement of bodies in time and the periods it takes for these movements to occur are independent variables.

72. Joshua 10.11–14.

73. O'Daly, *Augustine's Philosophy of Mind*, 152.

74. We must draw a distinction once more between recollection and illumination. Recollection presupposes continuity between what one has forgotten and what one recovers, while illumination adds the additional element of discontinuity that must be bridged by divine illumination. For a further discussion see Nash, "Some Philosophic Sources of Augustine's Illumination Theory," *Augustinian Studies* 2 (1971): 47–64.

75. Notice how Augustine begins his analysis of how to measure time with a spatial example that proves to be inadequate immediately.

76. See Descartes, *Meditations on First Philosophy*, vol. 2, trans. John Cottingham (Cambridge: Cambridge University Press, 1996), 16–23.

77. This vertical axis is part of the framework in terms of which we have analyzed the *Confessions*, and standing on the vertical axis is to exist all at once before God.

78. It is easy to hear echoes of Augustine, the rhetorician, in this example.

79. It is a well-known fact that two concepts are involved at this juncture, one of which pertains to meaning (intensionality) and the other of which pertains to action (intentionality). In the first case, a meaning can be the intention of a word or concept; and in the second, an action can be either intentional or inadvertent. Augustine makes what is at least an implicit use of this distinction here.

80. The last four Books of the *Confessions* are necessary conditions for the first four, and they are mirror images of them. This is true, even though many other principles of unity that bind the book together have been suggested, including Augustine's own.

81. Augustine can be read as an exegete, where this fact is expressed in his study of Scripture to preach to his parishioners and in his writings on biblical texts. This dimension of Augustine's life presupposes his participation in the community at Hippo and in the scholarly community of theologians and philosophers engaged in the study of Scripture.

82. See Edmund Husserl (*Formal and Transcendental Logic,* trans. by Dorian Cairns in *The Hague,* 110–11) for the concept of an *intentional synthesis* that binds together an entire life.

83. Philippians 3.12–14.

84. Again I am distinguishing two modes of the (finite-infinite) structure that human beings display; the first of which transcends itself toward God, and the second of which falls away from him.

85. For a view that stands in contrast with this one, see Teske, *Paradoxes of Time in Saint Augustine* (Milwaukee, WI: Marquette University Press, 1996), 29–30.

86. The image of God expresses itself at the existential level in the self-transcendence of the (finite-infinite) being toward God, where Augustine's characterization of the image in terms of rationality points in this direction. By stabilizing (stability$_1$) time, Augustine moves beyond the flux in a fashion that reflects this same analysis.

87. Dyson, "St. Augustine's Remarks on Time," *Downside Review* 100.340 (1982): 221–30.

88. The two modifications of the (finite-infinite) structure of the soul differ from the modifications of it that are involved in the concepts of creation and the fall. In the latter two cases, (finite-infinite) and (finite-infinite) modes provide the framework of the analysis, while in the first two, (finite-infinite) and (finite-infinite), modes become the central themes.

NOTES TO CHAPTER THREE

1. The framework within which I approach the *Confessions* involves an interplay among temporal, spatial, and eternal dimensions, all of which intersect in what might be called the "Place of places." This framework is presupposed by the community of images that I mention here.

2. Romans 8.31.

3. Matthew 5–7.

4. Augustine uses metaphors to bind the soul and the body together, and he uses analogies to hold them apart. As a consequence, Augustine's rhetoric permits him to move back and forth between unity and separation.

5. See Augustine, *Confessions* in *Augustine: Confessions and Enchiridion,* trans. Albert C. Outler (Philadelphia, PA: Westminster Press, 1955), 271, n. 3.

6. Augustine writes, "A sign is a thing which besides outward appearance that it presents to the sense causes something else to come out of it into one's knowledge." See *On Christian Doctrine,* 2.1. In addition, he claims that readers of the Bible can always strive for a better understanding of its contents (13.22.32). For further examples see *On Christian Doctrine,* 1.26–29, 3.10.14.

7. See *On Order,* 2.5.16. O'Donnell, *Augustine: Confessions,* vol. 3, 305–6. J. Van Winden, "Spiritual or Intelligible Matter in Plotinus and Augustine," *Vetera Christianorum* 16 (1962): 205–15; 18 (1964): 144–45.

8. This is both a clear reference to the fact that Augustine dictates the *Confessions* and one of the explanations for the rhetorical character of his presentation.

9. Plato, *Sophist* in *The Collected Dialogues of Plato*, ed. Edith Hamilton and Huntington Cairns (New York: Pantheon Books, 1961), 236c–237b.

10. Plotinus, *Enneads*, vol. 2, 2.4.8.

11. Ibid., 2.4.15.

12. Plotinus, *Enneads*, vol. 1, xiii.

13. Starnes, "Prolegomena to the Last Three Books," 16.

14. I also use the (finite-infinite) distinction throughout this chapter in understanding the transitions from creation to the fall, from the fall to conversion, and from conversion to fulfillment. These categories are not imposed on the text, but are ways of pointing to crucial distinctions that emerge from it. For analogous uses of this distinction see the works of Kierkegaard, *The Concept of Irony*, and Niebuhr, *The Nature and Destiny of Man*.

15. Richard Sorabji, *Time, Creation, and the Continuum* (Ithaca, NY: Cornell University Press, 1983), 32.

16. This is the first reference to the formlessness of the heaven of heaven (heaven$_2$) in the text. It remains to be seen how Augustine incorporates this kind of formlessness into his account.

17. Predication is transcategorial when the predicate in question is applied to a term that falls outside the genus of the things to which it applies in the strict sense of the term. In this case, "temporality" as it applies to things in time is extended to characterize the material (earth$_3$) out of which temporal things come into existence.

18. In Book X, Augustine refers to our simultaneous participation in the innocent and the unfallen Adams. This is the passage that I have in mind in making this claim (10.16.25).

19. For further discussion see, Bourke, *Augustine's Love of Wisdom*, 34–39.

20. O'Connell, *St. Augustine's Confessions*, 152–54.

21. For a justification of this way of understanding the issue, see Augustine, *The Literal Commentary on Genesis*, a book written soon after the *Confessions*.

22. The clearest place in the text where Augustine manifests this view is to be found in 10.20.29. In that context, he says that all of us have been happy either as individuals or insofar as we participate in the created Adam. This is not to deny that we also participate in original sin (13.20.17), but only to claim that original innocence must also be taken into account. Once more, the crucial problem is how to hold these aspects of a human being together. This can be done, not by adopting one of the four theories of the origin of the soul that Augustine never embraces, but by developing a sophisticated analysis of what it means for us to exist in Adam.

As Michael Mendelson says in his article about Augustine (see *The Stanford Encyclopedia of Philosophy* (Fall 2000 Edition), ed. Edward N. Zalta, http://plato.stanford.edu/archives/fall2000/entries/augustine/ [accessed 15 November 2004]), "it is . . . not surprising that there is an unofficial fifth hypothesis that can be found elsewhere in Augustine's works. In *The City of God*, for example, Augustine suggests that God created only one soul, that of Adam, and subsequent human souls are not merely genealogical offshoots (as in traducianism) of that original soul, but they are actually identical to Adam's soul prior to assuming their own individual, particularized lives (13.14). Not only does this avoid the mediation of the traducianist hypothesis, but it also manages to provide a theologically satisfying account of the universality of original sin without falling into the difficulties of God's placing an innocent soul into a sin-laden body, as would be the case in a general creationism. To what extent this constitutes a serious contender for Augustine's attention remains a matter of controversy (O'Connell, 1987, esp. 11–16; Rist, 1989; Rist, 1994, 121–29; and Teske, 1999, 810). The difficulty with these views is that they fail to mention the fact that Augustine considers this fifth hypothesis in the *Confessions* (10.20.29) and that when he does so, he sees it as a way of dealing with original innocence and original sin simultaneously.

23. It is interesting to note that Augustine embraces the concept of spiritual material (heaven$_3$) as a result of his interaction with other interpreters of the first chapter of Genesis (12.20.29).

24. Here we find another instance of transcategorial predication. In this case, we extend the concept of time to characterize the light that makes the formation of what is mutable, but which never mutates, possible.

25. The claim that conversion makes it possible to become a new creature in Christ is a familiar Pauline doctrine (II Corinthians 5. 21) and Augustine relies on it, just as he relies on Paul on so many other occasions (1.1.4; 1.3.3; 1.15.24; 2.23; 2.8.16; 3.7.12; 3.8.13; 4.41; 5.3.5; 5.4.7; 6.3.4; 6.4.5; 6.6.9; 7.3.4; 7.9.15; 7.10.16; 7.18.24; 8.5.7; 8.7.17; 8.10.22; 8.12.29; 8.12.30; 9.4.10; 9.4.11; 9.10.23; 9.10.24; 9.13.35; 10.1.1; 10.2.2; 10.3.3; 10.3.4; 10.4.5; 10.4.6; 10.5.7; 10.30.41; 10.31.43; 10.34.51; 11.7.9; 11.9.11; 11.30.40; 12.1.1; 12.15.18; 12.16.23; 12.19.28; 12.26.36; 13.2.2; 13.12.13; 13.13.14; 13.14.15; 13.18.22; 13.21.29; 13.29.30; 13.24.37; 13.25.38; 13.31.46). However, what is novel about Augustine's claim at this juncture is that he introduces the concept of creation as conversion to form and understands it by analogy with Paul's claim that conversion is creation.

26. In our discussion of Augustine's way of dealing with the problem of origins, it is important not to claim that we know more than he does about the issue in question. It is noteworthy that he never decides which theory of the origin of the soul to embrace throughout his lengthy philosophical career. See *On Free Choice of the Will*, 3.21.59; *The Retractations*, 1.1.3; *Select Letters*, 1.66; and *The Literal Meaning of Genesis*, 10.1. Augustine considers four explanations for the origin of the human soul. The first theory, traducianism, presupposes that the souls of human beings evolve from the one soul that God created. The second theory, creationism, suggests that souls are created individually at birth. The third theory maintains that God sends existing souls to bodies when they are born and that these souls govern individuals. Finally, according to the fourth theory, souls are not sent by God, but fall into bodies of their own accord.

27. It might be useful to compare my interpretation of this passage with that of O'Connell. See O'Connell, *St. Augustine's Confessions*, 152–54.

28. Josiah Royce, *The Problem of Christianity* (Chicago: University of Chicago Press, 1968), 92–98.

29. O'Connell has a view contrary to mine on this point as well. See O'Connell, *St. Augustine's Confessions*, 90–104.

30. O'Donnell expresses a contrary view in *Augustine: Confessions*, vol. 3, 328.

31. Though Augustine has hinted at the existence of spiritual matter (heaven$_3$) in contrast with corporeal matter (earth$_3$) before, this is the first time that he makes the distinction explicitly in the text. It is also important to notice that he does so first with reference to a position that some of his critics defend.

32. One of the chief difficulties with the view that the soul falls into time is that it ignores the fact that the soul and the body are created temporal creatures.

33. Gilson, 44–47.

34. See John K. Ryan, *The Confessions of St. Augustine* (New York: Doubleday, 1960), 319, n. 2.

35. Ibid.

36. "You shall love your neighbor as yourself" is found in Leviticus 19. 18, but the verse from the Old Testament is reformulated by Jesus, urging us to do the same thing in Matthew 22.39.

37. O'Donnell, *Augustine: Confessions*, vol. 3, 327.

38. Plotinus, 5.1.6.

39. Starnes, "Prolegomena to the Last Three Books," 16.

40. Ibid., 16–17.

41. Ibid.

42. Ibid.

43. In the first case, the entire cosmos is brought into existence, together with the material (heaven$_3$, earth$_3$) from which things are made. In the second case, a transition occurs from unformed material (heaven$_3$, earth$_3$) to finished products (heaven$_2$, earth$_2$).

44. The Christian community of charity is an illustration of what we have called, following Josiah Royce, "the beloved community." See Royce, 92–98. It stands in contrast with the hermeneutics of suspicion that expresses itself in the conviction that we can never succeed in understand an author's intentions and the nothing an author either says or implies can be taken at face value. See Paul Ricoeur, *Freud and Philosophy: An Essay on Interpretation*, 33.

45. For an additional and a more detailed account of what Augustine and his companions discuss at Cassiciacum see his first four works that were composed at the country house of Cassiciacum outside Milan. See *The Soliloquies*, *Answer to Skeptics*, trans. Denis J. Kavanagh, in *The Fathers of the Church*, vol. 1 (New York: CIMA, 1948); *The Happy Life*; *On Order*.

46. See Nash, *The Light of the Mind*, 48–51; Augustine, *The Teacher*, in *Philosophy in the Middle Ages*, 2.4.

47. Augustine asserts, "No part of truth is ever made the private property of anyone; rather, it is entirely common to all at the same time." See *On Free Choice of the Will*, 2.14.

48. In a number of passages in the text, Augustine says that the Truth is "in" our minds as a standard of judgment and that unless we know what it means, we cannot recognize it when we encounter it (10.6.9). On the other hand, Augustine also emphasizes the fact that God is above the mind, since otherwise, he could scarcely be the creator of heaven and earth (10.17.26). Yet perhaps the most accurate way to state Augustine's position is to say that he is both inside and outside the soul at the same time, however paradoxical this may seem (10.20.29).

49. Again, we find evidence in the text that Augustine's interest in the problem of the fallen soul is not a way of expressing a commitment to Neoplatonism, but a way of focusing on a distinctively Christian issue.

50. Plato, *Phaedrus*, trans. C. Rowe (Warminster: Aris and Philips, 1986).

51. As I have indicated before, Augustine defends the view that the soul is a substance, the body is a substance, and that the composite in which they are unified is a substance.

52. Concrete reflection occurs when conditions for and images of experience are bound together. I have developed this way of thinking in manuscripts about Books I–VI and Books VII–IX of the *Confessions*, and I am doing so again in this manuscript about Books X–XIII.

53. In two previous publications about Aristotle, I have developed the view that the matter of a substance is the substance itself in one of three senses of the term. I am making the same suggestion here with reference to Augustine. See Vaught, "Categories and the Real Order: Sellar's Interpretation of Aristotle's Metaphysics," *The Monist* 66 (1983): 438–49 and "The Quest for Wholeness and its Crucial Metaphor and Analogy: The Place of Places," *Ultimate Reality and Meaning* 7 (1984): 56–65.

54. This convergence of interpretations toward a standard is analogous to the convergence of meaning toward the meaning of a single term that Aristotle develops in his concept of *pros hen* predication. See Aristotle, *Metaphysics*, trans. Hippocrates G. Apostle (Bloomington: Indiana University Press, 1966), 1003a33–b18. It is also analogous to the convergence of inquiry toward truth that Peirce elaborates in his epistemology.

55. O'Donnell, *Augustine: Confessions*, vol. 3, 329–32.

56. This passage is a decisive indication that Augustine does not intend to interpret the whole of Scripture, as Courcelle suggests, but that he is simply construing the early words of Genesis as a microcosm of the macrocosmic journey from the creation to the appearance of the Holy City. See Courcelle, *Recherches sur les Confessions de Saint Augustin*.

57. As I have suggested already, Augustine regards the human being as a (finite-infinite) creature that is oriented toward God (finite-infinite), falls away from God (finite-infinite), can come back to itself (finite-infinite) , and can move

toward fulfillment (finite—infinite), . All four of these orientations are modification of the basic structure of the psyche.

58. O'Donnell, *Augustine: Confessions*, vol. 3, 347.

59. We find the concept of this kind of predication in Aristotle's *Metaphysics*, 1003a33–b18.

60. II Corinthians 5.17.

61. Just as there is an ontological continuum and a continuum of value that must be taken into account with reference to Augustine, there is a corresponding continuum of happiness.

62. One consequence of Augustine's view about this matter is that the doctrine of illumination that he elaborates with reference to crucial stages of his experience (7.10.16; 8.12.29; 9.10.24) is prefigured in his account of creation. This is one more indication that theoretical considerations serve as the conditions for and the images of Augustine's existential journey.

63. Romans 5.5, I Corinthians 12.1.

64. The angel in question is Satan, and the only serious question that arises at this point pertains to the relation between Satan, on the one hand, and the soul on the other. O'Connell argues that this passage, together with the passage about the lost sheep (12.15.21) that we have considered already, is a decisive indication that the soul preexists and that it falls into the body. (See O'Connell, *St. Augustine's Confessions*, 153–54.) Yet as I have argued on a number of occasions, Augustine never adopts the doctrine of the preexistence of the soul explicitly, preferring to remain open to four distinguishable options about the issue in question.

65. Rhetoricians educated in the Roman tradition are masters of contrast, where the contrast between the heaven of heaven (heaven$_2$) and the soul is the one to which Augustine calls our attention here. The more we pay attention to the "rhetorical" Augustine, the less likely we are to turn him into a Neoplatonist.

66. Augustine's shift to figurative discourse at this point is another indication of the rhetorical dimension of his procedure that we ought to take into account. Again, the point of comparing the soul with the heaven of heaven (heaven$_2$) is not to place the two alongside one another in a preexistent state, but to point to analogies that obtain between them.

67. See Augustine, *On Christian Doctrine*, 1.22.20.

68. Augustine uses metaphors to bind two terms together, and he uses analogies to hold two terms apart. The case before us is an example of his use of metaphorical discourse, just as the occasions when he separates the soul and the body (7.1.2; 10.10.16) is an example of his use of analogy.

69. See Augustine, *The Trinity*, trans. Edmund Hill, in *The Works of Saint Augustine: A Translation for the 21st Century* (Brooklyn, NY: New City Press, 1995), 14.4; 14.12; 15.11.

70. This is one more indication that Augustine is unifying his enterprise and is moving toward concrete reflection in terms of conditions for the possibility of experience, on the one hand, and images of the stages of experience on the other.

71. Augustine, *On Christian Doctrine*, trans. D. W. Robertson, Jr. (Indianapolis, IN: Bobbs-Merrill Educational Publishing, 1958), 43. This same distinction emerges later in the thought of Thomas Aquinas, where Thomas follows Augustine in the distinction he draws between literal and figurative discourse. See Aquinas, 1.12.

72. Romans 12.2.

73. Plotinus is occupied primarily with the necessary emanation of the Intellectual Principle from the One, of the soul from Nous, and so on all the way down to the pure potentiality of formless matter. Plotinus, 5.1.6; 5.1.7. By contrast, the Christian tradition reverses this process of necessary emanation and focuses our attention on the perfection we achieve when we see God.

74. Romans 8.23.

75. Contrast this view with the position of O'Connell (*St. Augustine's Confessions*, 145–57). We have seen already that Augustine commits himself to the resurrection of the body. See *On the Greatness of the Soul*, 33.76. This fact points to the Christian rather than the Neoplatonic strand in Augustine's thinking.

76. Genesis 3.22–24.

77. O'Donnell, *Augustine: Confessions*, vol. 2, 476–77; vol. 3, 365.

78. Ibid.

79. This distinction is developed most clearly in the *City of God*, 1.35, 11.1, 12.2, 18.49.

80. The distinction between *scientia* (rational judgments on the acts of God) and *sapientia* (delight in the grace of God) is fully explored by Augustine in Books XII–XIV of *The Trinity*.

81. I Corinthians 13.12.

82. Matthew 6.21.

83. Acts 2.2.

84. Matthew 5.14.

85. Genesis 1.24.

86. O'Donnell, *Augustine: Confessions*, vol. 3, 89–390.

87. Romans 12.2.

88. Ibid.

89. Genesis 1.26.

90. Romans 12.2.

91. II Timothy 1.16.

92. Matthew 10.41.

93. Matthew 10.41.

94. Matthew 10.42.

95. I Kings 17.10–13.

96. Augustine makes it clear in 4.12.19 that human beings die, not because of their nature, but because of their sin. He elaborates this point in the *The Literal Commentary on Genesis*, 8.2, 9.3, 11.16.

97. Genesis 2.3.

Bibliography

SELECTED ENGLISH TRANSLATIONS OF
AUGUSTINE'S WRITINGS, LISTED IN THE
APPROXIMATE ORDER OF THEIR COMPOSITION

Against the Academicians. Translated by Peter King in *Against the Academicians and The Teacher.* Indianapolis, IN and Cambridge, MA: Hackett, 1995.

The Happy Life. Translated by Ludwig Shopp in *The Fathers of the Church*, vol. 1. New York: CIMA, 1948.

Divine Providence and the Problem of Evil. Translated by Robert P. Russell in *The Fathers of the Church*, vol. 1. New York: CIMA, 1948.

Soliloquies. Translated with and introduction and notes by Kim Paffenroth in *The Works of Saint Augustine: A Translation for the Twenty-first Century*, vol. 2. Edited by John E. Rotelle. Brooklyn, NY: New City Press, 2000.

On the Immortality of the Soul. Translated with a preface by George G. Leckie in *Concerning the Teacher* and *On the Immortality of the Soul.* New York and London: D. Appleton-Century, 1938.

The Catholic and the Manichaean Ways of Life. Translated by Donald A. Gallagher and Idella J. Gallagher. Washington, DC, Catholic University of America Press, 1966.

The Greatness of the Soul. Translated and annotated by Joseph M. Colleran in *The Greatness of the Soul* and *The Teacher.* Westminster, MD: Newman Press, 1950.

On Free Choice of the Will. Translated by Anna S. Benjamin and L. H. Hackstaff. Englewood Cliffs, NJ: Prentice Hall, 1964.

On Genesis: Two Books on Genesis against the Manichees. Translated by Roland J. Teske in *On Genesis: Two Books on Genesis against the Manichees* and *On the Literal Interpretation of Genesis, an Unfinished Book.* Washington, DC: Catholic University of America, 1990.

The Teacher. Translated by Peter King in *Against the Academicians and The Teacher.* Indianapolis, IN and Cambridge, MA: Hackett, 1995.

On the Profit of Believing. Translated by C. L. Cornish in *Basic Writings of Saint Augustine*, vol. 1. Edited with an introduction and notes by Whitney J. Oates. New York: Random House, 1948.

On the Literal Interpretation of Genesis, an Unfinished Book. Translated by Roland
J. Teske in *On Genesis: Two Books on Genesis against the Manichees* and *On
the Literal Interpretation of Genesis, an Unfinished Book.* Washington, DC:
Catholic University of America, 1990.

Eighty-three Different Questions. Translated by David L. Mosher. Washington,
DC: Catholic University of America Press, 1982.

Teaching Christianity. Translated by Edmund Hill in *The Works of Saint Augustine:
A Translation for the Twenty-First Century,* vol. 1, Pt. 2. Edited by John
E. Rotelle. Brooklyn, NY: New City Press, 1996.

Confessions. Translated by Maria Boulding in *The Works of St. Augustine: A Trans-
lation for the Twenty-First Century,* vol. 1, Pt. 2. 2nd edition. Edited by John
E. Rotelle. Brooklyn, NY: New City Press, 1996; Henry Chadwick, Ox-
ford: Oxford University Press, 1991; Albert Outler in *Library of Christian
Classics,* vol. VII. Edited by Albert Outler, Philadelphia, PA: Westminster
Press, 1955; John K. Ryan, New York: Image Books, Doubleday, 1960;
and F. J. Sheed, revised edition, introduced by Peter Brown. Indianapolis,
IN and Cambridge, MA: Hackett, 1993.

The Trinity. Translated with an introduction and notes by Edmund Hill in *The
Works of Saint Augustine: A Translation for the Twenty-First Century.* Brooklyn, NY: New City Press, 1995.

The Literal Meaning of Genesis. Translated by John H. Taylor in *Ancient Christian
Writers,* vols. 41–42. New York: Newman Press, 1982.

The City of God against the Pagans. Translated by R.W. Dyson in *Cambridge Texts
in the History of Political Thought.* Cambridge: Cambridge University Press,
1998.

Select Letters. Translated by James Houston Baxter in *Loeb Classical Library,* vol. 239.
Cambridge, MA: Harvard University Press, 1980. In addition, there are
some important, recently discovered Letters numbered 1*–29*. Translated
by R. Eno in *The Fathers of the Church,* vol. 81. New York: CIMA, 1989.

The Retractations. Translated by Sister Mary Inez Bogan. Washington, DC: Catholic
University of America Press, 1968.

SELECTED GENERAL STUDIES

Bonner, Gerald. *Augustine of Hippo: Life and Controversies.* New York and Rome:
Canterbury Press, 1986.

Bourke, Vernon Joseph. *Augustine's Quest of Wisdom: Life and Philosophy of the
Bishop of Hippo.* Milwaukee, WI: Bruce, 1945.

Brown, Peter. *Augustine of Hippo: A Biography,* new edition with an epilogue.
Berkeley: University of California Press, 2000.

Burnaby, John. Amor Dei: *A Study of the Religion of St. Augustine.* Reissued with
corrections and a new forward. Norwich: Canterbury Press, 1991.

Chadwick, Henry. *Augustine.* In Past Masters Series. Oxford: Oxford University Press, 1986.

Clark, Gillian. *Augustine: The Confessions.* Cambridge: Cambridge University Press, 1993.

Clark, Mary T. *Augustine.* Washington, DC: Georgetown University Press, 1994.

Gilson, Etienne. *The Christian Philosophy of Saint Augustine.* Translated by L. E. M. Lynch. New York: Random House, 1967.

Kirwan, Christopher. *Augustine.* In *The Arguments of the Philosophers.* New York and London: Routledge, 1989.

Meagher, Robert E. *Augustine: An Introduction.* New York: Harper Colophon Books, 1979.

Mendelson, Michael. "Augustine." *The Stanford Encyclopedia of Philosophy.* Fall 2000 edition. Edited by Edward N. Zalta. http://plato.stanford.edu/archives/fall2000/entries/augustine/ (accessed 15 November 2004).

O'Donnell, James. *Augustine.* In *Twayne's World Author Series.* Boston: Twayne Publishers, 1985.

O'Meara, John J. *The Young Augustine, The Growth of St. Augustine's Mind Up to His Conversion.* Longmans, Green, 1954.

O'Meara, John Joseph. *Understanding Augustine.* Dublin, Ireland: Four Courts Press, 1997.

Portalie, Eugene. *A Guide to the Thought of Saint Augustine.* With an introduction by Vernon J. Bourke. Translated by Ralph J. Bastian. Chicago: H. Regnery, 1960.

Rist, John. *Augustine: Ancient Thought Baptized.* Cambridge: Cambridge University Press, 1994.

Scott, T. Kermit. *Augustine: His Thought in Context.* New York: Paulist Press, 1995.

Wills, Gary. *Saint Augustine.* New York: Viking, 1999.

SELECTED SECONDARY WORKS

Alfaric, Prosper. *L'évolution intellectuelle de Saint Augustin.* Nourry, 1918.

Armstrong, A. H., ed. *The Cambridge History of Later Greek and Early Medieval Philosophy.* Cambridge: Cambridge University Press, 1967.

Armstrong, Hilary. "St. Augustine and Christian Platonism." In *Collectanea Augustiniana.* Villanova, PA: Villanova University Press, 1967.

Augustine: A Collection of Critical Essays. Edited by R. A. Markus, Garden City, NY: Anchor Books, 1972.

Augustine, Saint, Bishop of Hippo: The Confessions of Augustine. Edited by John Gibb and William Montgomery. Cambridge: Cambridge University Press, 1908.

Augustine through the Ages: An Encyclopedia. Edited by Allen D. Fitzgerald. Grand Rapids, MI: Eerdmans, 1999.

Augustinian Studies. Villanova, PA: Villanova University Press.

The Augustinian Tradition. Edited by Gareth B. Matthews. Berkeley: University of California Press, 1999.

Babcock, William S. "Augustine's Interpretation of Romans (A.D. 394–396)." *Augustinian Studies* 10 (1979): 55–74.

Borresen, K. E. *Subordination and Equivalence: The Nature and Role of Woman in Augustine and Thomas Aquinas*. Translated by Charles H. Talbot. Lanham, MD: University Press of America, 1981.

Bourke, Vernon J. *Augustine's View of Reality*. Villanova, PA: Villanova University Press, 1963.

Bourke, Vernon J. *Augustine's Love of Wisdom: An Introspective Philosophy*, West Lafayette, IN: Purdue University Press, 1992.

Bubacz, Bruce. *St. Augustine's Theory of Knowledge: A Contemporary Analysis*. New York: E. Mellen Press, 1981.

Burkitt, F. C. *The Religion of the Manichees*. Cambridge: Cambridge University Press, 1925.

Burnaby, John. *Amor dei: A Study of the Religion of St. Augustine*. Reissued with corrections and a new foreword. New York and Rome: Canterbury Press, 1991.

Bussanich, John. "Plotinus' Metaphysics of the One." In *The Cambridge Companion to Plotinus*, edited by Lloyd P. Gerson, 38–65 (Cambridge: Cambridge University Press, 1996).

Chidester, David. *Word and Light: Seeing, Hearing, and Religious Discourse*. Urbana: University of Illinois Press, 1992.

Courcelle, Pierre. *Les confessions de Saint Augustin dans la tradition littéraire*. Études Augustiniennes, 1963.

Courcelle, Pierre. *Recherches sur les Confessions de Saint Augustin*. 2nd ed. Paris: E. de Boccard, 1968.

Dawson, D. "Transcendence as Embodiment: Augustine's Domestication of Gnosis." *Modern Theology* 1 (1994): 1–26.

Descartes, René. *Meditations on First Philosophy*. In *The Philosophical Writings of Descartes*, vol. 2, translated by John Cottingham, Robert Stoothoff, and Dugald Murdoch. Cambridge: Cambridge University Press, 1984.

Dyson, R. W. "St. Augustine's Remarks on Time." *The Downside Review* (1982): 221–230.

Findlay, J. N. *The Discipline of the Cave: Gifford Lectures Given at the University of St. Andrews*. New York: Humanities Press, 1966.

Gerson, Lloyd P. *The Cambridge Companion to Plotinus*. Edited by Lloyd P Gerson. Cambridge: Cambridge University Press, 1996.

Hartle, Ann. *Death and the Disinterested Spectator: An Inquiry into the Nature of Philosophy*. Albany: State University of New York Press, 1986.

Hegel, G. W. F. *Phenomenology of Spirit*. Translated by A. V. Miller. Oxford: Oxford University Press, 1977.

Heidegger, Martin. *Being and Time.* Translated by John Macquarrie and Edward Robinson. San Francisco: Harper Collins, 1962.

Johnstone, Henry. *The Problem of the Self.* University Park, Pa: Pennsylvania State University Press, 1970.

Kierkegaard, Søren. *The Sickness unto Death.* Translated by Howard Vincent Hong and Edna H. Hong. Anderson. Princeton, NJ: Princeton University Press, 1980.

Kierkegaard, Søren. *The Concept of Irony.* Translated by Edna H. Hong and Howard V. Hong. Princeton, NJ: Princeton University Press, 1992

Kristo, J. G. *Looking for God in Time and Memory: Psychology, Theology, and Spirituality in Augustine's Confessions.* Lanham, MD: University Press of America, 1991.

Luther, Martin. *Bondage of the Will* in *Luther and Erasmus: Free Will and Salvation.* Translated by E. Gordon Rupp. Philadelphia, PA: Westminster Press, 1969.

Matthews, Gareth B. "*Si Fallor, Sum.*" In *Augustine: A Collection of Critical Essays,* edited by R. A. Markus, 151–67 (Garden City, NY: Anchor Books, 1972).

Matthews, Gareth B. "The Inner Man." In *Augustine: A Collection of Critical Essays,* edited by R. A. Markus, 176–190 (Garden City, NY: Anchor Books, 1972).

Matthews, Gareth B. *Thought's Ego in Augustine and Descartes.* Ithaca, NY: Cornell University Press, 1992.

Matthews, Gareth B. "Augustine and Descartes on Minds and Bodies" in Matthews, 222–32.

McMahon, Robert. *Augustine's Prayerful Ascent: An Essay on the Literary Form of the Confessions.* Athens, GA: University of Georgia Press, 1989.

Mendelson, Michael. "The Dangling Thread: Augustine's Three Hypotheses of the Soul's Origin in the *De Genesi ad Litteram.*" *British Journal of the History of Philosophy* 3 (1995): 219–47.

Mendelson, Michael. "The Business of Those Absent, The Origin of the Soul in Augustine's *De Genesi ad Litteram* 10.6–26." *Augustinian Studies* 29 (1998): 25–81.

Mendelson, Michael. "*Venter animi/distentio animi*: Memory and Temporality in Augustine's *Confessions.*" *Augustinian Studies* 31 (2000): 137–63.

Mendelson, Michael. "Augustine." *The Stanford Encyclopedia of Philosophy.* Edited by Edward N. Zalta. Fall 2000 Edition. http://plato.stanford.edu/archives/fall2000/entries/augustine/ (accessed 15 November 2004).

Miles, Margaret R. *Augustine on the Body.* Missoula, MT: Scholars Press, 1979.

Miles, Margaret R. "Vision: The Eye of the Body and the Eye of the Mind in Saint Augustine's De Trinitate and Confessions." *Journal of Religion* 63 (1983).

Miles, Margaret R. *Desire and Delight: A New Reading of Augustine's Confessions,* New York: Crossroad, 1992.

Murphy, James J. *Rhetoric in the Middle Ages*. Berkeley: University of California Press, 1974.

Nash, Ronald H. *The Light of the Mind: St. Augustine's Theory of Knowledge*. Lexington: University Press of Kentucky, 1969.

O'Connell, Robert J. *St. Augustine's Early Theory of Man*. Cambridge, MA: Harvard University Press, 1968.

O'Connell, Robert J. *St. Augustine's Confessions: The Odyssey of Soul*. Cambridge, MA: Harvard University Press, 1969.

O'Connell, Robert J. "Action and Contemplation." In *Augustine: A Collection of Critical Essays*, edited by R. A. Markus, 38–58 (Garden City, NY: Anchor Books, 1972).

O'Connell, Robert J. *Saint Augustine's Platonism*. Villanova, PA: Augustinian Institute, Villanova University, 1984.

O'Connell, Robert J. *The Origin of the Soul in St. Augustine's Later Works*. New York: Fordham University Press, 1987.

O'Daly, Gerard. *Augustine's Philosophy of Mind*. Berkeley: University of California Press, 1987.

O'Donnell, James J. *Augustine, Confessions. Text and Commentary* in 3 vols. Oxford: Oxford University Press, 1992.

O'Meara, Dominic J. "The Hierarchical Ordering of Reality in Plotinus." In *The Cambridge Companion to Plotinus*, edited by Lloyd P. Gerson, 66–81 (Cambridge: Cambridge University Press, 1996).

Pepin, J. "Saint Augustin et la fonction protreptique de l'allegori." *Recherches Augustiniennes* 1 (1958): 243–86.

Plantinga, Alvin. "Augustinian Christian Philosophy." *Monist* 75 (1992): 291–320. Reprinted in Mathews, 1999, 1–26.

Plotinus, *Enneads*. Translated by A. H. Armstrong, 7 vols. In *The Loeb Classical Library*. Cambridge, MA: Harvard University Press, 1966–1984.

Poland, L. M. "Augustine, Allegory, and Conversion." *Journal of Literature and Theology* 1 (1988): 37–48.

Power, Kim. *Veiled Desire: Augustine's Writing on Women*. London: Darton, Longman, Todd, 1995.

Ricoeur, Paul. *Time and Narrative*, vol. 1. Chicago: University of Chicago Press, 1984.

Schroeder, Frekeric M. "Plotinus and Language." In *The Cambridge Companion to Plotinus*, edited by Lloyd P. Gerson, 336–355 (Cambridge: Cambridge University Press, 1996).

Severson, Richard James. *Time, Death, and Eternity: Reflecting on Augustine's Confessions in Light of Heidegger's Being and Time*. Metuchen, NJ: American Theological Seminary and the Scarecrow Press, 1995.

Sorabji, Richard. *Time, Creation, and the Continuum*. Ithaca, NY: Cornell University Press, 1983.

Starnes, Colin. *Augustine's Conversion: A Guide to the Argument of Confessions I–IX*. Waterloo, ONT: Wilfrid Laurier University Press, 1990.

Starnes, Colin. "Prolegomena to the Last Three Books." Paper presented at Celebrating Augustine's *Confessions*: Reading the *Confessions* for the New Millennium, Pruitt Memorial Symposium, Baylor University, Waco, TX, October 4, 2001.

Stock, Brian. *Augustine the Reader: Meditation, Self-knowledge, and the Ethics of Interpretation*. Cambridge, MA: Harvard University Press, 1996.

TeSelle, Eugene. *Augustine, the Theologian*. New York: Herder and Herder, 1970.

TeSelle, Eugene. "Pelagius, Pelagianism." In *Augustine through the Ages: An Encyclopedia*, edited by Allan D. Fitzgerald, 633–640 (Grand Rapids, MI: Eerdmans, 1999).

Teske, Roland. "The World-Soul and Time in St. Augustine." *Augustinian Studies* 14 (1989).

Teske, Roland J. *Paradoxes of Time in Saint Augustine*. Milwaukee, WI: Marquette University Press, 1996.

Teske, Roland J. "Soul." In *Augustine through the Ages: An Encyclopedia*, edited by Allan D. Fitzgerald, 807–812 (Grand Rapids, MI: Eerdmans, 1999).

Vaught, Carl G. *The Quest for Wholeness*. Albany: State University of New York Press, 1982.

Vaught, Carl G. "Signs, Categories, and the Problem of Analogy." In *Semiotics*, edited by John Deely, 64–82. Lanham, MD: University Press of America, 1986.

Vaught, Carl G. "Metaphor, Analogy, and the Nature of Truth." In *New Essays in Metaphysics*, edited by Robert C. Neville. Albany: State University of New York Press.

Vaught, Carl G. "Participation and Imitation in Plato's Metaphysics." In *Contemporary Essays on Greek Ideas: The Kilgore Festschrift*, edited by Robert M. Baird, William F. Cooper, Elmer H. Duncan, and Stuart E. Rosenbaum, 17–31. Waco, TX: Baylor University Press, 1987.

Vaught, Carl G. "Hegel and the Problem of Difference: A Critique of Dialectical Reflection." In *Hegel and His Critics*, edited by William Desmond, 35–48. Albany: State University of New York Press, 1989.

Vaught, Carl G. "Categories and the Real Order: Sellar's Interpretation of Aristotle's Metaphysics." *The Monist* 66 (1983): 438–49.

Vaught, Carl G. "The Quest for Wholeness and Its Crucial Metaphor and Analogy: The Place of Places." *Ultimate Reality and Meaning* 7 (1984): 156–65.

Vaught, Carl G. "Metaphor, Analogy, and System: A Reply to Burbidge." *Man and World* 18 (1984): 55–63.

Vaught, Carl G. "Semiotics and the Problem of Analogy: A Critique of Peirce's Theory of Categories." *Transactions of the Charles S. Peirce Society* 22 (1986): 311–26.

Vaught, Carl G. "Subject, Object, and Representation: A Critique of Hegel's Dialectic of Perception." *International Philosophical Quarterly* 22 (1986): 117–35.

Wetzel, James. *Augustine and the Limits of Virtue*. Cambridge: Cambridge University Press, 1992.

Zepf, Max. "Augustine's *Confessions*." *Lutheran Church Quarterly* 21 (1948).

Index

265